AYATULLAH IBRAHIM AMINI

Imamate and the Imams

Copyright © 2010 by Ayatullah Ibrahim Amini

All rights reserved. No part of this publication may be reproduced, stored or transmitted in any form or by any means, electronic, mechanical, photocopying, recording, scanning, or otherwise without written permission from the publisher. It is illegal to copy this book, post it to a website, or distribute it by any other means without permission.

First edition

Contents

1 Author's Preface   1
2 Translator's Preface   5
3 Characteristics of the Imam   7
4 The Ahlul Bayt in the Quran and the Traditions   49
5 The Arguments for Imamate   83
6 Brief Biographies of the Infallible Imams   94
   The Shi'ah Opinion about the Infallible Imams   94
   The First Imam; Ali Ibn Abi Talib   101

One

Author's Preface

Imamate is not a dated ineffective issue so that it would be said, "It is not related to our time; discussing it is only a waste of time and increases old religious differences. It does not make any difference if Imam Ali ('a) is the Prophet's successor or the fourth Caliph after him. Such issues have no influence on our current lives."

It can be said in reply that the importance of Imamate, as a vital Islamic issue, will be proved later on in this book. It has a leading role now and in all eras, in all aspects of life. It also brings about a kind of responsibility for every Muslim. That is why various traditions cite recognition of the Imam in every age as a major Islamic duty and a sign of the belief. This duty is so important that ignoring it is regarded as going astray.

The Messenger of Allah (s) stated, "Anyone who dies without having an Imam has died as a pagan."[1]

He also said, "Anyone who dies while he has not recognized his Imam has died a pagan death."[2]

Ibn Abi Ya'fur said that he asked Imam Sadiq ('a) about this tradition of the Prophet (s), "Does it mean death as an infidel?" Imam Sadiq ('a) replied, "It means dying in deviation." He asked Imam ('a) again, "Therefore, has someone who dies while he has no Imam died as a pagan?" Imam Sadiq ('a) answered, "Sure he did."[3]

Fuzayl Ibn Yasar has narrated from Imam Sadiq ('a) that the Messenger of Allah (s) stated, "Anyone who dies without having an Imam has died a pagan death." Fuzayl asked Imam Sadiq ('a), "Has the Messenger of Allah (s) stated this?" Imam ('a) answered, "Yes, by Allah." The narrator asked again, "So if someone dies while he has no Imam, has he died a pagan death?" Imam Sadiq ('a) stated, "Surely he did."[4]

Various other traditions have also been narrated with the same theme. Such traditions reveal that recognition of the Imam is one of major Islamic obligations. Two important questions come to mind in this regard. The first one is that what is meant by recognition of the Imam? Does it mean knowing the identifications of the Imam or a deeper recognition?

The second question is that what is the advantage of recognizing the Imam? Why is it so emphasized in traditions of Prophet of Islam ('a) and his Household, the infallible Imams ('a)? This question arises especially since the Imamate age has apparently terminated; no one is supposed to be Imam today, so that we have no duty to search for and find the true Imam. In these conditions, isn't it better to leave

---

[1] Musnad Ahmad, Vol 4, p. 96.

[2] Biharul Anwar, Vol 23, p. 67.

[3] Kafi, Vol 1, p. 376.

[4] Kafi, Vol 1, p. 376.

the Imamate issue and the controversy about it and attend to more important Islamic issues?

In answer to the first question it can be said that as will be proved later in the present book, Imamate and leadership are high positions in Islam, which cannot be occupied by regular people. Only qualified persons, with the following characteristics, can reach the Imamate position:

1. The Imam should know all the Divine sciences, teachings, and verdicts that are revealed to Prophet Muhammad (s) by Allah. In other words, the Imam is and should be the inheritor of the Prophet's knowledge.

2. The Imam should be away from mistakes and forgetfulness (be infallible) in gaining, recording, maintaining, and publishing religious sciences and teachings.

3. The Imam should also be away from committing sins and transgressing religious rules. He should follow religious rules and verdicts so that the people follow his Islamic speech, behavior, and morality.

Therefore, the recognition of Imam, mentioned in the traditions, is not merely being familiar with his identification; rather it is recognition of his brilliant scientific, practical, ethical, and virtuous personality.

The answer to the first question clears the answer to the second question too. In other words, if we consider the Imam as the source of all religious sciences, teachings, and verdicts, every Muslim should refer to the Imam –as an original reliable source– for learning his religious duties. As a result, research for recognizing the true Imam –for acquiring religious sciences– is a major duty of every Muslim, who thinks of his salvation in this world and the Hereafter. It is clear that such an important duty does not belong to a certain age and is necessary in all times. In fact, Muslims in all eras should attempt to recognize the infallible Imam of their age –introduced by Prophet Muhammad (s) along with the Holy Quran as two reliable scientific sources– and benefit from his virtuous speech and behavior. Moreover, since only an infallible Imam is introduced from Allah to rule the Islamic Ummah (nation), as the Prophet's true successor, people in all ages should discover the true Imam and ruler and help establish the Islamic government. The government issue does not belong to a certain time and place either. In fact, the need for legitimate Islamic government has always been a preliminary need of the Islamic Ummah.

The present book is written for the youth about the same topics in four chapters:

The first chapter is about definition of Imamate and privileges of the Imams. The second chapter is about Prophet Muhammad's (s) Household, as mentioned in the Holy Quran and the traditions. The third chapter discusses the Imamate reasons. Finally, chapter four introduces the infallible Imams ('a), specific reasons for Imamate of each of them, virtues, ethical values, knowledge, worship, and moral journey of these selected servants toward the Exalted Allah. This is the most important part of the book, so that we may follow the pattern of the infallible Imams ('a).

I hope the Islamic Ummah, especially the youth, attend to spiritual lives of the infallible Imams ('a), learn lessons for life, and set them as their leaders everywhere and every time. In fact, this is the true way of being a real Shiah.

Ibrahim Amini
11/22/1387 (2/12/2008)

Two

Translator's Preface

Praise be to Allah, Lord of the worlds, Who bestowed me with the knowledge and perseverance necessary to translate this valuable work of Ayatollah Amini into English. Translation of Islamic works is a demanding job, especially when the assigned work is lengthy. Keeping the same tone and style throughout the work requires outstanding attention and concentration. It will be very much appreciated for the readers to point out their viewpoints on my translation, including any constructive criticism.

I'd like to express my thanks to my father, Hujjatul Islam Elahinia, for helping me with jurisprudential issues and Arabic terms.

I am very much indebted, also, to my husband, Mr. Seddighian, for his constant help and support during this translation project.

I sincerely dedicate this little attempt in propagating Islamic beliefs to the presence of infallible Imams ('a) of the Shi'ah. May Allah accept their intercession for us in the Last Day; **"The day when We call every person with their Imams"**[5] *and* **"The day on which property will not avail, nor sons."**[6]

---

[5] Surah Al-'Isra' (17): 71.

[6] Surah Al-Shu'ara' (26): 88.

Three

Characteristics of the Imam

Lexical Definition of Imamate

Imamate means leadership and Imam is attributed to someone –either righteous or vicious– whose conduct and ideas are followed by the people. The leader of the pious and the leader of the evildoer are both called Imam. Both meanings are mentioned in the Holy Quran too.

The Holy Quran states,

> *"And We appointed, from among them, leaders, giving guidance under Our command, so long as they persevered with patience and continued to have faith in Our Signs."*[7]

---

[7] Surah Al-Sajdah (320: 24.)

"And we made them (but) leaders inviting to the Fire; and on the Day of Judgment no help shall they find."[8]

Definition and Position of Imamate

Imamate has been a fundamental Islamic belief since Early Islamic Era. It has divided the Islamic Ummah (nation) into two group; the Sunni and the Shiah, each of which having different definitions of Imamate. Abdur Rahman Lahiji, a Sunni scholar, defines Imamate as:

Imamate is not an Islamic fundamental for us; rather it is one of obligatory commandments, unlike the Shiah that consider it as an Islamic principle. Some have defined Imamate as the leadership of the public in worldly and religious issues. However, a better definition of it is the caliphate of Prophet Muhammad (s) in establishing the religion and maintaining the Muslims' unity. Obeying such a caliph is then obligatory for all the Muslims.[9]

As is clear, the Sunni Muslims consider Imamate a worldly position, and an Islamic fundamental. They regard the necessity of appointing Imam a jurisprudential issue and appointment of him the duty of Islamic Ummah, unlike the Shiah, who know Imamate as an Islamic fundamental, after Prophethood. The Shiah define Imamate as succession and caliphate of the Messenger of Allah (s) in all prophetic duties and ranks, except relation with the invisible world and receiving revelation, which are only for the prophets ('a).

The Prophet's Positions

It is proved in kalam[10] books that Prophet of Islam (s) had several positions during his lifetime:

---

[8] Surah Al- Qasas (28): 41.

[9] Sharhul Mawaqif, Vol 8, p. 344.

[10] Speculative theology.

1. Having relation with the invisible world and getting revelation from the Almighty Allah,

2. Maintaining religious knowledge, teachings, commandments, and laws descended as revelation,

3. Propagating this heavenly collection among the people, answering their questions, and fighting superstition,

4. Enforcing political, social, judiciary, economic, legal, and punitive Islamic commandments, defending Islam and the Muslims, and establishing Islamic government.

Prophet Muhammad (s) was always away from mistakes and forgetfulness in fulfilling these duties. He was also infallible and away from committing sins and crimes. If a prophet is not infallible, religious commandments and rules are not guaranteed and Divine Mercy is not accomplished.

This is, in fact, the Shiah viewpoint, who believe that just as human being needs Divine knowledge, teachings, and rules revealed to prophets ('a) for reaching material and spiritual perfection, he needs to have an infallible leader who undertakes the Prophet's ('a) responsibilities and follow his goals in the absence of the Prophet (s) throughout history. Otherwise, the prophets' (s) mission in guiding human beings will remain incomplete. Human need for religious sciences and teachings is not limited to the Prophet's (s) age; humans need this Divine Source of knowledge in all ages. The short time of Prophet Muhammad's (s) prophetic mission did not secure this continual need; especially because of termination of prophetic missions ever.

The Shiah Muslims know the Imam as a brilliant complete human, who succeeds the Prophet of Islam (s) and undertakes all his duties, except receiving revelation.

The Duties of the Imam

The characteristics and duties of the Imam are as follows.

1. He knows all sciences, teachings, commandment, and rules of the religion, not from revelation, but through the Prophet's (s) training and other sources that will be mentioned later.

2. He tries to propagate Islamic teachings and commandments and fight religious deviations.

3. He enforces political, social, judiciary, legal, punitive, and economic rules of Islam; that is he continues the Prophet's (s) Islamic government based on Islamic criteria.

4. The Imam, like the Prophet (s), is completely away from mistakes, forgetfulness, and intentional wrongdoing. He is, in fact, infallible; otherwise, Allah's purpose of guiding humans and introducing the true path toward perfection would remain incomplete and His Mercy would not be accomplished.

The Shiah argue for human need to the Imam, his knowledge and infallibility, and the necessity of his appointment by the Almighty Allah based on the famous Mercy (lutf) principle, considering the existence and appointment of the Imam as a sign of Allah's Mercy.

The late Allamah Hilli writes, "The existence of Imam is because of Allah's Mercy and appointing the Imam is obligatory upon the Exalted Allah, so that His purpose is accomplished![11]"

The Imamiyyah (Shiah) Muslims know the Imam a noble person, who is the best one in his age in regard to belief, commitment to ethical virtues, true knowledge of Islamic commandments and rules, and devoutness, after the Messenger of Allah (s). He is infallible and away from mistakes, forgetfulness, wrongdoing, and sins. Only such a person can be the Prophet's (s) successor and the people's leader.

The Sunni Muslims, however, do not necessitate these conditions for the successor of Prophet Muhammad (s). They even do not nullify

---

[11] Sharhi Tajrid, p. 284.

the probability of mistakes or wrongdoing for him. They think that qualification for ruling and managing worldly issues suffices for the Imam. The Sunni Muslims consider obeying the Imam obligatory for the people and opposing him forbidden.

The Imam as Mentioned in Traditions

There are many traditions, which define the Imam and Imamate, one of which we mention here. The eighth infallible Imam of the Shiah, Imam Riza ('a) stated,

Imamate is the position of the prophets (s) and the heritage of their successors. Imamate is caliphate of Allah and His Messenger and the position of Amiral Mu'minin, Imam Ali ('a), (Imam) Hassan ('a), and (Imam) Hossein ('a). Imamate is governing Muslims' religion and system, worldly prosperity and honor. Imamate is the basis of blossoming tree of Islam and its young branches. The Imam manages well the issues related to salat (regular prayers), sawm (fasting), zakat (statutory Islamic levy), hajj (pilgrimage of the ka'bah), jihad, developing government properties, sadaqat (alms), execution of commandments and hudud (Islamic punishment defined for specific sins), and guarding the boundaries.

The Imam is Allah's trusted servant among the people, His hujjat (sign) for the servants, His caliph in lands, inviter to Allah's religion, and protector of Allah's sanctuary. The Imam is infallible and away from sins and vices. He is abound with knowledge and patience, the pillar of religion, honor of Muslims, and the cause of anger and perish of the infidel and the heterodox. The Imam is a unique personality in his own age; no one can replace him and no scholar reaches his scientific stance. The Imam's virtues and goodness are not obtainable; rather he has reached such a position by Allah's Mercy.[12]

---

[12] Usul Kafi, Vol 1, p. 200.

Characteristics of the Imam

According to the tradition of Imam Riza ('a), the Imam is a noble personality with the following characteristics:

1. He is completely away from committing sins; he is infallible.
2. He has unobtainable sciences, which are granted to him by the Exalted Allah.
3. He is patient in dealing with the people and fulfilling his duties.
4. His position is the position of the prophets (s).
5. He is Allah' caliph and the successor of the Messenger of Allah.
6. His government organizes Muslims' affairs and gives them honor and prosperity.
7. Islamic rules and commandments are enforced in his government; salat, sawm, zakat, hajj, and jihad. Religious hudud are executed and Islamic country's boundaries are protected.
8. The Imamate is steady tree of Islam, whose branches are always spreading in the world.
9. The Imam is Allah's trustee and His hujjat for the servants. He invites the people toward Allah and defends Allah's commandments.
10. The Imam is a unique person in his own age; no one is like him, nor can anyone reach his position.
11. The Imam honors Muslims, but angers and perishes the infidel and the heterodox.

The Necessity of Obeying the Imam

The Holy Quran has placed obeying the Imam in the same rank as obeying the Almighty Allah and His Messenger (s);

> *"O ye who believe! Obey God, and obey the Messenger, and those charged with authority among you. If ye differ in anything among yourselves, refer it to God and His Messenger, if ye do believe in God and the Last Day: That*

is best, and most suitable for final determination.[13] "

In this verse, obeying three ones is considered obligatory for the believers:

1. The Almighty Allah has created humans and all the blessings for them, so appreciating the Creator is a logical issue.

One of the Divine blessings is sending the prophets ('a) along with Divine guidelines. Allah's Mercy necessitates that He regulate guidelines and plans for humans' worldly and spiritual perfection and send them by His messengers, so that the people are guided to the true path and warned against evilness and wrongdoing. In other words, following the Divine commandments and obeying the prophets (s) are to the benefit of the servants, hence logically obligatory.

2. The Prophet of Islam (s) is the second one whose obeying is considered obligatory in the mentioned Quranic verse. Prophet Muhammad (s) received messages from Allah through revelation and declared them to the people. Moreover, the Almighty Allah had allowed him to issue commandments in two cases. First he was allowed to issue commandments in various jurisprudential fields based on heavenly revelations and propose them to the believers. Second, since he was the Muslims' leader and managed their social and political issues, he was permitted to make rules based on the expediency of the Islamic Ummah and in framework of general Islamic commandments and execute them. These rules are literally called 'governmental commandments'.

Based on the mentioned Quranic verse, obeying the Prophet (s) is obligatory in this case too. This verse is also a proof for Prophet Muhammad's (s) infallibility, or else obeying him absolutely was unjustified.

---

[13] Surah Al-Nisa' (4): 59.

3. The Ulul Amr (those charged with authority). Although ulul amr apparently includes all the leaders and rulers, it should only mean the infallible rulers, because obeying them is considered absolutely obligatory. As mentioned before, obeying the fallible is religiously and logically baseless. As a result, ulul amr –as mentioned in the Quranic verse under discussion- means the Prophet's (s) successors or the infallible Imams ('a), who are responsible for ruling the Islamic ummah after the Messenger of Allah (s) and manage the Islamic country. Some traditions interpret ulul amr as the infallible from the Prophet's (s) Household.

Hussayn Ibn Abil 'Ala' says, "I asked Imam Sadiq ('a), 'Is obeying the successors of Messenger of Allah (s) obligatory?' Imam Sadiq ('a) answered, 'Yes. They are the people about whom the Exalted Allah said,

'Obey Allah and obey the Apostle'

And He stated,

'(Your (real) friends are (no less than) God, His Apostle, and the (fellowship of) believers,- those who establish regular prayers and regular charity, and they bow down humbly (in worship).[14])"[15]

Therefore, the infallible Imams ('a) were the possessors of the Prophet's (s) sciences and attempted in circulating them. Moreover, Prophet

---

[14] Surah Al-Ma'idah (5): 55.

[15] Usul Kafi, Vol 1, p. 189.

Muhammad (s) had allowed them to make necessary laws in case there was no explicit text in Holy Quran, based on Muslims' expediency and time and place requirements and execute these so called 'governmental laws'.

The Imam's Knowledge from a Logical Point of View

The main goal of Prophet Muhammad's (s) mission was training and refining humans. In addition to reciting and teaching the Holy Quran, the Messenger of Allah (s) interpreted Quranic verses and explained vague points when necessary. He mentioned transformer and obsolete, general and specific, absolute and conditional verses. He presented religious commandments and rules that he obtained from revelation to the people. He spread true beliefs and fought superstition and wrong ideas. He invited the people to moral virtues and prohibited from vices. He had necessary knowledge about all these teachings and sciences from revelation or logic; hence he could accomplish these duties well, directing his followers to the right path.

The Imam, who is the successor to the Prophet (s) and continues his path, should possess all these sciences to be able to fulfill his responsibilities; otherwise there will be no valid guarantee for continuation of religion. In other words, the Imam should have all the sciences of the Prophet (s), except that the Prophet gets them directly via the Divine revelation but the Imam gets them from the Prophet (s).

The Imam's Knowledge in Traditions

In various traditions, knowing religious sciences, teachings, and commandments is considered a necessary condition of the Imam. Imam Riza ('a) has stated, "In fact, the Almighty Allah grants success to the prophets and Imams and benefits them from His treasure of sciences and maxims like no one else. Therefore, their knowledge is superior to that of the people in their own age. The Holy Quran states,

"Is then He Who gives guidance to truth more worthy to be followed, or he who finds not guidance (himself) unless he is guided? What then is the matter with you? How judge ye?"[16]

And also,

He to whom wisdom is granted receiveth indeed a benefit overflowing; but none will grasp the Message but men of understanding.[17]

When the Almighty Allah selects one of His servants for managing other servants, He grants him patience, fills his heart with knowledge, and continuously reveals His sciences to him. Therefore he is not disabled from answering questions and does not become bewildered in finding the truth."[18]

Imam Ali ('a) stated, "O people! The most deserving person for Imamate is the most powerful one among you in managing the issues and the most learned one in Divine commandments. If someone was going to plot sedition after taking oath of allegiance, he is asked to leave it and if he did not accept, he is fought with.[19]"

Amiral Mu'minin, Imam Ali ('a), also stated, "The Imam is aware of the lawful and the unlawful, the obligatory and recommended deeds and Allah's commandments. He is needless to the people and everyone needs him."[20]

He has also stated, "Learn the true path to salvation from those who know this path (the Ahlul-Bayt). They are revivers of knowledge and

---

[16] Surah Al-Yunus (10): 35.

[17] Surah Al-Baqarah (2): 269.

[18] Usul Kafi, Vol 1, p. 202.

[19] Nahjul Balaghah, Sermon 173.

[20] Biharul Anwar, Vol 68, p. 389.

removers of ignorance. Their commandments reveal their knowledge to you. Their silence shows their speech style. Their appearance is the sign of their inside. They never oppose the religion and have no controversy over it."[21]

The first infallible Imam of the Shi'ah also described the Prophet's (s) Ahlul-Bayt this way, "They pondered in the religion as they should, learned it, and used it, not merely hear it and transfer to others. The narrators of knowledge are numerous, but safe guarders of it are little."[22]

Conclusion of Prophethod and Accomplishment of Religion

As the Holy Quran explicitly states, the Prophet of Islam is the last prophet and there will be no prophets after him.

> *"Muhammad is not the father of any of your men, but (he is) the Apostle of God, and the Seal of the Prophets: and God has full knowledge of all things."*[23]

The end of prophet hood is a fundamental idea in Islam and the Islamic Ummah has consensus over it. Therefore, Islam is a religion forever and suffices human need for a religion in all times and all places. Moreover, since Prophet Muhammad (s) is the last prophet, revelation has ended after him. This is explicitly stated in Nahjul Balaghah of Imam Ali ('a) and some traditions.

Amiral Mu'minin ('a) stated, "The Exalted Allah sent Prophet Muhammad (s) at a time when there were no prophets and the people were in controversy. Therefore, He sent the Prophet (s) after other

---

[21] Nahjul Balaghah, Sermon 147.

[22] Ibid, Sermon 239

[23] Surah Al-Ahzab (33): 40.

prophets and the revelation ended after him." [24]

As a result, at the time of Prophet Muhammad's (s) demise all religious commandments and rules should have been presented to the people and the religion been completed, as is explicitly stated in the Holy Quran.

The Holy Quran says,

> "*This day have I perfected your religion for you, completed My favor upon you, and have chosen for you Islam as your religion.*"[25]

There is controversy among Quran interpreters about the important day mentioned in this verse, in which Islam is completed and stabilized and the infidels got disappointed of nullifying it. After precise detailed discussions and reviewing some traditions, the late Allamiyi Tabataba'i concludes that the important day mentioned in the Quranic verse is eighteenth of Zil Hajjah (the last lunar month) and during Prophet Muhammad's Hajjatul Wida' (the last hajj pilgrimage)[26]. As mentioned in traditions and history books, the Messenger of Allah (s), who was returning from his last hajj pilgrimage, gathered the pilgrims in Ghadir land on this day. After performing a sermon, he formally appointed Ali Ibn Abi Talib ('a) to the Imamate position and during a long tradition he said, "Anyone whose Imam is I, so now Ali ('a) is his Imam. O Lord! Love those who love him and dislike those who dislike him!"

The Messenger of Allah (s) did two things in that historical day. First, he introduced the Holy Quran and his Household (the Ahlul-Bayt)

---

[24] Nahjul Balaghah, Sermon 133.

[25] Surah Al-Ma'idah (5): 3.

[26] Al-Mizan Exegesis, Vol 5,s pp. 214-277.

as two valid scientific sources, saying, "Anyone who follows these two sources will not go astray." Second, he introduced Imam Ali ('a) as his first successor and Imam from the Ahlul-Bayt ('a). Since the Prophet of Islam (s) had chosen Ali ('a) as the guardian of prophet hood sciences during his prophecy and attempted well in training him, Islam was completed by appointing him as the Imam of the ummah; a trustworthy guardian and executer of religious sciences. In such conditions, the mentioned verse was revealed to the Messenger of Allah (s).

How the 'completion of religion' by the Almighty Allah is justified, except that the Prophet (s) taught all religious commandments and rules part by part or wholly to Imam Ali ('a) during his lifetime and to other Imams ('a) via Imam Ali ('a). It should also be remembered that the rules and commandments mentioned in the Holy Quran or left from Prophet Muhammad (s) do not satisfy the needs of people in that age and later eras. That is why the Sunni jurisprudents were forced to use qiyas (analogy), istihsan (using Imams' speech), or other principles for deducting religious commandments.

The Range of Imam's Knowledge

The range of Imam's knowledge is similar to that of prophet hood knowledge for fulfilling the prophet hood mission and conveying Allah' guidance to human beings. It is understood from the Mercy Theorem that since human is not able to provide his own physical and spiritual salvation he needs divine guidance sent by the prophets (s). Therefore, the prophet receives from Allah everything humans need for seeking the path toward Allah and presents them to humans. The Imam, as the prophet's (s) successor, continues the prophet's (s) mission, hence he should know the prophet's sciences. The necessary prophet hood and Imamate sciences can be divided to six parts, as follows:

First, worshipping issues have the greatest role in guaranteeing heavenly salvation. These are, in fact, religious obligatory and recommended deeds, such as prayer, fasting, hajj, supplication, almsgiving, jihad, etc. The Prophet (s) and the Imams ('a) are completely aware of the quality, prelude, conditions, and other related issues of performing these worshipping duties and they guide the people in this regard.

Second, unlawful worshipping deeds are considered obstacles to seeking the path to salvation. Examples of such deeds are usury, bribery, drinking wine, oppression, usurp, dishonesty in transactions, adultery, etc. The Prophet (s) and Imams ('a) are quite aware of these vices and forbid people from committing them.

Third, belief principles –that are theology and Resurrection– are the basis of the Prophet's (s) and Imams' ('a) mission. Although attention to Allah and Resurrection is set in human temperament and can be discovered by thinking, they are often neglected and need to be revitalized and completed in human nature by the Prophet (s) and the Imams ('a). This way Allah's hujjah (reasoning) is completed for the servants. To this end, the first human on the earth was a prophet. Therefore, the prophet and the Imam should have a firm belief in belief principles and know the related issues to be able to guide the people to it too.

Fourth, attending to ethics as well as avoiding the vices have a major role in human worldly and heavenly salvation. Though, understanding goodness of morality and obscenity of evilness is set in human temperament, he needs a guide in recognizing good and evil and having a desirable behavior, because of his powerful carnal instincts. That is why refinement of the soul has been considered a major purpose of the prophets. The prophet and the Imam should be familiar with virtues and vices. They should be adorned with virtues and away from vices to lead the people in this way by their knowledge and behavior.

Fifth, political and social issues or government-related rules and commandments, such as judgment, retaliation (qisas), hudud, diyat (blood money), ta'zirat (Islamic punishment limits), jihad, defense, khumus (Islamic one-fifth tax), zakat (Islamic statutory levy), war booties, state property, etc. One of the jobs of Prophet Muhammad (s) was governing the Islamic society. This needed certain rules, some of which were descended by revelation and he was allowed by the Exalted Allah to deduct some others and then execute them based on expediency of Islamic system. This type of rules called governmental rules was obligatory for Muslims. After the Prophet's (s) demise, this duty was put to his successor, who was permitted to deduct and execute necessary rules according to the interests of Islamic ummah. Therefore, the Imam should know all the social and political rules.

Sixth, customary issues that are related to different transactions, heritage, will, matrimony, divorce, etc. Although such issues are customary and have existed in all ages including the Prophet's (s) era, they are considered Islamic commandments because they have been rejected, validated, modified, or completed by the Messenger of Allah (s). As a result, the Imam should know the related issues. Certainly the Imam can modify such issues too, considering the interests of Islamic ummah and time and place necessities.

The Prophet's (s) Traditions as Source of Imams' Knowledge

The main source of infallible Imams' sciences is the traditions presented by Messenger of Allah (s) to Imam Ali ('a) and Imam Ali ('a) recorded. He then presented these to his successor, Imam Hassan ('a), and later to other infallible Imams ('a) in the same way.

Here is how this tradition collection was compiled: Islamic rules and commandments were revealed to Prophet Muhammad (s) during his 23-year mission in two ways; first, in the form of the Holy Quran, whose illuminating verses were descended to Prophet's (s) heart and second, as traditions, whose phrases were revealed to his heart in various instances. The Messenger of Allah (s) recited the very Quranic verses to the Muslims and especially to Imam Ali ('a). He recommended Imam Ali ('a) –who was able to read and write– record and maintain Quranic verses for future Muslims. There were, of course, other people, who wrote all Quranic verses or memorized them. Still there were some others who wrote or memorized only some of the verses.

The traditions were, however, dealt with differently. Though Prophet Muhammad (s) conveyed the rules and commandments he received through revelation for his companions, they were not committed to write or memorize the exact words of the Prophet (s) and transmit them to others. They either quoted from the Prophet's (s) traditions approximately or ignored them and forgot them later. Of course there were people among the companions who were committed to writing or memorizing the traditions of the Prophet (s), but unfortunately they were scarce. Islamic general issues and jurisprudential minor points were very enormous. They should have been kept for Muslims outside Medina –Prophet Muhammad' city– and later generations. Moreover, many jurisprudential issues were not related to simple life of the people in that age to be asked from Prophet Muhammad (s) and answered by him. That is while Islam is the everlasting religion and should respond to human needs in all ages and places.

The Messenger of Allah (s) who was aware of present and future conditions of Islamic ummah should have found a solution for this scientific problem; maintaining all religious rules, commandments, teachings, and sciences in a safe position, which was immune from mistakes and forgetfulness. This position was not but the luminous heart of Imam Ali ('a). Prophet Muhammad (s) attended to this important duty –by Allah's revelation and support– from the outset of his mission to his demise. He transmitted whatever he received from revelation to Imam Ali ('a). Imam Ali ('a) in turn attempted at exact recording and maintaining the information and was supported by the Almighty Allah in this major duty.

Imam Ali ('a) stated, "Once, the Messenger of Allah (s) embraced me and said, 'The Exalted Allah has ordered not to distance you from myself so that you hear my words and remember them.' Then this Quranic verse was revealed,

> *"...And that ears (that should hear the tale and) retain its memory should bear its (lessons) in remembrance.*[27] "[28]

Ibn Abbas has quoted from the Prophet (s), "When the holy verse '**And that ears retain its memory should bear its in remembrance**' was revealed, I asked my Lord to set that retaining ear Ali's ear." Ibn Abbas then says, "Therefore, Ali ('a) recorded and kept what he had heard from Allah's Messenger and never forgot it."[29]

> *Imam Ali ('a) says, "I visited Messenger of Allah (s) everyday. We were alone for an hour or so. I followed him everywhere he went. The Prophet's (s) companions know that he did not behave so with others. Sometimes he came to my house and sometimes I went to him. We then went to a solitude place. Prophet Muhammad (s) even sent his wives out. When he came to my house, however, Hadrat Fatimah (s) and my children were*

---

[27] Surah Al-Haqqah (69): 12.
[28] Biharul Anwar, Vol 35, p. 327; Hilyatul Awliya', Vol 1, p. 108; Manaqib Kharazmi, p. 199.
[29] Manaqib Kharazmi, p. 99

*present. I asked him questions and he answered. When my questions finished, he began speaking. He recited all newly-revealed Quranic verses for me and I wrote them down. He explained exegesis, transformer, outdated, strong, similar, specific, and general of the verses. He had asked Allah to grant me ability to understand and memorize them; therefore, I did not forget any Quranic verse or scientific information I had written down. Prophet Muhammad (s) taught me the whole knowledge Allah had taught him, including halal and haram, recommended and prohibited, past and future information, all the heavenly Books of past prophets (s), and any worship and wrongdoing. I memorized them all and forgot not even a letter of them. The Messenger of Allah (s) put his hand on my chest and prayed that the Almighty Allah replete my heart with knowledge, understanding, wisdom, and light. Then I told him, 'O Messenger of Allah! I did not forget anything from the time you prayed for me. Do you fear that I forget something?' He said, '**No, I do not fear that you may be forgetful or ignorant.**"*[30]

Imam Ali ('a) was asked, "Why is it that you have quoted more traditions from the Messenger of Allah (s) than other companions?" He answered, "Because when I asked him questions he answered and when I became silent he began speaking."[31]

Imam Ali ('a) also said, "By Allah that no verse is revealed except that I know where and about which subject or person it is revealed. My Lord has granted me conscious mind and fluent speech."[32]

---

[30] Kafi, Vol 1, p. 64.

[31] At Tabaqatul Kubra, Vol 3, p. 338.

[32] Ibid, p. 33.

The Prophet Confirms Ali's Scientific Mastery

Imam Ali ('a) could acquire all Islamic sciences, teachings, rules, and commandments in Prophet Muhammad's (s) 23-year mission due to his extraordinary talent, Allah's support, and the Prophet's especial attention to him. This way he became the treasurer of prophet hood sciences, as confirmed by the Prophet (s) in various occasions too. The Prophet (s) stated, "O Abal Hassan[33]! You have drunk out of science beverage and you have drunk it much."[34]

The Messenger of Allah (s) also stated, "I am the house of wisdom and Ali is its door."[35]

Anas Ibn Malik has quoted from the Prophet, who told Imam Ali ('a), "You will state the truth whenever the ummah has controversy over something after me."[36]

Salman Farsi has quoted from Prophet Muhammad (s), "Ali Ibn Abi Talib is the most learned one in my ummah."[37]

Inscription Order

Although Imam Ali ('a) was away from mistakes and forgetfulness in keeping traditions, Prophet of Islam (s) ordered him to write down the sciences the Prophet (s) taught him in a book to be left for next Imams ('a).

Amiral Mu'minin ('a) has quoted, "The Prophet (s) told me, 'Write down what I tell you.' I said, 'O Messenger of Allah! Do you fear that I may forget?' He said, 'I am not afraid of your forgetfulness, because I have asked the Almighty Allah to set you as guardian of sciences. But

---

[33] Imam Ali's (a.s) nickname
[34] Dhakha'irul 'Uqba, p. 78.
[35] Yanabi'ul Mawaddah, p. 82.
[36] Mustadrak Hakim Niyshaburi, Vol 3, p. 122.
[37] Ibid, p. 80.

write them down for the Imams from your progeny.'"[38]

Transmission of Science Books to Other Imams

By Imam Ali's ('a) constant attempt and Prophet Muhammad's (s) supervision, prophet hood sciences and religious rules and commandments were recorded in some books, inherited to each of the infallible Imams ('a) and used by them. The infallible Imams ('a) sometimes made reference to these books in their speeches, calling the books 'Ali's book', 'sahifah', or 'jami'ah'.

Various traditions include this fact, some of which are pointed out here:

Abu Maryam has quoted from Imam Baqir ('a), "The jami'ah book is with us (the Prophet's Ahlul-Bayt). It is a script as long as seventy dhara'[39]; everything is recorded in it even the diyah (compensation) of a scrape on the skin. This book is dictated by Messenger of Allah (s) and hand written by Imam Ali ('a). Another book is owned by us called jafr that is written on a piece of tanned skin. Past, present, and future sciences until the Hereafter are recorded in it."[40]

Abdullah Ibn Sanan has narrated that Imam Sadiq ('a) said, "There is a piece of skin of seventy dhira' with us, dictated by Prophet Muhammad (s) and in Imam Ali's ('a) handwriting. Whatever the people need exists in it, even the compensation for a scrape on someone's skin."[41]

Mu'alli Ibn Khanis has narrated from Imam Sadiq ('a) who stated, "The books were with Imam Ali ('a). When he traveled to Iraq, he entrusted them to Ummi Salamah. After his demise, they were given to Imam Hassan ('a). After Imam Hassan ('a), they were given to Imam

---

[38] Mustadrak Hakim Niyshaburi, Vol 3, p.22.

[39] Plural of dhar', a measure of length equal to 104 centimeters.

[40] Jami' Ahadith Al-Shi'ah, Vol 1, p. 185.

[41] Jami' Ahadith Al-Shi'ah, Vol 1, p. 186.

Hussayn ('a) and after his martyrdom to Ali Ibn Al-Hussayn ('a), the fourth infallible Imam. After his demise, they were with my father."[42]

Jabir Ibn Hayyan says that Imam Muhammad Baqir ('a) told him, "O Jabir! By Allah that if we narrated traditions with our own opinion, we were certainly perished. Rather, we state traditions from what we have inherited from Messenger of Allah (s). Just as the people save gold and silver, our fathers have saved traditions to leave them for us."[43]

Ibn Hayyan considers Ja'far Ibn Muhammad, Imam Sadiq ('a), as a trustworthy narrator, saying, "He is among the nobles of Ahlul-Bayt regarding jurisprudence, knowledge, and virtues; his traditions are reliable. I examined the traditions I narrated from him and found all of them true. I found nothing opposing the reliable traditions in them." [44]

Conclusion

Some points can be understood from mentioned traditions and many other similar ones:

1. Islam was completed during Prophet Muhammad's ('a) lifetime and all required sciences, teachings, and rules were received through revelation.

2. The Messenger of Allah (s) attempted in publicizing and imparting the commandments in two ways; first, imparting them to the people and recommending they maintain and follow the commandments and second, saving all of the commandments in a secure place completely immune to forgetfulness and mistakes, that is Imam Ali's ('a) luminous heart.

---

[42] Ibid, p. 195.

[43] Ibid, p. 195.

[44] Jami' Ahadith Al-Shi'ah, Vol 2, p. 104.

3. Prophet Muhammad (s) recommended Imam Ali ('a) to record and write the traditions and leave them for the following Imams ('a).

4. Therefore, some books were compiled by Imam Ali ('a), who used them after Prophet Muhammad's (s) demise. After Imam Ali's martyrdom the books were given to Imam Hassan ('a) and to other infallible Imams ('a) successively.

Reference to the Books

The mentioned books were with the infallible Imams ('a) and they attributed their knowledge to them. Each of the Imams ('a) transmitted religious sciences and commandments to his successor in two ways; verbal training and granting of books and permission to narrate from them. Each of the Imams attributed his traditions to the Prophet (s) through his fathers, as is seen in traditions.

Husham Ibn Salim, Hamad Ibn Uthman, and other people have narrated from Imam Sadiq ('a), "My tradition is the tradition of my father and his tradition is the tradition of my grandfather. The tradition of my grandfather is the tradition of Imam Hussayn ('a) and his tradition is the tradition of Imam Hassan ('a), whose tradition is the tradition of Amiral Mu'minin ('a). The tradition of Amiral Mu'minin ('a) is the tradition of Messenger of Allah (s) and his tradition is the speech of the Exalted Allah." [45]

Jabir says, "I told Imam Baqir ('a), 'When you recite a tradition for me, please mention its document.' Imam Baqir ('a) said, 'My father has narrated traditions from my grandfather and he from Gabriel and he from the Almighty Allah. Every tradition I recite for you has the same document. O Jabir! If you acquire a tradition from a truthful narrator, it will be better than the whole world for you.'" [46]

---

[45] Kafi, Vol 1, p. 53.

[46] Jami' Ahadith Al-Shi'ah, Vol 1, p. 181.

Hafs says, "I told Imam Sadiq ('a), 'I have heard a tradition, which I am not sure is from you or your father.' He stated, 'What you hear from me you can narrate from my father and the Messenger of Allah (s).'"[47]

With regard to above-mentioned discussion it can be said that a major source of knowledge of infallible Imams ('a) is the traditions compiled from Prophet Muhammad's speech by Imam Ali ('a), which is transmitted to infallible Imams ('a). As a result, although the Imams ('a) were deprived of direct revelation, they benefited from revelation sciences indirectly. Each of the Imams ('a) narrated traditions with the most reliable documents –all whose narrators were infallible– from direct revelation. What an honor!

The Contents of the Books

Unfortunately, the content of the books is not completely known to us. We do not know if they only included jurisprudential issues and commandments or other religion-related issues such as ethics and mental teachings, or they contained all sciences. We do not know if all jurisprudential trivial points were recorded in detail in those books or they only contained principles of jurisprudence, from which the infallible Imams ('a) deducted the minor points. Some traditions imply that all required issues of the Muslims existed in the books.

Muhammad Ibn Muslim says, "I asked Imam Sadiq ('a), 'Does your scientific heritage of the Prophet (s) include main principles or the exegesis of all the topics people need, such as divorce and legacy as well?' Imam Sadiq ('a) replied, 'Imam Ali ('a) has written all scientific issues, even divorce and legacy in that book. If our Imamate be accepted, we have a tradition in every field, which will be executed.'"[48]

---

[47] Ibid, p. 181

[48] Jami' Ahadith Al-Shi'ah, Vol 1, P. 192.

Traditions similar to above-mentioned ones reveal that everything, even the compensation ('arsh) for a scrape on body skin is recorded in those books.

Nevertheless, it is improbable that the mentioned books also include all minor issues in all jurisprudential topics. Everyone familiar with extensive Islamic jurisprudence confirms that including all related issues in a single book –even if it is seventy dhara'– is impossible, especially if it contains other religion-related sciences too. In sum, the exact content of the books is not known.

The Holy Quran

The second source of infallible Imams' sciences is the Holy Quran. This heavenly book is the main most valid source of Islamic sciences, teachings, commandments, and rules. The reliability of Holy Quran is certain, because successive narrations and Muslims' consensus throughout history prove that the present text of Quran has revealed from Almighty Allah to Prophet Muhammad's (s) luminous heart. He has recited it –with its rich content– and Imam Ali ('a) and other revelation writers have recorded it and transmitted to Muslims in that era and finally to us. The Holy Quran has a very rich content to the extent that whatever human being needs for his salvation in this world and the Hereafter –and has necessitated sending of the prophets (s) for the Generous Al-wise– exists in it. The sciences and teachings mentioning which have been necessary because of Allah's Mercy as pointed out in Holy Quran are: major principles about the world Creator, theology and the Almighty Allah's Attributes, some of His blessings, the after-death life, Resurrection, reckoning human deeds in the Hereafter, the Paradise and rewards of good deeds, the Hell and punishment of evil deeds, Prophet Muhammad (s) and other prophets (s) and their role in guiding mankind throughout history, good conduct and its result in human salvation, bad behavior and its harm, duties of the servants before the Creator, and the methods of worshipping and thanking Him. Human should know these issues, ignoring which brings about irreparable harms. Therefore, common sense necessitates that the All-Merciful never leaves human without guiding him; rather He sends prophets (s) equipped with sciences to guide people to the true way.

The Prophet of Islam (s) was appointed to prophet hood for the same reason and his mission plan is mentioned in the Holy Quran. Prophet Muhammad (s) is the last messenger and there will be no prophet with a heavenly book after him. Since human mind is always progressing, reaching new findings everyday and evolving his life, sciences and teachings of the Holy Quran should be so comprehensive that they fulfill religious requirements of all times, places, and conditions. The Holy Quran introduces itself this way,

> "And We have sent down to thee the Book explaining all things, a Guide, a Mercy, and Glad Tidings to Muslims." [49]

In other words, all sciences and teachings that are related to religion and human beings need are present in the Quran.

It should be borne in mind, however, that though the Holy Quran is an explanatory guiding book from which every human can benefit as much as his understanding, it has a very deep inside, which is not captured by everyone. Different people have different understandings from the Quran internal meanings, which have led to appearance of Quranic exegesis (tafsir). The Quranic verses are not alike; there are indisputable and analogous verses, cancelling and cancelled verses, general and specific verses, and absolute and conditional verses.

---

[49] Surah Al-Nahl (16): 89.

The exegetists of Holy Quran can compare the verses, ponder, use related sciences, and refer understanding of analogous verses to the indisputable ones, thus finding the truth of verses. An expert exegetist is someone who is completely familiar with Arabic language, literature, and minute linguistic points, speculative theology (ilmul kalam), philosophy, and other related sciences, as well as all Quranic verses and traditions of Prophet Muhammad (s). However, not all exegetists have equal knowledge in these fields. Everyone can benefit from deep meanings of this heavenly book to the extent of his innate genius and curiosity.

The honorable Prophet of Islam (s) was a brilliant Quran exegetist. He was quite aware of indisputable vs. analogous, cancelling vs. cancelled, general vs. specific verses, and absolute vs. conditional verses, revelation reason of verses, and minute literary points of Quranic verses. Moreover, he was familiar with interpretation of verses and was considered a pioneer in Quranic sciences. His understanding of Quranic themes was chiefly different from other exegetists; ordinary exegetists get Quranic teachings by their apparent or inner senses and are not aware of objective realities, while Prophet Muhammad (s) –the first addressee of Holy Quran– observed Quranic realities through his inner sense in their own places, which helped have mental understanding of them too. This unseen means of understanding was always a powerful aid for him. The secret of his infallibility is also rooted in this important privilege.

As a result, Prophet Muhammad's (s) understanding of theology, theism, or Allah's attributes is different from and much deeper than our understanding of these themes, because his knowledge is intuitive while ours is acquirable. When the honorable Messenger of Allah (s) gave news of the after-death life, Resurrection, the Paradise, and the Hell, he had already witnessed their true setting; his mental understanding resulted from objective realities.

The Prophet's (s) understanding of enjoining and forbidding, obligations and prohibitions, religious rules and commandments was different from our understanding. During revelation, Prophet Muhammad (s) saw true expediency or imperfection of religious rules and their sources and roots –which show the true path to humanity and guarantee salvation in this world and the Hereafter– through his insight. Moreover, he witnessed the goodness of good deeds and evilness of wrongdoing directly.

Considering this background about Prophet Muhammad's (s) sciences, we can conclude that some commandments –which are not mentioned as revelation– have been general revelation. Or they have been issued by the Prophet (s); he was religiously allowed to issue verdicts because of his known purified conduct.

Transmission of Quranic Sciences to the Infallible Imams

The honorable Messenger of Islam (s) attempted to teach Quranic sciences and teachings as well as exegesis of the verses to Imam Ali ('a) to be left for later Muslims. Imam Ali ('a) recorded this information exactly and transmitted to other Imams ('a). Therefore, all infallible Imams ('a) can be considered knower of Quranic exegesis and truth and pioneers in Quranic sciences, as was Prophet Muhammad (s). The difference, however, was that the Prophet (s) received the revelation –and Quranic sciences– directly, while the Imams ('a) acquired the sciences through Prophet Muhammad's (s) guidance and Allah's especial attention –which is a key necessity for being an Imam.

In sum, the Holy Quran is a major source of infallible Imams' sciences and the Imams ('a) are knower of Quranic sciences and exegesis, as is mentioned in many traditions.

Abus Sabah says, "By Allah that Imam Baqir ('a) stated, 'The Almighty Allah taught Quranic sciences and exegesis to His Prophet (s). The Prophet (s) taught them to Ali ('a). By Allah that Ali ('a) taught them to us.'"⁵⁰

Imam Sadiq ('a) said, "I know Allah's Book by heart completely. The news of heaven and the earth from the past to the future are in it. The Almighty Allah stated, 'Everything is mentioned in the Quran.'"⁵¹

Barid Ibn Mu'awiyyah has narrated Imam Sadiq ('a) or Imam Baqir ('a) who said about the Quranic verse,

> *"No one knows its hidden meanings except God and those who are firmly grounded in knowledge."*⁵²,

"The Messenger of Allah (s) was the best pioneer in science. The Almighty Allah taught him whatever He had revealed to other prophets (s) in addition to their exegesis, not leaving anything untold. The Prophet's (s) successors know all these too. Those who are now aware of Quranic exegesis say that they believe in what Allah has revealed when they hear it from a scholar (Prophet's successor). The Holy Quran has absolute and conditional, cancelling and cancelled, and specific and general verses. Pioneers in science know them all." ⁵³

Abdur Rahman Ibn Kathir has quoted from Imam Sadiq ('a), "The pioneers in science are Amiral Mu'minin ('a) and the Imams ('a) after him."⁵⁴

The mentioned traditions and many other similar ones indicate that the infallible Imams ('a) knew Quranic exegesis, the scientific sources, the real advantages and reasons for issuing religious commandments and rules, just like Prophet Muhammad (s). The difference, of course,

---

⁵⁰ Jami' Ahadith Al-Shi'ah, Vol 1, p. 184.

⁵¹ Kafi, Vol 1, p. 229.

⁵² Surah 'ali 'Imran(3) 7: .

⁵³ Kafi, Vol 1, p. 113.

⁵⁴ Usul Kafi, Vol1, p. 213.

was that the Prophet (s) received the revelation directly, while infallible Imams ('a) were deprived of it. Therefore, what was mentioned about the commandments issued by the Prophet (s) is true about the commandments issued by the Imams ('a), which are not seen in Holy Quran and Prophet's (s) tradition. In other words, they are issued by the Imams; they were allowed to issue verdicts because of their known purified conduct. And Allah knows best.

The Infallible Imams ('a) and Mental Sciences

Human being is wise. He uses his wisdom and logical measurement to discover some unknown things from his definite general data. Human, for instance, understands the cause-effect relationship and that everything requires a cause. Therefore, when he sees something, he is certain that it has a cause and seeks that cause. This is a privilege for human being, which is idiomatically called theoretical mentality. Such mental reasoning is used in proving belief principles, such as theology, Resurrection, or prophet hood. All humans have the Divine blessing of mentality, but their intellectual levels are very different. The prophets (s) and the infallible Imams ('a) have been the wisest of the people in their own age.

The Messenger of Islam (s) states, "The Almighty Allah did not send a prophet or messenger except when his wisdom was perfect and superior to that of his people." [55]

The honorable Messenger of Allah (s) used his perfect wisdom in understanding belief principles, such as theology, Resurrection, and human need to prophets' guidance sent by the Almighty. In fact, he believed in these facts through his mentality. Therefore, he had certainly believed in Allah even before his appointment and hated disbelief and polytheism. It should be pointed out that mental belief

---

[55] Mizanul Hikmah, Vol 3, p. 2034.

–the belief that is acquired by pondering– is not beyond conception and acquirable knowledge, even if it reaches certainty.

After being appointed to prophet hood, direct relationship with the unseen world, and receiving revelation, however, Prophet Muhammad's (s) mental belief got beyond meaning and reached the level of intuition. In this level, he observed the facts that cannot be understood with conceptual knowledge. Intuitive knowledge and heavenly observations of Prophet Muhammad (s) can be considered as a support for his mental sciences. The belief and heavenly sciences have special effects that do not exist in case of mental sciences. The infallible Imams ('a) –as testified in the history and their traditions– have been the wisest of the people in their own age. Therefore, they perceived sciences related to Creation and the Resurrection by their perfect mentality. They were away from disbelief and infidelity even before being appointed for Imamate. These chosen people did not receive the revelation directly, but they benefited from the Prophet's (s) heavenly sciences indirectly due to Allah's especial blessings and Prophet Muhammad's (s) guidance. As a result, their knowledge about the Creation and the Resurrection was above conceptual science and had reached the level of intuition and certainty. They sometimes talked about Creation- or Resurrection-related facts in a way as if they directly observed them. Some examples of this manner can be studied in tradition, biography, or history books.

Amiral Mu'minin, Imam Ali ('a) stated about knowledge of the infallible Imams ('a), "Knowledge has been perceived by their insight and they have touched certainty. They have easily accepted what is considered difficult by the mollycoddle and are accustomed to what the unwise fear. They relate with the bodies whose souls have ascended to the Heavens. They are Allah's caliphs on the earth and inviters to

His religion. How much I desire meeting them!"[56]

Imam Ali ('a) also stated about the sciences of infallible Imams ('a), "They revitalize knowledge and perish ignorance. Their patience reveals their knowledge and their appearance shows their inside. Their silence is a sign of their strong logic. They do not oppose the truth and have no difference about it. They are pillars of the religion and refuge of the people. They replace the falsehood with the truth, drive falsehood away and abandon it forever. They ponder on and use the religion as it deserves, not merely hearing it and narrating for others. In fact, narrators of science are many, but its guardians are few."[57]

The infallible Imams ('a), just as prophet Muhammad (s), used mental and logical methods in inviting people to the belief principles, as is seen in their traditions and discussions. They talked to everyone as much as his recognition and understanding. Some of their words are so deep and complicated that are only understandable for the scholars. However, they sometimes speak so simply for the ordinary people. These different speech styles can be found in Imam Ali's ('a) Maxims in Nahjul Balaghah as well as various traditions of infallible Imams ('a).

As a result, the wisdom of the infallible can be considered a science source of the Prophet (s) and Imams ('a). Mental and logical reasoning is their propaganda method too. Of course, they were way from fallacy and wrong doing in deploying these tools.

The Role of Mind in Recognizing Ethics

Human being has an innate power that –if used properly– can recognize moral codes and follow them in the interest of the society and perfection of his soul. It knows wrongness too and considers it to

---

[56] Nahjul Balaghah, Maxim 147.

[57] Ibid, Maxim, 239.

the detriment of his life in this world and the Hereafter as well as the society. This precious innate power is called practical wisdom or the conscience. The Holy Quran considers this recognition as an innate sense.

"By the Soul, and the proportion and order given to it; And its enlightenment as to its wrong and its right; Truly he succeeds that purifies it, And he fails that corrupts it!"[58]

This invaluable force exists more or less in all humans and can be used in ordinary conditions, provided inhumane forces have not overcome human wisdom. Unfortunately, some people are so much surrendered to carnal instincts, such as selfishness, lust of position and property, greediness, wrath, hatred, and revenge that they forget their human spirit. Therefore, the light of their pure instinct is darkened and they cannot recognize virtues and vices; they even sometimes consider vices as virtues. That is why human being always needs the guidance of selected infallible individuals to brighten his nature and help him know virtues and vices.

These selected people are the prophets (s) and infallible Imams ('a). Since the infallible Imams ('a) have perfect mentality and are away from faults and wrongdoing, they completely recognized ethical values and their outcomes in this world and the Hereafter. They followed these values and invited others to them too. They also knew ethical vices and their undesirable consequences in this world and the Hereafter. They avoided the vices and forbade others from them too. Therefore, practical wisdom and ethical conscience –in addition to the Holy Quran and Prophet's (s) traditions– can be considered a source of

---

[58] Surah Al-Shams (91): 7-10.

infallible Imams' ('a) ethical knowledge. The thousands of traditions about ethics, which are recorded in tradition books, are rooted in this rich infallible source.

The Prophet (s) and Guardianship Commandments

The commandments issued by Prophet Muhammad (s) were of two types; religious and guardianship. The religious commandments are the ones directly issued from the Exalted Allah and revealed to the Prophet (s). The Prophet (s) was ordered to convey them to the people. These commandments form the religion of Islam and no one except Allah has the right to issue them. Such commandments are either mentioned in Holy Quran or revealed to the Messenger of Allah (s) in different occasions and presented to the people.

The guardianship commandments, however, are the commandments that are not directly issued by the Almighty Allah. Rather Prophet Muhammad (s) –who was the guardian and ruler of Islamic government– was allowed to issue and execute the commandments necessary for managing social affairs of the society, such as defining tax for the expenses of Islamic government, issuing the order of jihad (the holy war) or peace, relations with other Islamic or non-Islamic governments, judicial commandments, the limits of personal or governmental ownership, expropriating or limiting personal ownership in certain cases, and ordaining necessary commandments for various fields of Islamic government. In fact, since the ruling was given to the Prophet (s), wide authority was given to him too.

The Holy Quean states,

"The Prophet is closer to the Believers than their own selves."[59]

---

[59] Surah Al-Ahzab (33): 6.

What was mentioned above was about government-related commandments.

According to some traditions, Prophet Muhammad (s) was permitted to ordain commandments in minor religious issues too and even in case of worships and present them to the people.

Abu Basir says, "I asked Imam Sadiq ('a) about the Quranic verse:

'Obey God, and obey the Messenger, and those charged with authority among you.'

The Imam ('a) said, 'This verse is revealed about Ali Ibn Abi Talib, Imam Hassan ('a), and Imam Hussayn ('a).' I said, 'People wonder why the names of Imam Ali ('a) and the Ahlul-Bayt are not mentioned in the Holy Quran.' Imam Sadiq ('a) replied, 'Tell people that salat (the prayer) is mentioned in the Quran, but not the number of rak'ahs (unites); the Messenger of Allah defined it. Zakat (statutory Islamic levy) is mentioned in the Holy Quran, but its amount –which is one dirham in every forty dirhams– was defined by Prophet Muhammad (s). The hajj issue is mentioned in Quran, but the obligation of seven rounds of tawaf (circumambulation around the ka'bah) was only mentioned by the Prophet (s). The mentioned verse was revealed about Imam Ali ('a), Imam Hassan ('a), and Imam Hussayn ('a) and then Prophet Muhammad (s) said about Imam Ali ('a) in hajjatul wida' (the last hajj), 'Everyone whose leader is I, now Ali is his leader.'"[60]

Based on such traditions, it can be said that the guardianship commandments go beyond governmental commandments and include issuing obligatory commandments too. All the commandments issued by Prophet Muhammad (s) are so, unless they are mentioned in Holy

---

[60] Jami' Ahadith Al-Shi'ah, Vol 1, p. 247.

Quran or the Prophet (s) had announced them as revelation. Anyway, if such commandments are narrated with true document, they are religiously valid and should be followed by the Muslims. According to the text of Holy Quran, obeying Prophet's order and avoidance is obligatory for the believers.

We read in the Holy Quran,

> *"Obey God, and obey the Messenger, and those charged with authority among you."*[61]

It should be said that guardianship commandments of Messenger of Allah (s) were never issued out of carnal desires and without criterion. Being aware of real interest of the Muslims –through revelation– and away from fault or wrongdoing, he issued necessary commandments to maintain these interests. The Holy Quran states,

> *"Your Companion is neither astray nor being misled. Nor does he say (aught) of (his own) Desire. It is no less than inspiration sent down to him: He was taught by one Mighty in Power."*[62]

Therefore, intuitive awareness of real interests and detriments can be considered a source of the Prophet's sciences.

Fuzayl Ibn Yasar said, "I heard from Imam Sadiq ('a), 'The Almighty Allah trained His Prophet with the best method. When his learning completed, Allah told him,

---

[61] Surah Al-Nisa' (5): 59.

[62] Surah Al-Najm (53): 2-5.

'And thou (standest) on an exalted standard of character.'[63]

Then He presented the command of religion and the Ummah (Islamic nation) to the Prophet (s) to guide the people. Allah then told the people,

'So take what the Apostle assigns to you, and deny yourselves that which he withholds from you.'[64]

The Messenger of Allah (s) was supported by Ruhul Qudus (Gabriel). He was away from fault in managing people's issues and observed Allah's rules. Next Allah religiously set the prayers two units by two units until they were ten units a day. The Messenger of Allah (s) added another two units to all the two-unit prayers and one unit to the Evening Prayer (salatul Maghrib). What was added by Prophet Muhammad (s) was included in wajib (obligatory) prayers, whose leaving is not permitted unless in travel. The one unit added to Evening Prayer should not be left even in travel. The Exalted Allah confirmed these alterations, therefore, the wajib prayers became seventeen units (rak'ahs).

Afterward, the Messenger of Allah (s) set the nawafil (recommended prayers) 34 units –twice the unit of obligatory prayers– which was confirmed by Allah too. This way the obligatory and recommended prayers became 51 units; nafilah of Night Prayer (Salatul 'Isha') is two units that is performed while sitting and is considered one unit. The Almighty Allah obliged the sawm (fasting) of Ramadan and His Messenger (s) recommended the fasting of Sha'ban month and

---

[63] Surah Al-Qalam (68):4.

[64] Surah Al-Hashr (59): 7.

three days in every month, which were confirmed by the Almighty. The Almighty Allah prohibited drinking wine, but the Prophet (s) prohibited every intoxicating drink and was supported by Allah's confirmation. Prophet Muhammad (s) prohibited the Muslims from doing some deeds in the form of undesirability not complete forbiddance, giving option to the people. Therefore, the servants should use the options, but avoid the prohibited deeds altogether. The Messenger of Allah (s) did not permit avoiding the obligations and doing the prohibitions. One such prohibited deed is drinking any intoxicating drink, which is forbidden for everyone. The Prophet (s) did not allow the people to abandon the two units he added to all the obligatory prayers, except while in travel, so they should be stuck to. As a result, Prophet Muhammad's (s) enjoining and forbidding is obligatory to be obeyed by the servants just as Allah's enjoining and forbidding.'"[65]

Moreover, Imam Sadiq ('a) has stated, "The Exalted Allah trained His Prophet (s) until he reached perfection. Then Allah told him, 'And thou (standest) on an exalted standard of character.', presented the religion to him, and said, 'So take what the Apostle assigns to you, and deny yourselves that which he withholds from you.' Allah defined the heritage shares of family members, but set nothing for the forefather. The Prophet (s) defined one-sixth of the dead property for the forefather and Allah verified it. That is why Allah said,

> *'Such are Our Bounties: whether thou bestow them (on others) or withhold them, no account will be asked.*[66] "[67]

---

[65] Kafi, Vol 1, p. 266.
[66] Surah Al-Sad (38): 39.
[67] Kafi, Vol 1, p. 267.

Imam Baqir ('a) stated, "The Messenger of Allah (s) defined the compensation for eye loss and murder and prohibited wine and any intoxicating substance." The narrator asked Imam ('a), "Did the Prophet (s) issue any commandments without being first revealed by Allah?" Imam Baqir ('a) said, "Yes. It was for recognizing those who obeyed and those who disobeyed the Prophet (s)." [68]

> Imam Sadiq ('a) stated, "By Allah that the Exalted Allah relegated the religious issues to no one but His Messenger (s) and the Imams ('a). Allah stated, '**We have sent down to thee the Book in truth, that thou mightest judge between men, as guided by God: so be not (used) as an advocate by those who betray their trust.**[69] The same is true about the Prophet's (s) successors." [70]

The Imams and Guardianship Commandments

The Imams ('a) are successors to Prophet Muhammad (s). They have all the Prophet's (s) duties and the necessary authority. The Prophet (s) ruled the people and was permitted to issue commandments in the same filed. An Imam, too, has the government position and can issue and execute the necessary commandments related to ruling. Although, none of the infallible Imams ('a) –except Imam Ali ('a)– were formally in office, they were religiously the rulers of Islamic country and had guardianship. They were also permitted to issue commandments in the field of their guardianship. The traditions about minor issues of judgment, testimony, hudud, diyat, qisas, ta'zirat,

---

[68] Ibid.
[69] Surah Al- Nisa' (4): 105.
[70] Kafi, Vol 1, p. 268.

duties, authority, and qualifications of rulers and judges, jihad, defense, khumus, and zakat, which are narrated from infallible Imams ('a) and have no similar theme in Quran or traditions of Prophet Muhammad (s), are considered guardianship commandments of infallible Imams ('a). Rulers and officials of government should follow these guidelines. The Muslims should ask the rulers to execute these useful principles. This is the least of what infallible Imams ('a) could do in the hard conditions of oppressed governments in their ages to show the true image of Islamic government.

Some jurisprudential commandments transferred to us from infallible Imams ('a), which are not mentioned in Holy Quran or Prophet Muhammad's (s) traditions. They may be guardianship commandments too. One may say, "Just as the Prophet (s) was permitted to issue these commandments from Allah, the infallible Imams ('a) are allowed to do so from Prophet Muhammad (s). Such commandments are rooted in their guardianship, which is mentioned in Holy Quran and approved by the Prophet (s). If these kinds of commandments are narrated to us with valid religious documents, they are religiously reliable and should be obeyed."

It should be said that guardianship commandments of infallible Imams ('a) were not issued without regulation and out of carnal desires; rather they were based on real personal and social interests of Muslims in this world and the Hereafter. The Imams ('a) had received general regulations for issuing commandments from Prophet Muhammad (s) and issued necessary commandments based on time and place requirements and presented them to the people. They benefited from Divine support and their infallibility –as a strong aid– and were away from faults and wrongdoing.

The Infallibility of Imams ('a) and its Limits

One of the brilliant characteristics of the Imams ('a) is infallibility.

Infallibility means being safe. An infallible person is someone who is completely safe from committing faults, forgetfulness, and wrongdoing. Just as the Prophet (s) should be infallible, the Imam should be infallible, since he is the Prophet's (s) successor. If the Prophet's (s) successor is not infallible, there will be no guarantee for execution of religious commandments revealed for people' guidance and Allah's blessings will not be completed. Various qualities of an infallible person are:

1. He has no superstitious or wrong opinion.

2. He commits no fault in understanding religious facts and issues.

3. He is away from fault and forgetfulness in recording and maintaining religious commandments, sciences, and teachings.

4. He commits no fault in presenting religious commandments, sciences, and teachings to the people.

5. He commits no unlawful or irreligious deed.

The Secret of Infallibility

The infallibility of the Prophet (s) and the Imams ('a) does not mean that they do not have the factors for or ability to commit sins. It does not mean that if they intended to commit sins, the Almighty Allah directly or through His angels avoided them. Rather, the infallible Imams ('a) –like other people– had lust and anger and could do wrong, but they avoided it. The secret of their infallibility is twofold; first, their strong belief in Allah, the Hereafter, the Hell and the Paradise, the Reckoning, and punishments and rewards, and second, inner intuition of outcomes of wrongdoing, which is granted to them by the Almighty Allah.

The secret of infallibility of the Imams from faults and forgetfulness is their knowledge type. The Imams' ('a) knowledge of religious facts is intuitive, which originates from their insight. They intuitively know the true path to humanity and the sources of religious commandments and rules without any forgetfulness. Moreover, their physical structure is created by the Exalted Allah in a way that they can state their intuitive knowledge in words for the people. This in another Devine blessing and support from the Almighty Allah.

Infallibility in Traditions

The main reason for the infallibility of the Imams ('a) is the very mental reason, which was mentioned before. Furthermore, infallible Imams ('a) have considered infallibility as a brilliant characteristic of an Imam in their traditions. As an example, Imam Riza ('a) stated, "The Imam is away from faults and wrongdoing. He possesses especial knowledge and patience. He causes the organization of religion, the honor of Muslims, anger of the heterodox, and perishing of the infidel."[71]

Imam Riza ('a) also stated in the same tradition, "When the Exalted Allah selects a servant to manage others, He grants the selected servant an open chest for this duty, illuminates his heart with wisdom, and inspires the necessary sciences to him, so that he will be able to answer any question and tell the truth. This selected person will thus be away from sins or faults and supported by the Almighty. Allah has given him these qualifications to be as a reason for other servants. This is Allah's blessing that grants everyone He wishes. And Allah possesses great blessings."[72]

Imam Sadiq ('a) described the Imam this way, "The Imam is a selected person from the Household of Prophet Muhammad (s), who is always observed and supported by Him. Allah guards him, saves him from Satan's deceits, bad reputations, and calamities. He is away from all faults and wrongdoing."[73]

---

[71] Usul Kafi, Vol 1, p. 200.
[72] Usul Kafi, Vol 1, p. 202.
[73] Usul Kafi, Vol 1, p. 204.

Amiral Mu'minin ('a) stated, "The greatest level of wilayat (guardianship) of the Imam –whose obedience is obligatory– is considering him as infallible from faults, slip, and intentional offense. He does not commit major (kabirah) or minor (saqhirah) sins, nor does he commit irreligious deeds or debauchery."[74]

---

[74] Biharul Anwar, Vol 68, p. 389.

Four

The Ahlul Bayt in the Quran and the Traditions

The Infallibility of Ahlul Bayt in the Holy Quran

For proving the infallibility of the Imams ('a), the famous Tat'hir verse from the Holy Quran is mentioned here:

> *"And God only wishes to remove all abomination from you, ye members of the Family, and to make you pure and spotless."*[75]

Some points are mentioned here regarding the exegesis of this verse and explaining this reason.

Revelation Reason of Tat'hir Verse

Undoubtedly, the mentioned verse has been revealed about Messenger of Allah (s), Imam Ali ('a), Hadrat Fatimah (s), Imam Hassan ('a),

---

[75] Surah Al-Ahzab (33): 33.

and Imam Hussayn ('a). There are numerous facts in this regard in the Shi'ah and Sunni books. For instance, ªyishah says, "One morning the Messenger of Allah (s) came out wearing a black wool cloth. Then Hassan ('a), Hussayn ('a), Fatimah (s), and Ali ('a) came. Then Prophet Muhammad (s) placed them beneath his cloak and said, "And God only wishes to remove all abomination from you, ye members of the Family, and to make you pure and spotless."[76]

Ummi Salamah says, "The verse, And God only wishes to remove all abomination from you, ye members of the Family, and to make you pure and spotless was revealed to the Prophet (s) in my house. Then Hadrat Fatimah (s) brought a container of food for him. Messenger of Allah (s) told her, 'Invite your husband Ali ('a) and your sons Hassan ('a) and Hussayn ('a) to have food with me.' When all of them came and were eating, the verse was revealed. So Prophet Muhammad (s) placed all of them beneath his cloak and said three times, 'O Lord! These are my household; take away pollution and sins from them and make them pure.'"[77]

Umar Ibn Abi Salamah says, "The verse And God only wishes to remove all abomination from you, ye members of the Family, and to make you pure and spotless was revealed in the house of Ummi Salamah. Then Messenger of Allah (s) called Fatimah (s), Hassan ('a), and Hussayn ('a), spread his cloth on them, and said, 'O Lord! They are my household. Take away pollution from them and purify them.' Ummi Salamah stated, 'O Messenger of Allah! Am I included with them?' He replied, 'You have your own place. You are good too.'"[78]

Ziynab says, "When the Messenger of Allah (s) saw that blessings are descending from the heaven he stated, 'Who will invite Ali ('a), Fatimah

---

[76] Sahih Muslim, Vol 4, p. 1883.

[77] Yanabi'ul Mawaddah, p. 125.

[78] Ibid, p. 125.

(s), Hassan ('a), and Hussayn ('a)?' I said, 'I do.' When they gathered, the Messenger of Allah (s) spread his cloak on them and joined them beneath it. Then Gabriel was descended with this verse."[79]

Abu Sa'id Khidri says, "This verse (Tat'hir) was revealed about five people; the Prophet (s), Ali ('a), Fatimah (s), Hassan ('a), and Hussayn ('a)."[80]

Imam Hassan ('a) stated in his sermon, "We –the Prophet's (s) Household– are the people about whom the verse: And God only wishes to remove all abomination from you, ye members of the Family, and to make you pure and spotless was revealed."[81]

The gathering of as'habi kisa' (people of the cloak) and revelation of Tat'hir verse is one of the main events of Prophet Muhammad's (s) mission.

As'habi kisa' were five; the honorable Prophet (s), Imam Ali ('a), Fatimatal Zahra' (s), Imam Hassan ('a), and Imam Hussayn ('a).

As is revealed from the traditions, when Tat'hir verse was revealed to the Prophet (s), he sent someone to Imam Ali ('a), Hadrat Fatimah (s), Imam Hassan ('a), and Imam Hussayn ('a) and invited them to his house. Then he placed all of them on a carpet and sat beside them.

Afterward, the Prophet (s) spread his cloak or a cloth on them and joined them himself. Then he recited the Tat'hir verse and said, "O Allah! They are my Household. Take away pollution and sins from them." Apparently, this event has happened in the house of Ummi Salamah, the Prophet's (s) wife. The same five people have narrated the happening for others. Moreover, 'ayishah and Ummi Salamah, the Prophet's (s) wives, 'Umar, the son of Abi Salamah –who was trained in Prophet Muhammad's (s) house– Ziynab –who was raised in

---

[79] Ibid, p. 126.

[80] Ibid.

[81] Ibid.

Prophet's (s) house– as well as Thawban, the freed slave of the Prophet (s) and Wasilatibni Asqa', the Prophet's (s) maid have narrated this for other people. All these individuals were among close companions of Messenger of Allah (s). They can be considered eye witnesses of the event.

Some other companions of the Prophet (s), such as Anas Ibn Malik, Abul Hamra', Abu Sa'id Khidri, and Ibn Abbas have also narrated this event, though they have not witnessed it directly.

For six or seventeen months, the Messenger of Allah (s) recited the Tat'hir verse loud in front of Hadrat Zahra's (s) house, every morning he was going to the mosque for Morning Prayer and said, "O Ahlul-Bayt! Prepare for establishing the prayer!"[82] He wanted to inform the companions of it and confirm the event.

Instances of the Ahlul Bayt

The Ahlul-Bayt means the members of the promised house. According to the traditions, the promised house is the house of Ummi Salamah –Prophet Muhammad's (s) wife. The Tat'hir verse was revealed in this house, in which the Prophet (s) invited Imam Ali ('a), Hadrat Fatimah (s), Imam Hassan ('a), and Imam Hussayn ('a), throw a cloak on them and himself, and recited the Tat'hir verse. He placed only these four people beneath the cloak with himself, not letting Ummi Salamah to accompany them, to exclude any other one from the Ahlul-Bayt, who were five. Prophet Muhammad (s) did so for fear that someone in the future claims to be included among the Ahlul-Bayt. He always stipulated that the Tat'hir verse was only revealed about Ali, Fatimah, Hassan, and Hussayn ('a).[83]

Imam Ali ('a), Imam Hassan ('a), and Imam Hussayn ('a) always

---

[82] Majma'ul Zawa'id, Vol 9, pp. 168 & 169.

[83] Ibid, p. 167.

referred to the Tat'hir verse for proving their virtues and were never denied in this case.

Exegesis of the Tat'hir Verse

Two points need mentioning for clarification of the verse:

1. Rijs (abomination) lexically means filth and is used in two meanings in Holy Quran. The first meaning is apparent religious impurity. The Holy Quran states,

> *"Say: "I find not in the Message received by me by inspiration any (meat) forbidden to be eaten by one who wishes to eat it, unless it be dead meat, or blood poured forth, or the flesh of swine,- for it is an abomination* [84]*"*

The second meaning is internal carnal impurity that is disbelief, transgression, and sin. The Holy Quran states,

> *"But those in whose hearts is a disease,- it will add doubt to their doubt, and they will die in a state of Unbelief."*[85]

2. Obviously, the disbelievers do not suffer from apparent filth and the Almighty Allah has not asked them to avoid outward impurity. Rather, carnal impurities, such as disbelief, dissension, and malice are considered disobeying Allah.

The question now is that if the rijs mentioned in the Tat'hir verse is used in the first meaning or the second one. The advantage pointed out for the Ahlul-Bayt is used with the word innama (surely), which

---

[84] Surah Al-'An'am (6): 145.

[85] Surah Al-Tawbah (9): 125.

shows specialty in Arabic. If this characteristic of the Ahlul-Bayt was only purity of superficial filth, it could be for all the Muslims, and not an advantage for the Ahlul-Bayt ('a) to be praised by the Exalted Allah and honored in many instances.

Will in the Holy Quran

Human will is an inner state and a prerequisite of optional acts. Human will sometimes brings about accomplishment of wishes and sometimes not. Not everything human wishes is objectively realized. Allah' deeds are out of knowledge, will, and option. Allah' will, however, differs from human will and always accomplishes ambitions. The Holy Quran points out two kinds of will for the Almighty Allah; Will of the genesis and Will of the religion. Allah's Will of the genesis means realization ambitions by knowledge and option with no exception.

The Holy Quran states,

> *"Verily, when He intends a thing, His Command is, 'be', and it is!"*[86]

Allah's religious Will does not command realization of things; rather He regulates certain rules and verdicts and wants the servants to follow them, so that His command will be externally realized.

The Holy Quran states about Ramadan fasting,

> *"So every one of you who is present (at his home) during that month should spend it in fasting, but if anyone is ill, or on a journey, the prescribed period (should be made up)*

---

[86] Surah Yasin (36): 82.

by days later. God intends every facility for you; He does not want to put to difficulties.[87]

Allah's Will in this case is Will of religion. In other words, since the Almighty Allah has willed not to take the servants into trouble for sawm (the Ramadan fasting), He has permitted the patients and travelers not to fast in Ramadan and perform it in other months.

The question now is that if Allah's Will mentioned in the Tat'hir verse is of genesis or of religion. If this Will is of religion, the verse would mean that Allah has wished to purify the Prophet's Ahlul-Bayt ('a) from carnal impurities, hence regulating necessary verdicts and presenting them to the Ahlul-Bayt. This assumption is not logically acceptable, since such verdicts are not only dedicated to the Ahlul-Bayt, but to all the Muslims. Moreover, this assumption is not compatible with the word innam (verily), which has a limiting meaning. If the mentioned assumption was true, Prophet Muhammad (s) could allow Ummi Salamah to come beneath the cloak too to be included in the Tat'hir verse. She was at least among the believers. As a result, Allah's Will in this verse is Will of the genesis. In other words, the Almighty Allah has originally wished to purify the Ahlul-Bayt ('a) from carnal impurities, such as disbelief, polytheism, and sins, creating them this way. They are, in fact, completely away from carnal impurities and are infallible.

Based on the same exegesis of this verse, being among the Ahlul-Bayt is considered a virtue and honor by the infallible Imams ('a) and they were never denied.

Therefore, numerous traditions have mentioned the Tat'hir verse for proving the Imams' ('a) infallibility, such as the ones below:

Ali Ibn Abi Talib ('a) stated, "Allah says in Holy Quran, 'And God

---

[87] Surah Al-Baqarah (2): 185.

only wishes to remove all abomination from you, ye members of the Family, and to make you pure and spotless.' Therefore, He purified us from inner and outer vices and led us in the path of truth."[88]

The Messenger of Allah (s) after reciting the Tat'hir verse said, "My Ahlul-Bayt (Household) and I are purified from sins."[89]

Imam Hassan ('a) stated, "We are the Prophet's (s) Ahlul-Bayt. Allah honored us by Islam, selected us, and cleaned us from filth and sin. Rijs means doubt. So we have no doubt in Allah and His religion. He purified us from any impurity and deviation."[90]

The Itrat (Household); Most Valid Religious Source

The honorable Messenger of Islam (s) was commissioned by the Almighty to introduce his Household (itrat), as a source of Islamic sciences, to the Muslims. The Messenger of Allah (s) did so when returning from his last Hajj pilgrimage (hajjatul wida') at Ghadir Khum (Ghadir pool). When he reached Ghadir on his way back to Medina, Gabriel descended with this verse,

> *"O Apostle! proclaim the (message) which hath been sent to thee from thy Lord. If thou didst not, thou wouldst not have fulfilled and proclaimed His mission. And God will defend thee from men (who mean mischief). For God guideth not those who reject Faith."*[91]

Although it was very hot, Prophet Muhammad (s) stopped in that desert for performing Allah's order. He sent for the hajjis, who had

---

[88] Ghayatul Maram, Vol 3, p. 199.

[89] Al-Badayah wan Nahayah, Vol 2, p. 136; Biharul Anwar, Vol 35, p. 213, Bab 5.

[90] Biharul Anwar, Vol 10, Bab 9, p. 138.

[91] Surah Al-Ma'idah (5): 67.

proceeded, to come back and called on those, who were behind, to travel faster. When all the hajjis gathered in one place, the Prophet (s) ascended a pulpit –made from camels' saddles– and performed a long sermon, called the Ghadir sermon. This event is narrated in various traditions, one of which is cited here:

Ziyd Ibn 'Arqam says, "When Messenger of Allah (s) was returning from hajjatul Wida', he stopped in Ghadir Khum. First he ordered to remove brush hood from beneath the trees. Then he performed a sermon and said, 'It is as if I am invited by the Exalted Allah and I have accepted it. I trust two precious things among you, one of which is better than the other; Allah's Book and my itrat (Household). Beware of maintaining these two trusts. They will not separate until the Resurrection.' Then he continued, 'The Exalted Allah is my Lord and I am the master of all the believers.' He then held Ali's ('a) hand and said, 'Anyone whose guardian is I, Ali ('a) is his guardian. O Lord! Befriend those who accept Ali's guardianship and dislike his enemies.'"[92]

Bara' Ibn 'Azib has narrated the same tradition, adding this sentence, "Prophet Muhammad (s) began his speech this way, 'Am I not more deserved to interfere in the believers' issues than themselves?' The congregation said, 'O Messenger of Allah! In fact you are so.' So the Prophet (s) stated, 'He (Ali) is the guardian of anyone whose guardian is I.'"[93]

Bara' has added after this tradition, "Then Umar Ibnil Khattab met Ali ('a) and told him, 'O Ali! May this position be pleasant for you! Now you are the guardian of every man and woman.'"[94]

The Ghadir tradition has been recorded in valid Shi'ah and Sunni books with different statements and texts and has always been referred

---

[92] Mustadrak Hakim Niyshaburi, Vol 3, p. 109.

[93] Al-Bidayah wan Nahayah, Vol 5, p. 229.

[94] Ibid.

to by Imam Ali ('a) and other infallible Imams ('a). This tradition is mutiwatir (narrated successively) and with an authentic document. Many great companions of Messenger of Allah (s) have related this tradition, such as:

Abu Harirah, Abul Ali Ansari, Abul Hiytham Ibnil Tihan, Abu Bakr Ibn Abi Qahafah, Umar Ibn Khattab, Uthman Ibn Affan, Ali Ibn Abi Talib, Hassan Ibn Ali, Hussayn Ibn Ali, Fatimatal Zahra', Usamatibni Ziyd, Ummi Salamah, Prophet Muhammad's (s) wife, Anas Ibn Malik, Bara' Ibn ªzib, Jabir Ibn Samarah, Jabir Ibn Abdullah Ansari, Hazifatibni Asid, Hisan Ibn Thabit, Khazimatibni Thabit Ansari, Zubiyr Ibn Awam, Ziyd Ibn Arqam, Ziyd Ibn Thabit, Abu Sa'id Khidri, Salman Farsi, Miqdad Ibn Amri Kandi, Abbas Ibn Abdul Mutallib, Abdullah Ibn Ja'far Ibn Abi Talib, Abdullah Ibn Abbas, Abdullah Ibn Umar Ibn Khattab, and Ammar Ibn Yasir[95], may Allah be content with them all!

The Content of the Ghadir Tradition

Some facts are understood from the Ghadir tradition:

1. The Messenger of Allah (s) introduced the Holy Quran and the itrat (his Household) as two precious entities in presence of a great number of Muslims, saying, "I trust these two things among you to see what you will do with them." And according to some narrations he said, "If you seek help from them, you will never go astray."

2. Prophet Muhammad (s) also said, "The Holy Quran and the itrat will be together until the Day of Judgment." No one can say that there is no need to the itrat when the Quran exists or vice versa.

3. As the Holy Quran is the greatest and richest source of religious sciences, teachings, verdicts, and rules, the Muslims are obliged to benefit from it for solving their religious issues. The Prophet's (s) itrat

---

[95] Al-Ghadir, Vol 1.

is also a source of religious sciences and teachings and the Muslim should use it for acquiring religious knowledge, following the infallible Imams' ('a) behavior and speech.

Resorting to the Holy Quran and Prophet Muhammad's (s) itrat, which is stressed in ghadir (or thaqalayn) tradition and other traditions, is realized this way, not by superficial respect or rituals.

The Itrat and its Instances

Itrat lexically means the progeny and includes Prophet Muhammad's (s) Household or the Ahlul-Bayt ('a), about whom the Tat'hir verse is revealed, as some texts of thaqalayn tradition has quoted the phrase, "my itrat, my Ahlul-Bayt". It is narrated from Imam Hussayn ('a), "Amiral Mu'minin ('a) was asked, 'What is the meaning of itrat in the words of Messenger of Allah (s)?' Imam Ali ('a) replied, 'The itrat are I, Hassan, Hussayn, and nine Imams from Hussayn's progeny, the ninth of which is Mahdi, Qa'im of the Ahlul-Bayt. They will not separate from Allah's Book and the Book will not separate from them until they are presented to Messenger of Allah (s) in the hawz (Khawthar fountain in the Paradise) on the Last Day.'"[96]

Imam Sadiq ('a) has quoted from his father and grandfathers ('a) from Prophet Muhammad (s), "I leave two precious trusts among you; Allah's Book and the itrat, my Ahlul-Bayt. They will not separate from each other until they will be presented to me in the Kawthar fountain." Then he stuck his two thumbs together and said, "This way." Then Jabir Ibn Abdullah Ansari stood up from the crowd and asked, "O Messenger of Allah! Who are your itrat?" Prophet Muhammad (s) answered, "Ali, Hassan, Hussayn, and the Imams from the progeny of Hussayn until the Resurrection."[97]

---

[96] Biharul Anwar, Vol 23, p. 147.

[97] Ibid.

Appointment of Imam Ali ('a)

The most important part of Ghadir sermon is appointment of Imam Ali ('a) to guardianship and caliphate. Ziyd Ibn Arqam, after the mentioned tradition, has quoted from the Prophet (s), "The Exalted Allah is my Lord and Guardian and I am the master and guardian of all the believers." Then he caught Ali's hand and stated, "Anyone whose master and guardian is I, now Ali is his master and guardian."

Obviously, the Messenger of Allah (s) has introduced Imam Ali ('a) as the guardian or ruler of the Muslims in this tradition. Both the words wali and mawla (mentioned in various forms of this tradition) mean the same; that is someone who deserves to interfere in others' affairs.

Ziyd Ibn 'Arqam says, "The honorable Prophet (s), after performing the sermon, asked the people to take oath of allegiance with Ali ('a). The people said, 'We heard and obey the command of Allah and His Messenger (s).' The first people to take oath of allegiance with Prophet Muhammad (s) and Ali ('a) were Abu Bakr, 'Umar, and 'Uthman as well as Talhah and Zubayr."[98] It was then that 'Umar shook hands with Imam Ali ('a) and said, "May this be pleasant for you! From now on you are the guardian of every believing man and woman."[99]

Prophet Muhammad's Recommendations about Imam Ali ('a)

The honorable Messenger of Allah (s) had pointed out inner virtues and scientific stance of Imam Ali ('a) for the Muslims many times during his prophetic mission, stating the obligation of following and obeying him. This way he prepared people's minds for acceptance of Imam Ali's ('a) guardianship and Imamate. There are thousands of traditions recorded in the Shi'ah and Sunni books in this regard, some of which are mentioned here:

---

[98] Al-Ghadir, Vol 1, p. 508.

[99] Al-Bidayah wan Nahayah, Vol 5, p. 229.

Ibn Abbas says, "The Messenger of Allah (s) said, 'If you like to live and die like me and live in the Paradise my Lord has prepared, you should accept Ali's ('a) guardianship after me, befriend his friends, and follow the Imams after me. They are my itrat, are created from the same essence as I was, and possess my understanding and knowledge. Woe to those who deny the Imams and ignore my kinship right; my intercession will not include them.'"[100]

Hadhifat Ibni Yaman said, "Some of the companions told the Prophet (s), 'O Messenger of Allah! Don't you appoint Ali ('a) as caliph?' The Prophet (s) stated, 'If you accept his guardianship, he will guide you to the right path.'"[101]

Abu Sa'id Khidri has narrated that Messenger of Allah (s) stroke Ali's shoulder and said, "O Ali! You have seven characteristics, about which no one can argue in the Last Day; you are the first believer in Allah, you are the most loyal to Allah's promises, you are the most firm of all in performing Allah's orders, you are the kindest to the people, the most just in dividing properties, the most learned in judging, and the best in the Resurrection."[102]

Ummi Salamah said, "I heard from Messenger of Allah (s) who said, 'Ali is with the Quran and the Quran is with Ali and they will not separate until the Day of Judgment.'"[103]

The Messenger of Allah (s) stated, "I am the city of knowledge and Ali is its gate. If someone seeks knowledge, he should enter the gate."[104]

'Ayishah said, "I heard the Messenger of Allah (s) saying, 'Ali accompanies the truth and the truth accompanies Ali; they will not

---

[100] Hilyatul Awliya', Vol 1, p. 128.

[101] Hilyatul Awliya', Vol 1, p. 104.

[102] Hilyatul Awliya', Vol 1, p. 106.

[103] Nurul Absar, p. 80.

[104] Yanabi'ul Mawaddah, Vol 1, p. 75.

separate until the Resurrection.'"[105]

The Messenger of Allah (s) stated, "Everyone who likes to resort to my religion and be on board of the salvation ship should follow Ali Ibn Abi Talib, befriend his friends, and dislike his enemies. He will be my successor and caliph after my demise. Ali is the Imam of Muslims and hope of the believers. His speech, orders, prohibition, follower, and companion are just like those of mine. Not helping him is not helping me."[106]

These and tens of other traditions, which can be considered successive in meaning, reveal that the honorable Prophet (s) has had a mission from the Almighty Allah to introduce Imam Ali ('a) as the Imam and successor after himself to the Muslims and prepare the conditions for formal appointment of Imam Ali ('a), which was finally realized in Ghadir Khum.

Recommendation about the Ahlul Bayt ('a)

The honorable Prophet of Islam (s) always attempted to attract Muslims' attention to his Ahlul-Bayt ('a) by using the terms 'kindness', 'love', 'friendship', etc. during his mission. An instance of such speech is:

Ibn Abbas said, "When the verse, Say: "No reward do I ask of you for this except the love of those near of kin."[107] was revealed, some of the Prophet's (s) companions asked him, 'O Messenger of Allah! Who are the people that the Almighty Allah has ordered loving them?' Prophet Muhammad (s) replied, 'Ali and Fatimah and their progeny.'"[108]

Ibn Abbas has also narrated from the Messenger of Allah (s), "Allah's

---

[105] Ghayatul Maram, Vol 5, p. 283.

[106] Ikmalud Din, Vol 2, p. 376.

[107] Surah Al-Shura (42): 23.

[108] Ghayatul Maram, Vol 3, p. 233.

servant does not move in the Hereafter except that he is asked of four things; how he has spent his lifetime, how he has used his body, how he has gained and spent his property, and of the affection of the Ahlul-Bayt ('a)."[109]

Ibn Abbas has narrated from Prophet Muhammad (s) who said, "The example of my Ahlul-Bayt is like Noah's ship; the one who boards it will be saved and the one who resorts to it will get salvation and the one who denies it will be drowned."[110]

Prophet Muhammad (s) had not merely meant expressing superficial verbal –or even hearty– affection. This is not the remuneration of his hardships in prophetic mission; rather, he had meant encouraging the Muslims to follow the Ahlul-Bayt ('a) and learn religiousness from them, as is explicitly stated in Safinah (the No'ah ship) tradition.

Affection for the Ahlul Bayt ('a)

Affection means loving. It is used in the same meaning in the traditions too. Affection for the Ahlul-Bayt ('a) is so important in Islam that the Holy Quran introduces it as the remuneration of Prophet Muhammad's (s) mission.

> The Messenger of Allah (s) is addressed in the Holy Quran and asked to tell the believers, Say: **"No reward do I ask of you for this except the love of those near of kin."**

Prophet Muhammad (s) has enjoined the Muslims to loving his Ahlul-Bayt ('a) –including Ali ('a)– in many traditions, considering it the best means of salvation.

The Messenger of Allah (s) stated, "Anyone who wants to resort to

---

[109] Ibid, p.92.

[110] Dhakha'irul Uqba, p. 20.

Allah's firm knob should have affection for Ali and my Ahlul-Bayt." [111]

The Prophet of Islam (s) stated, "The first thing which is asked about in the Hereafter is affection for the Ahlul-Bayt."[112]

The Messenger of Allah (s) stated, "Anyone who loves my Ahlul-Bayt will be resurrected with me in the Hereafter."[113]

Prophet Muhammad (s), holding Ali's hand, said, "Someone who thinks he loves me, but he does not love Ali, is a liar." [114]

Amiral Mu'minin, Imam Ali ('a), has quoted from the Prophet (s), "I will mediate for four groups in the Resurrection; the lovers of my Ahlul-Bayt, those who have accepted guardianship of my Ahlul-Bayt and hated their enemies, those who fulfill requests of my Ahlul-Bayt, and those who help my Ahlul-Bayt in their affairs."[115]

As is observed, the Holy Quran and Prophet's (s) traditions have strongly emphasized the affection for Prophet Muhammad (s) Ahlul-Bayt ('a), considering it as a way to reach salvation. Now we should see who the Prophet's (s) Ahlul-Bayt are. Are they all his close relatives or certain people among them? Some traditions can help clarify the issue.

> 'Isma'il Ibn Abdul Khallaq says, "Imam Sadiq ('a) asked me, 'What do the people say about the Quranic verse, Say: **No reward do I ask of you for this except the love of those near of kin."** I answered, 'May I sacrifice for you! They say the verse is about the Prophet's (s) close relatives (zil qurba).' Imam Sadiq ('a) stated,

---

[111] Biharul Anwar, Vol 27, p. 79.

[112] Ibid.

[113] Biharul Anwar, Vol 27, p. 79.

[114] Ibid.

[115] Biharul Anwar, Vol 27, p. 79.

'They lie. The verse is revealed about us, the Ahlul-Bayt; Ali, Fatimah, Hassan, and Hussayn; people of the cloak.'[116]

Abdullah Ibn 'Ajlan has narrated from Imam Baqir ('a), who said about the exegesis of mentioned verse, "The close relatives (zil qurba) are the Imams ('a)."[117]

These and many other traditions –about the Tat'hir verse– imply that Prophet Muhammad's (s) close relatives (zil qurba), mentioned in this verse are Imam Ali ('a), Fatimatal Zahra' (s), Imam Hassan, Imam Hussayn, and other infallible Imams ('a) from Imam Hussayn's progeny.

These noble Imams ('a) always introduced themselves as zil qurba, Ahlul-Bayt, and source of Prophetic sciences and were never denied by anyone. Therefore, according to the verse under discussion, all the Muslims oblige themselves to love the Prophet's (s) Ahlul-Bayt, showing this affection by composing poems, eulogizing, and visiting their shrines and tombs.

Now we should see what real affection is, how it is realized, and what consequences it has?

Affection means loving someone. It is an inner sense in which the lover is attracted to the beloved; a sense that is perceivable but not describable. Affection has different levels, the highest level of which is called love. Affection can be for the people or the objects, but it certainly has a criterion. This criterion may be the beloved one's beauty, handsomeness, good ethics or behavior, or his usefulness.

One of the results of affection is that a lover always tries to honor and satisfy the beloved and even sacrifices himself for his beloved, which is a sign of real affection. Expression of affection may be unreal

---

[116] Rawzatul Kafi, p. 80.

[117] Kafi, Vol 1, p. 413.

without a practical sign.

> The Holy Quran and the traditions mention Allah's affection for the servants, who have at least one virtue, such as, **"Surely Allah loves the pious", "Surely Allah loves the purified", "Surely Allah loves the good-doers", "Surely Allah loves the repentant", "Surely Allah loves the reliers on Allah", "Surely Allah loves the patient", "Surely Allah loves the just."** The Exalted Allah, who has created the servants and granted them all the blessings, wants the servants to obey His orders and forbiddances, so that their salvation in this world and the Hereafter is guaranteed.

Allah' affection for His servants, however, is not a carnal sense, since He is away from occurrence of phenomenon. Allah's affection means His granting Mercy to the servants for reaching perfection.

The Holy Quran also mentions the servants' affection for the Almighty Allah.

> *"O ye who believe! If any from among you turn back from his Faith, soon will God produce a people whom He will love as they will love Him,- lowly with the believers, mighty against the rejecters, fighting in the way of God, and never afraid of the reproaches of such as find fault. That is the grace of God, which He will bestow on whom He pleaseth. And God encompasseth all, and He knoweth all things."*[118]

The Almighty Allah suggests mutual affection to the believers in this

---

[118] Surah Al-Ma'idah (5): 54.

verse and introduces jihad in Allah's path as a sign of believers' real affection for Allah.

In another verse, obeying the Prophet's (s) orders is considered a sign of true fondness. The Holy Quran states,

> **Say: "If ye do love God, Follow me: God will love you and forgive you your sins: For God is Oft-Forgiving, Most Merciful."** [119]

As a result, the believers who claim to love Allah, but do not emphasize it by practicing religious duties and the Prophet's commands, do not have a real affection and their affection for the Almighty is not useful for them.

Affection for zil qurba (the Prophet's close relatives) and his Ahlul-Bayt is the same. Since the Prophet' (s) Ahlul-Bayt –the infallible Imams ('a)– were guardians of the religion and promoters of Prophet Muhammad's (s) mission, the Muslims are asked to accept their guardianship and follow them. Our affection for the infallible Imams ('a) is real in case we set them our leaders and follow their speech, behavior, and ethics. The people who claim to be the Imams' ('a) lovers, but do not perform their commands, deceive themselves and such superficial affection will not save them. The infallible Imams ('a) have always emphasized this point, as will be mentioned in the future.

The Imamate Position

True recognition of Imamate position and defining the people who filled this position is an important issue for the Muslims, as mentioned

---

[119] Surah 'ali 'Imran (3): 31

in many traditions. The science of kalam[120] discusses if certain characteristics are necessary for Imamate position, or if everyone can get it. If the former is true, what are these qualities? In other words, is Imamate an innate position or a conventional one –obtained by being appointed? Can it decay? The same discussions exist in case of prophet hood, but it is proved that prophet hood is a real innate position for attaining which inborn qualifications are necessary. If Prophet Muhammad (s), for instance, was appointed as prophet, it was because of his own virtues. No other person could be appointed to that position by the Exalted Allah. Prophet hood means direct relation of a selected person with the unseen world and obtaining Divine sciences and teachings from the Almighty Allah. Not everyone deserves such an important duty.

Some issues are proved about prophet hood that are briefly mentioned here:

1. Human life is not limited to this world; there will be another life after death with bliss or misery.

2. Human salvation or misfortune in the Hereafter is the result of his deeds and ethics in this world.

3. Human being is unable to recognize the best plan for his life and needs Allah's guidance.

4. The All-Knowing All-Wise Allah, who has created human beautiful and delicate, has had a purpose. Allah knows well human material and spiritual needs and the secret of his salvation or unluckiness. The Exalted Allah never leaves His servants in deviation, rather He has sent prophets (s) for guiding humans with the necessary sciences, teachings, plans, and duties, so that the signs are completed for the servants. This way, the necessity of sending the prophets (s) is confirmed.

The same theorem affirms the prophets' (s) science and infallibility.

---

[120] Speculative Theology.

In other words, Allah's purpose of sending the prophets (s) is fulfilled only if all the necessary sciences are presented to them and the prophets (s) are completely away from mistakes and wrongdoing in acquiring, maintaining, and declaring the revelation sciences to the people. It is also proved in philosophy and kalam that revelation sciences are not like acquirable and conceptual sciences, which are acquired by our senses from the outside world. Revelation sciences are illuminating facts revealed to the Prophet's (s) soul and he observes them with his inner sight and hears with his inner hearing. That is why the Prophet (s) does not commit mistakes and sins and is infallible. Such a person should be followed and can be 'the best pattern' (Uswatul hasanah) for the people. Denying or doubtfulness about the necessity of the prophet's sciences and infallibility is like denying the necessity of existence of the prophet.

In sum, the prophet is a complete, noble, and selected human in terms of spiritual aspects. He can make relations with the unseen world, acquire religious sciences, teachings, and commandments, and convey them to the people exactly. This is the lofty position of prophet hood, which ordinary people cannot attain. However, the prophet is like other people in terms of material aspects. He needs Allah in his essence and all his behaviors and deeds. His sustenance is provided by the Almighty Allah. He may get tired and ill and he needs medicine for getting well. He gradually ages and cannot help his appointed death.

The real position and advantages of the prophets become clear from above discussion.[121]

The lofty position of the Imams can be understood from what was mentioned about the prophet's position, since Imamate is continuation of prophet hood. Some points should be born in mind in this regard, which have been proved elsewhere:

---

[121] For more information, you can refer to kalam and philosophy books.

1. Prophet Muhammad (s) was the last prophet and Islam is the ever-lasting religion until the Resurrection.

2. The Prophet's (s) mission was only 23 years. He had to solve the problems of new Muslims and could not teach all Islamic sciences, teachings, and commandments to all the Muslims to be maintained for the future Muslims.

3. A great amount of Islamic commandments are political, social, judiciary, economical, etc. which were executed by the Messenger of Allah (s) among the ummah. He had the guardianship of ummah and defended Islam.

As a result, a person or some persons should accept all the Prophet's (s) duties and attempt in realizing his purposes. Such people are called the Prophet's caliphs or Imams and have guardianship on the people and continue the Prophet's (s) path. The Imamate is completion of the religion and an organization for the Muslims. As human being needs a prophet, he needs an Imam. Allah's purpose of sending the prophets (s) for guiding the people is fulfilled well only in case the prophet is followed by the Imams to pursuit his goals; otherwise the prophet's (s) mission will not be accomplished.

It is concluded that the Imam should be fully aware of religious teachings, sciences, and commandments just like the prophet, so that the people access true commandments of Islam in prophet's (s) absence throughout the ages.

The Imam should also be away from mistakes, forgetfulness, and wrongdoing in maintaining religious commandments and declaring them to the people, just as the prophet is; otherwise Allah's blessings for the servants will not be completed. Such an infallible learned person should be obeyed and is people' leader and Imam from Allah.[122]

---

[122] The same issue is understood from many Quranic verses and traditions. For more information on this, you can refer to kalam books about "Imamate".

The major difference between the Prophet (s) and the Imams is that the Prophet (s) met the revelation angel and received religious commandments and rules from Allah, but the Imams do not benefit from revelation and direct relation with the Exalted Allah; they receive religious sciences, teachings, rules, and commandments from the Prophet (s).

In sum, the Imam is a perfect selected person, aware of religious sciences, teachings, and commandments, and away from fault, sin, and forgetfulness. His knowledge and deeds are so perfect that all human virtues are materialized in his personality and he can be the people's Imam and leader. Denying or doubting about any of these innate advantages equals denying the necessity of existence of Imam and hence denying the necessity of existence of the Prophet (s).[123]

Material Aspects

It should be emphasized again that the Imam –just like the Prophet (s) – is materially an ordinary person, created by Allah. He needs the Almighty in his essence, deeds, sustenance, and other wishes. If he gets sick, he goes to the doctor to be cured. He ages by the passage of time and surrenders to the death when its appointed time comes.

As Allah states in the Holy Quran,

> **Say: 'I have no power over any good or harm to myself except as God willeth. If I had knowledge of the unseen, I should have multiplied all good, and no evil should have touched me: I am but a warner, and a bringer of glad**

---

[123] All the issues related to "Imamate" are authored in detail in the book General Issues of Imamate and the book Patterns of Excellence, as well as former sections of the pr sent book.

tidings to those who have faith."[124]

The conduct of the Prophet (s) and infallible Imams ('a) was this way; they asked their requests from Allah, not others. They thought resorting to others prevents granting of the prayers. They never told the people, "Resort to us for answering your requests!" Rather, they recommended the people to be hopeful only of Allah and ask their requests from Him, because everything is in Allah's hands. No one is able to fulfill the requests except the Almighty. The conduct of the Prophet (s) and infallible Imams ('a) was so when praying. Some instances of this manner are cited here:

Amiral Mu'minin, Imam Ali ('a), told his son, Imam Hassan ('a), "Only ask your Lord, since granting and depriving is only in His power." [125]

He also stated, "You ask something from His treasures of Mercy no one else can grant you. You ask him long life, health, and abundance of sustenance and no one but He can grant them." [126]

Moreover, Imam Ali ('a) said, "Only resort to the One who has created you, gives you provisions, and has created you beautiful." [127]

The fourth infallible Imam, Imam Sajjad ('a), states in his prayer, "Praise be to Allah, Who I ask, whenever I want, for granting my request and to Who I talk privately for saying my request whenever I wish, without any mediator. So He grants me my request. Praise be to Allah, Who I only pray to, and if I prayed to others, my prayer would not be granted. Praise be to Allah, Who I am hopeful of, and if I were hopeful of others, I would become disappointed." [128]

---

[124] Surah Al-'A'raf (7): 188.

[125] Nahjul Balaghah, Book 31.

[126] Ibid.

[127] Ibid.

[128] Mafatihul Janan, Du'a Abu Hamzah Thumali.

Imam Sajjad ('a) stated in another prayer, "Anyone who attends to Your servants for his request or consider one of them the means to success has deprived himself from goodness... And You have stated, 'How is a needy asks from another needy and a poor attends to another poor?'"[129]

According to mentioned traditions and prayers as well as hundreds of other prayers in du'a collections, such as Sahifah Nabawiyyah, Sahifah Alawiyyah, Sahifah Sajjadiyyah, and Sahifah Kazimiyyah, the lifestyle of Prophet Muhammad (s) and infallible Imams ('a) has been direct requesting from the Exalted Allah when having a request, with no mediator. This conduct was the result of their powerful belief and pure monotheism; they clearly knew that no one can do anything for them, but Allah.

We, the Shi'ah, follow the Messenger of Allah (s) and infallible Imams ('a), when praying. We know Allah the All-mighty in the world and ask Him when in need. If we pray and weep in the Imams' ('a) shrines, vowing to Allah by them, we do not mean that they have an independent effect. It is because we have a better spiritual mood to pray to Allah in shrines and mosques. Our avow, cries, resorts, and mourning are for the same reason too.

The Real Position of the Imam with three Advantages

As mentioned before, prophet hood and Imamate are two real positions with three characteristics:

1. Awareness the religiousness sciences, teachings, commandments, and rules, ethics, worshipping and non-worshipping duties, and in sum awareness of all that is revealed to Prophet Muhammad (s) and effects human salvation in this world and the Hereafter.

2. Infallibility of mistakes, forgetfulness, and sins in maintaining

---

[129] Sahifah Al-Sajjadiyah, Du'a 13.

religious commandments and conveying them to the people.

3. Infallibility of wrongdoing or ignoring religious rules.

The mentioned characteristics are truly the prerequisites of prophet hood and Imamate positions, by which the Muslims can recognize their Prophet and Imams and believe in them.

Two Devious Beliefs
Taqsir

If someone is doubtful about some or all of the characteristics of the Prophet or the Imams, he has not known them well and has committed taqsir (delinquency) and is called muqassir. A muqassir person is the one who denies the Prophet's (s) or the Imams' ('a) comprehensive knowledge, is doubtful about their infallibility of mistakes, sins, or forgetfulness, knows them fallible like other humans, or attributes a wrongdoing to them. Such devious beliefs are wrong, with whatever reason. The argument against this wrong belief, as pointed out before, is that any of such beliefs means denying necessity of sending prophets (s) or necessity of appointment of Imams ('a).

Ghuluw

Ghuluw (hyperbole) means extravagance in a belief. The late Allamah Majlisi defines ghuluw this way, "Ghuluw about the prophet or the Imam is belief in their Divinity, their being Allah's partner in worshipping, creation, or granting sustenance to the servants, or manifestation of the soul of one of them in another person's body and uniqueness of these two. It may also be the belief that the Prophet and Imams are aware of the unseen without Allah's help, that Imams are Messengers, or that recognizing the Imams is enough and the servants do not need obey Allah or avoid sins." Then he continues, "All these beliefs are infidelity and going out of the religion, as emphasized by logical reasons, Quranic verses, and many traditions. The infallible Imams ('a) have rejected the people with such beliefs and announced their infidelity."[130]

Qulat (those who believe in quluw) go to extremes in believing in Imamate, consider the Imams, Allah's selected servants, beyond humans, and sometimes assign Allah's specific attributes to them.

The qulat consider the Imams ('a) Allah's partners in managing world issues, such as granting sustenance to the servants, granting people's wishes, descending the rain, healing the patients, removing calamities, or forgiveness of the sins, slaughtering livestock in their path. Some of claimers of shi'ism replace performing religious deeds, doing the obligatory deeds and avoiding the unlawful deeds with superficial expression of affection to the Prophet's (s) Ahlul-Bayt.

Such devious beliefs are not only in contrast with logical reasons, Quran's text, and infallible Imams' ('a) conduct, but also considered infidelity. Sometimes the holders of such beliefs are religiously doomed to murder.

Abu Hashim says, "I asked Imam Riza ('a) about the qulat and mufawizzah. Imam ('a) stated, 'The qulat are infidels and the mufawwizah are polytheists. Anyone who interacts with and accompanies them, has food or drink with them, marries them, trusts them, confirms their speech, or helps them even by saying a single word, will go out of guardianship of Allah, His Messenger (s) and the Ahlul-Bayt.'"[131]

Mufazzal Ibn Yazid says, "Imam Sadiq ('a) mentioned the companions of Abul Khattab[132] and the qulat and said, 'O Mufazzal! Do not accompany them, nor eat or drink water with them, nor shake hands

---

[130] Biharul Anwar, Vol 25, p. 346.

[131] Biharul Anwar, Vol 25, p. 273.

[132] Abul Khattab ,a head of the qulat, lived in Imam Sadiq's (a.s) age. He deceived a group of the masses and founded an invalid religion. His full name was Muhammad Ibn Ta'las and his nickname Abul Khattab and Abu Ziynab. He was originally from Kufah, but lived in Medina for acquiring knowledge and the traditions of Imam Sadiq (a.s), as his companion.

At first he had no deviation; therefore some traditions are narrated by him. However, he was a fool person. Imam Sadiq (a.s) has stated about him, "Abul Khattab was a fool, ..." Then he left Medina, went to other cities, and gathered some stupid people around himself by deceiving them, fabricating incorrect traditions, and attributing them to Imam (a.s). Then he founded an invalid religion with superstitious infidel beliefs. First he claimed that Imam Sadiq (a.s) has taught him Allah's Grand (A'zam) Name and has set him his successor. Then he went even further and claimed prophet hood and then prophetic mission. He said, "Ja'far Ibn Muhammad (Imam Sadiq) is Allah and I am the Messenger of Allah, so obey me!" He and his father recommended some unlawful deeds, such as adultery, theft, and wine-drinking. They did not oblige prayer, fasting, and zakat. At the beginning, they gave Imam Sadiq (a.s) and other infallible Imams positions beyond their real positions, introducing them as prophets and messengers. Then they even claimed the Imams are Allah. They said, "The Imam is not merely the person you can observe; rather he has been a superior light, which has come to this world after passing some levels, and materialized in the form of a human." When his void beliefs and deeds were reported to Imam Sadiq (a.s), the Imam (a.s) raised his hands toward the heaven and said, "May Allah, His angels, and all the people curse Abul Khattab. By Allah that he is infidel and polytheist. He will accompany the pharaoh in the Hell." Later, Abul Khattab and some of his followers were killed and the remnant was divided into several groups, continuing their deviant practice for years. For more information, you can refer to the book Al-Milal wan Nihal by Shahristani and firaqush Shi'ah by Nubakhti and rijal books.

The authors of rijal books have controversy over Mufazzal Ibn 'Umar Kufi mentioned in the same tradition. Some consider him one of the qulat and follower of Abul Khattab, rejecting the traditions he has quoted. Some others regard him a real Muslim and a companion of Imam Sadiq (a.s), considering his ghuluw belief a scandal. The reason for this controversy is various traditions attributed to infallible Imams (a.s) and recorded in tradition books, either rejecting or approving him. A group of rijal scientists have found a solution; he has been one of qulat and follower of Abul Khattab at first, but accepted the truth, abandoned Abul Khattab, and joined Imam Sadiq (a.s) later.

Therefore, the traditions Mufazzal has narrated when being a ghali are denied and the ones narrated after his repenting are valid.

Assessment of this issue needs a long discussion in rijal science, which is not possible in the present book. For more information, you can refer to Mu'jam Rijal Al-Hadith by the late Ayatollah Sayyid Abul Qasim Khu'i, Majma'ur Rijal by 'Inaytullah Ali Qahbali, Qamusur Rijal by Muhammad Taqi Tastiri, Bahjatul Maqal by Mulla Ali Alyari, and other rijal sources.

with them, nor receive their heritage.'" [133]

Two companions of Imam Sadiq ('a) came to him and said, "Mufazzal Ibn 'Umar says that you –the Ahlul-Bayt– define the servants' sustenance." Imam Sadiq ('a) stated, "By Allah that no one defines the servants' sustenance except Allah. I once could not provide my family's provisions and got upset. I thought about it until I could provide food for my family, then I became relaxed. May Allah curse Abul Khattab who attributes lies to us." The two companions said, "Should we curse Abul Khattab and avoid him?" Imam ('a) replied, "Yes." So his companions did so and said, "Allah and His Messenger (s) hate Abul Khattab too." [134]

Zararah says, "I told Imam Sadiq ('a), 'One of the children of Abdullah Ibn Sanan believes in tafwiz (devolving).' Imam ('a) asked, 'What is tafwiz?' I said, 'They believe that the Exalted Allah created Muhammad (s) and Ali ('a), then devolved the world issues to them. Now they create, give sustenance, and give death and life.' Imam Sadiq ('a) stated, 'He is Allah's enemy and lies. If you saw him, recite this verse:

> *'Or do they assign to Allah partners who have created (anything) as He has created, so that the creation seemed to them similar? Say: "Allah is the Creator of all things: He is the One, the Supreme and Irresistible."'*[135]

Zararah says, 'When I recited the verse for that person it was as if there was stone in his mouth (He could not defend his belief anymore).'"[136]

---

[133] Ibid, p. 296.

[134] Ibid, p.301.

[135] Surah Al-Ra'd (13): 16.

[136] Biharul Anwar, Vol 25, p. 343.

Abdur Rahman Ibn Kathir says, "Imam Sadiq ('a) told his companions, 'May Allah curse Mughayrat Ibn Sa'id and the Jew woman, who visited him and learned magic and odd things from him. Mugayrah attributed lies to my father, so the Almighty Allah took his belief from hims. Some other people attributed lies to me. Allah will make them taste the heat of iron.'

By Allah, we are only His servants; He created and selected us. We have no power to bring advantage or disadvantage for ourselves. If the Almighty has Mercy on us, it is from He and if He punishes us, it is because of our own deeds.'

By Allah that we have no argument against Allah! We cannot free ourselves from the Fire. We die like other people and will be placed inside a grave. Then we will be resurrected and reckoned about our deeds in the Hereafter. Woe be to them! May Allah curse them! They upset Him. They upset Messenger of Allah (s), Amiral Mu'minin ('a), Fatimah (s), Hassan ('a), Hussayn ('a), Ali Ibn Hussayn ('a), and Muhammad Ibn Ali ('a) in their graves. I am the son of Prophet Muhammad (s). You see that I am fearful of Allah's wrath in my bed, while they sleep comfortably in their beds. I beg Allah and weep from His fear, but they are asleep. I am frightened of Allah's punishment in mountains and deserts. I take refuge to Allah from this stupid man (Abul Khattab). May Allah curse him!'"[137]

Imam Sadiq ('a) stated, "Be careful that the qulat do not lead your youth astray! The qulat are the worst creatures of Allah, because they belittle Allah's greatness and consider divinity for His servants."

By Allah that qulat are worse than the Jews, the Christians, and the infidels. If they come to us, we do not accept to see them, but we will accept a muqassir." The Imam ('a) was then asked, "O son of Messenger of Allah! What is the reason?" Imam Sadiq ('a) replied, "Because a ghali

---

[137] Biharul Anwar, Vol 25, p. 289.

is used to abandoning prayer, fasting, zakat, and Hajj and cannot leave his habit. A muqassir, however, will practice his obligatory deeds when he finds out his fault."[138]

Imam Riza ('a) said in his prayers, "O Lord! I take refuge in You for changing the states and abilities. Wa la hawla wa la quwwata illa bik (And there is no power except from You) O Lord! I take refuge in You and hate the people who lie about us. O Lord! I take refuge in You from the people who say things about us that we do not say."

"O Allah! Creation is done by You and You grant sustenance. I worship You and ask help from You. You are the Creator of us and our fathers; from the first one to the last one. O Allah! Divinity is for You and does not deserve anyone else. I curse the Christians who belittle Your magnitude and the people who attribute greatness to Your other servants. O Lord! We are your creatures and servants, not owners of our advantage and disadvantage, nor our life and death. We avoid anyone who thinks we are his Lord or supposes that the servants' creation or sustenance is in our hands, just like the avoidance of Jesus from the Christians."

"O Lord! We have not invited them to this belief, so do not scold us for what they say and save us from such invalid qualities. Perish them from the earth; if they remain on the earth they will lead Your servants astray and make them infidels."[139]

Abu Basir Says, "I told Imam Sadiq ('a), 'People say some things about you.' Imam ('a) asked, 'What do they say?' I said, 'They say that you know the number of rain drops, stars, trees' leaves, sands, and the weight of seas' water and deserts' soil.' Imam Sadiq ('a) raised his head to the sky and stated, 'Subhana Allah! Subhana Allah! (Glory be to

---

[138] Ibid, p. 265.

[139] Biharul Anwar, Vol 25, p. 343.

Allah!) By Allah not! Only Allah knows these things.'"[140]

Ibn Mughayrah says, "Yahya Ibn Abdullah and I visited Imam Abul Hassan ('a). Yahya told Imam ('a), 'May I be sacrificed for you! People think that you know the unseen.' Imam ('a) replied, 'Glory be to Allah! Put your hand on my head; by Allah that my hair bristled from hearing this. By Allah that everything I say I narrate from the Messenger of Allah (s).'"[141]

The Motives of Ghuluw (Hyperbole)

The qulat and their supporters have had different motives, some of which are mentioned in the traditions as follows:

1. Ignorance. We read in a letter from Hadrat Sahibul 'Amr, Imam Mahdi ('a), 'O Muhammad Ibn Ali! The ignorant from the Shi'ah and the people who do not value their religion as much as a fly wing tease us. I take Allah, the Prophet (s), the angels, and Allah's prophets and Imams as well as anyone who hears this witness that I take refuge in Allah and His Messenger (s) from the people who say that we know the unseen sciences or are Allah's partner in His sovereignty, or attribute positions to us other than what Allah has defined for us. Surely, Allah, the angels, the prophets (s), and the Imams ('a) avoid such people.'[142]

2. Material misuses. Imam Muhammad Baqir ('a) stated about three of the qulat, namely Abul Ghamar, Ja'far Ibn Waqid, and Hashim Ibn Abi Husham, "They misuse people's property by our names and invite people to what Abul Khattab invites. May Allah curse Abul Khattab and the people who invite others to Abul Khattab and anyone who invited people to him before."[143]

3. Extravagance in affection. Imam Ali Ibn Al-Hussayn ('a) stated,

---

[140] Ibid, p. 394.

[141] Biharul Anwar, Vol 25, p. 293.

[142] Ibid, p. 267.

[143] Biharul Anwar, Vol 25, p. 319.

"The Jews attributed what they believed in to 'Uzayr, out of extreme affection. Therefore, 'Uzayr is not one of them and they are not like him. The Christians, too, attributed what they believed in to Christ, so Christ is not one of them, nor are they his followers. The same is true about us (the Ahlul-Bayt). A group of the Shi'ah love us so much that they attribute what the Jews said about 'Uzayr and what the Christians said about Jesus to us; therefore, they are not our followers, nor are we from them." [144]

Summary and a Warning

As was mentioned, one of the major problems of infallible Imams ('a) and Shi'ism has been the creation of two devious trends of ghuluw and tafwiz. These invalid beliefs harmed the Imams' ('a) honor and Shi'ism sect, making the people pessimistic about them. Unfortunately, this danger was plotted by pretenders of Imams' ('a) affection, who belittled the Exalted Allah's greatness because of ignorance, untrue expression of affection, or due to financial misuses, considering the Imams' ('a) Allah's partners in some of His attributes. They deceived some gullible people by publicizing these ideas, thus threatening the Shi'ism sect. In such conditions, the infallible Imams ('a) did not remain silent before these invalid eulogies and struggled with superstitious opinions behind them. They introduced the heads of these fabricated beliefs as infidels, cursing, abandoning, and even allowing their murder, in order to inform their simple-minded followers. Thanks to this conscious step by the infallible Imams ('a), this major plot was removed in a way that there is no remnant of the ghulat and mufawwizah today. Of course, the Shi'ah scholars have always attempted to guard true Islamic beliefs and campaign devious opinions.

It is worth mentioning that religious scholars and dignitaries should

---

[144] Biharul Anwar, Vol 25, p. 288.

be aware of misusers, now and in future, who plot to deceive the masses especially at the time of social crises. They do so by telling hopeful stories, groundless dreams, unreliable quotations, and doing some untrue deeds and eulogies.

It may also be possible that the mentioned people propagate ghuluw or tafwiz beliefs consciously or unconsciously. Therefore, religious authorities should always be conscious of and campaign against invalid opinions, just as their predecessors.

Five

The Arguments for Imamate

The Methods of Selecting the Prophet's (s) Caliph or the Imam

One of the major controversial issues among the Muslims from Early Islamic Era has been the true and legitimate method of selecting the Prophet's (s) caliph or the Imam of the Muslims. The question is that who is allowed to define the Prophet's (s) caliph and introduce him to the people. Is the Divine guidance needed in recognition and appointment of the Imam or is this task devolved to the Islamic ummah? This controversy has divided the Muslims into two sects of Sunnism and Imamiyyah (Shi'ism). The Shi'ah Muslims believe that no one can recognize and introduce the Imam, except the Almighty Allah and Prophet Muhammad (s); therefore, the Imam is appointed by Allah and His Messenger (s). The Sunni Muslims, however, claim that there is no need to introduction and appointment of the caliph by the Prophet (s); rather, recognition and selection of the Imam is put to the Muslims and they are qualified to do so.

The root of this difference among the two major Islamic sects is another difference about conditions and characteristics of the caliph and the Imam. The Shi'ah Muslims consider two qualities necessary for the caliph of Messenger of Allah (s); first, complete knowledge of Islamic sciences and teachings, values and disvalues, virtues and all Islamic rules and commandments revealed to Prophet Muhammad (s), and second infallibility of faults, forgetfulness, wrongdoing, sins, and transgression of Divine regulations. The Imamiyyah or Shi'ah have proved these two necessary qualities of the Prophet's (s) caliph in kalam books, using logical arguments and the traditions. [145]

Regarding the necessity of these two characteristics, it is said that the introducer of Prophet's (s) caliph should be able to recognize the infallible individuals and the Divine scholars among other people. Only Allah and His Prophet (s) can do so, because it is He Who has created humans and knows well their innate essence. The Almighty has created the Prophet (s) and the Imams ('a) and is aware of their infallibility. Therefore, only the Imam who is selected by Prophet Muhammad (s) possesses the Divine sciences and guidance. This way, an infallible Imam can be known in one of these three ways; first, introduction and appointment by the Prophet (s), second, introduction by the previous infallible Imam, who holds Prophet Muhammad's (s) sciences and knowledge, and third, showing a miracle that is the sign of Allah's support.

The Sunni Muslims, however, do not consider knowledge of Islamic sciences and infallibility as necessary conditions of the Prophet's (s) caliph. They believe that selecting the caliph is devolved to the people; anyone, who is selected by the people and the people take the oath of allegiance with him, is the Prophet's (s) caliph and should be

---

[145] The issues of Imam's knowledge and infallibility are discussed in detail early in this book and also in the book Review of General issue of Imamate.

obeyed. They define three methods in this regard. One is people's consensus, as happened in case of Abu Bakr's caliphate. The other method is introduction of previous fallible caliph, just as Abu Bakr introduced 'Umar, as the next caliph, before his demise. One other method is selection by the nobles' council, like what happened in selecting Uthman, the third Sunni caliph after Prophet Muhammad (s).

The Imamiyyah Shi'ahs

The Imamiyyah Shi'ahs are the people who believe in the successive caliphate and Imamate of Ali Ibn Abi Talib ('a) and eleven of his progeny after Prophet Muhammad (s). They are also called Ithna 'Ashari (Twelver). The Shi'ah believe that these Imams are inheritors of the Prophet's (s) sciences and infallible of mistakes and sins and should all be obeyed.

The Names of Twelve Imams
1. Ali Ibn Abi Talib ('a)
2. Hassan Ibn Ali ('a)
3. Hussayn Ibn Ali ('a)
4. Ali Ibn Hussayn ('a)
5. Muhammad Ibn Ali ('a)
6. Ja'far Ibn Muhammad ('a)
7. Musa Ibn Ja'far ('a)
8. Ali Ibn Musa ('a)
9. Muhammad Ibn Ali ('a)
10. Ali Ibn Muhammad ('a)
11. Hassan Ibn Ali ('a)
12. Hujjat Ibn Al-Hassan (May Allah hasten his reappearance)

Each of these Imams reached the imamate position and were martyred or passed away after a while, except the twelfth Imam, who is alive but hidden from sight. He will remain absent until the world is ready for accepting his worldwide government and Allah orders his reappearance. This important issue will be explained in detail later in the present book.

The Reasons for Imamate of the Imams ('a)

It was proved in previous sections that recognition and appointment of the Imam is impossible without Divine guidance. Since the Imam should be away from mistakes, forgetfulness, and sins, only Allah and His Messenger (s) who can recognize the infallibles from among the servants can introduce Prophet's (s) successor. As a result, the infallible Imam can be recognized in either of three ways:

1. Identifying and appointing by the Prophet (s) who is aware of revelation sciences.

2. Identifying and appointment by the previous Imam, whose Imamate is proved before, and has been aware of the Prophet's (s) sciences.

3. Bringing a miracle, that is a sign of Divine support.

The First Reason; Prophet Muhammad's (s) Traditions

The honorable Messenger of Allah (s) has mentioned the number of twelve Imams and their names in the traditions recorded in books of the Sunni and Shi'ah narrators. These traditions are of several types:

The first type; twelve people and All from Quraysh

There are some traditions of this type, some of which are cited here. Jabir Ibn Samarah said, "I heard from Messenger of Allah (s), 'People's affairs are managed well so long as twelve people rule them.' Then the Prophet (s) said something that I could not hear. I asked my father what the Prophet said. He told me that Prophet Muhammad (s) said, 'All of them are from Quraysh.'[146]"[147]

---

[146] Prophet Muhammad's (s.a) tribe.

[147] Sahih Muslim, Vol 3, p. 1452.

Sammak Ibn Harb has quoted Jabir Ibn Samarah who said, "I heard from Prophet Muhammad (s), 'Islam will be honored as long as twelve caliphs will rule the Muslims.' The Messenger of Allah (s) then said something that I did not hear. I asked my father about it and he said, 'The Prophet (s) stated, 'All of them will be from Quraysh.'"[148]

'amir Ibn Sa'd Ibn Abi Waqqas said, "I wrote a letter and sent it to Jabir Ibn Samarah by my slave Nafi'. I asked him to inform me of what he had heard from messenger of Allah (s). He wrote in reply, 'On a Friday, the Prophet (s) stated, 'This religion will last until the Resurrection or until twelve caliphs, who are all from Quraysh, rule you.'"[149]

Prophet Muhammad (s) has declared the existence of twelve righteous caliphs from Quraysh after himself. They will honor Islam and the Muslims as rulers. The researchers know well that this number of caliphs is not compatible with caliphs of Rashidin, the Umayyid, Bani Marwan, the Abbasid, or combining some of them with some others. The only twelve-caliphs that remain are the Imamiyyah infallible Imams ('a), who are all from Quraysh.

The Second Type; Twelve People and All Infallible

Abdullah Ibn Abbas said, "I heard from Messenger of Allah (s), 'In addition to me, Ali, Hassan, Hussayn, and nine people from Hussayn's progeny are purified and infallible.'"[150]

The Messenger of Allah (s) told Hadrat Fatimah (s), "Do not cry or be upset! You are the Mistress of the ladies in Paradise, your father is the master of prophets, your cousin (Ali) is the master of caliphs, and your two sons (Hassan and Hussayn) are masters of the youth in Paradise.

---

[148] Sahih Muslim, Vol 3, p. 1453.

[149] Sahih Muslim, Vol 3, p. 1453.

[150] Ghayatul Maram, Vol 2, p. 162.

Nine Imams from Hussayn's progeny will be appointed, all of which are infallible. Mahdi ('a) of this nation will be from us too."[151]

Abu Tufayl has narrated from Imam Ali ('a), "The Messenger of Allah (s) told me, 'You are my successor and guardian to anyone who dies from the Ahlul-Bayt and my caliph among my ummah. War with you is war with me and peace with you is peace with me. You are the father of Imams; eleven Imams from your progeny are infallible and purified. Mahdi of my ummah, who fills the world with justice, is one of them. Woe be to their enemies!'"[152]

Based on what was stated before in proving the necessity of infallibility for the Imams, the above-mentioned traditions and many other similar ones confirm the Imamate of twelve Imams ('a). Except for these twelve people from the Prophet's (s) Ahlul-Bayt, about who tat'hir verse is revealed, no one has claimed infallibility nor has anyone's infallibility ever been proved.

The Third Type; Twelve People and the Names of the First and Last Ones

In many traditions, the number twelve for the Imams and the names of their first and last ones are mentioned. As an instance, Salman Muhammadi said, "I went to Prophet Muhammad (s), who had placed Hussayn ('a) on his lap, kissing his eyes and mouth. The Prophet (s) then told him, 'You are sayyid, son of sayyid, and father of sayyids. You are the Imam, son of the Imam, and father of the Imams. You are the hujjat, son of the hujjat, and father of nine Imams, the ninth of which will be Qa'im.'"[153]

Abdullah Ibn Abbas has quoted from the Messenger of Allah (s), "The caliphs, successors, and Allah's hujjats after me are twelve; the first

---

[151] Ibid, p. 239.

[152] Ghayatul Maram, Vol 1, p. 193.

[153] Ibid, p. 103.

one is my brother, Ali, and the last one will be one of my progeny too." The Prophet (s) was then asked, "O Messenger of Allah! Who is your brother?" He replied, "Ali Ibn Abi Talib." The Prophet (s) was asked, "Who is your last progeny?" Prophet Muhammad (s) answered, "Mahdi, who will fill the earth with justice after being filled with injustice and oppression."[154]

Imam Hassan Ibn Ali ('a) has quoted from the Messenger of Allah (s), "The number of Imams after me will be as the number of the Israelite leaders and apostles of Jesus (twelve). Anyone who likes them is believer and anyone who dislikes them is hypocrite. They are Allah's hujjats for the people and like flags of guidance."[155]

The Fourth Type; Twelve People in Order of Imamate

Jabir Ibn Abdullah Ansari told the Messenger of Allah (s), "O Messenger of Allah! Who are the Imams from the progeny of Ali Ibn Abi Talib?" Prophet Muhammad (s) stated, "Hassan and Hussayn; the masters of youth of Paradise, then Ali Ibn Hussayn; Sayyidul 'abidin (master of the worshippers) in his own age, then Baqir Ibn Ali, who you will see. Say my greetings to him. Then Sadiq; Ja'far Ibn Muhammad, then Kazim; Musa Ibn Ja'far, then Riza; Ali Ibn Musa, then Taqi; Muhammad Ibn Ali, then Naqi; Ali Ibn Muhammad, then Zakiyy; Hassan Ibn Ali, and then his son Qa'im; Mahdi, who will fill the earth with justice as it would filled with injustice. O Jabir! These are my successors, caliphs, sons, and the 'itrat. Everyone who obeys them has obeyed me and everyone who denies one or all of them has denied me. The heaven does not collapse on the earth nor does the earth swallow its occupants for their sake."[156]

Sahl Ibn Sa'd Ansari said, "I asked Hadrat Fatimah (s), the daughter of

---

[154] Ghayatul Maram, Vol 1, p. 106.

[155] Ibid, Vol 1, p. 113.

[156] Ghayatul Maram, Vol 1, p. 163.

Messenger of Allah (s) from the Imams. She said that the messenger of Allah (s) told Imam Ali ('a), 'O Ali! You are the Imam and caliph after me; you are more deserved to interfere in believers' affairs than themselves. When you pass away, your son Hassan will be more deserved and after him Hussayn will be more deserved. After Hussayn's demise, his son Ali Ibn Hussayn will be more deserved. When Ali Ibn Husayn passes away, his son Muhammad will be more deserved. When Muhammad passes away, his son Ja'far will be more deserved. After Ja'far's demise, his son Musa will be more deserved. When Musa passes away, his son Ali will be more deserved. After Ali's demise, his son Muhammad will be more deserved. When Muhammad passes away, his son Ali will be more deserved. After Ali's demise, his son Hassan will be more deserved. When Hassan passes away, his son Qa'im and Mahdi will be more deserved; he will conquer the East and the West.'"[157]

Ali Ibn Abi Talib ('a) has quoted from Messenger of Allah (s), "Everyone who likes to meet Allah and be attended by Him should resort to your guardianship (wilayat). Everyone who likes to meet the Almighty Allah without fearing Him should accept the guardianship of your son Hussayn. If anyone likes to meet Allah while his sins are forgiven, he should accept the guardianship of Ali Ibn Hussayn, since the Almighty said about him,

> '*On their faces are their marks, (being) the traces of their prostration.*'[158]

Everyone who wants to meet the Exalted Allah while his eyes are illuminated should accept the guardianship of Muhammad Ibn Ali.

---

[157] Ghayatul Maram, Vol 1, p. 216.

[158] Surah Al-Fat'h (48): 29.

Anyone who likes to meet his Lord with his Letter of Deeds in his right hand should know Ja'far Ibn Muhammad Sadiq as his guardian. Everyone who wants to meet Allah while he is purified should take Musa Ibn Ja'far Kazim guardian. Everyone who likes to meet Allah delighted should accept the guardianship of Ali Ibn Musa Riza. Everyone who likes to meet Allah with high spiritual degrees and removed sins should accept the guardianship of Muhammad Ibn Ali. If someone likes to meet the Almighty while his reckoning is easy and go to the paradise, that is wider than the heavens and the earth, along with the pious servants, he should accept the guardianship of Ali Ibn Muhammad. Everyone who wants to meet Allah with salvation should accept the guardianship of Hassan Ibn Ali. Everyone who likes to meet the Almighty with perfect belief in Islam should accept the guardianship of the waited Imam Mahdi; Sahib Al-Zaman. These are guidance lights in darkness, Imams of guidance, and flags of piety. I guarantee going to the Paradise for everyone who likes them and accepts their guardianship."[159]

Imam Hassan Ibn Ali ('a) stated, "I heard from the Messenger of Allah (s) who told Ali Ibn Abi Talib ('a), 'You are the inheritor of my knowledge and wisdom and the Imam after me. When you get martyred, your son Hassan will be the Imam. When Hassan will be martyred, your other son Hussayn will be the Imam. After Hussayn's martyrdom, his son Ali will be the Imam. After him nine people from Hussayn's progeny will become the Imams.' Hassan Ibn Ali ('a) then said, 'O Messenger of Allah! What are the names of these nine Imams?' Prophet Muhammad (s) answered, 'Ali, Muhammad, Ja'far, Musa, Ali, Muhammad, Ali, Hassan, and Mahdi, from Hussayn's progeny. Mahdi will fill the earth with justice after being filled with oppression and

---

[159] Jami' Ahadith Al-Shi'ah, Vol 17, p. 103.

injustice.'"[160]

The Second Reason; Appointment by the Previous Imam

The main reason for the Imamate of twelve Imams ('a) is being appointed by their previous Imam. The Imam, who is appointed by the Prophet (s), can recognize the Imam after himself and introduce him to the people, just like the Prophet (s). Since the Imams ('a) possess Prophet Muhammad's (s) sciences, information, and necessary recommendation directly from him or from their earlier Imam ('a), they can identify the infallible among the people. The Imamate of twelve Imams (s) is done in the same way, as recorded in hadith and kalam books. The same method is used in the present book.

As pointed out before, the honorable Messenger of Allah (s) was infallible himself, supported by the Almighty Allah, and recognizer of the infallible. He had prepared the conditions and people's minds for Imamate of Imam Ali ('a) by emphasizing his virtues, innate qualities, scientific stance, and infallibility. Finally, Prophet Muhammad (s) selected and appointed Imam Ali ('a) to Imamate in Ghadir Khum in presence of tens of thousands of hajj pilgrims. This way his Imamate was confirmed for the audience. Prophet Muhammad (s) gave necessary recommendations to Ali ('a) for continuation of his Imamate. Imam Ali ('a), too, selected and appointed his son, Hassan, for the Imamate position in his lifetime. Imam Hassan ('a) selected and appointed Imam Hussayn ('a) as Imam, before his death. Imam Hussayn ('a) selected and appointed his son, Ali Ibn Hussayn, for Imamate. The same method was continued until the appointment of the twelfth Imam ('a).

The Third Reason; Miracles

---

[160] Ghayatul Maram, Vol 1, p. 193.

The infallible Imams ('a) have had some miracles in their lifetimes for proving their Imamate, which are cited in hadith, history, and kalam books. We do not cite them here not to prolong the discussion.

Six

Brief Biographies of the Infallible Imams

The Shi'ah Opinion about the Infallible Imams

Based on mental reason for necessity of existence of the Imam, mentioned before, and some Quranic verses about the Imamate as well as many traditions from Prophet Muhammad (s) and infallible Imams ('a) regarding the issue of Imamate, our belief about the twelve Imams ('a) is that:

1. They are completely away from any sins, faults, and wrongdoing and are infallible.

2. They are the most perfect humans in knowing the Almighty Allah and His Attributes. They deeply believe in Allah's uniqueness, the Resurrection, and prophet hood. They see the unseen world intuitively.

3. They are adorned with all ethical virtues and away from all vices.

4. They are completely aware of religious rules, commandments,

fundamental and minor issues, obligatory, undesirable, recommended, and prohibited deeds. They did not receive the revelation or make religious rules; rather they deducted their knowledge directly from the Holy Quran or indirectly from the Prophet (s) or the books inherited from Messenger of Allah (s).

5. They knew well all governmental rules and regulations. They benefited from especial authority too.

The infallible Imams ('a) had two major duties as well:

Guarding the Divine Commandments

The honorable Imams (s) of the Shi'ah possessed the necessary sciences and were prepared for safeguarding religious rules and commandments, circulating Islamic teachings and sciences, and pursuing Prophet Muhammad's (s) purposes. As mentioned before, the Messenger of Allah (s) had trained them for this important duty. He introduced his 'itrat or Ahlul-Bayt as the most valid scientific source to the Muslims and recommended benefitting from their knowledge. But unfortunately Prophet Muhammad's (s) purpose was not fully realized; the seekers of property and worldly positions not only removed the Ahlul-Bayt from caliphate of the Prophet (s), but also hindered their scientific authority, depriving the Islamic ummah from authentic prophet hood sciences. Each of the Imams ('a) attempted in publicizing Islamic sciences, teachings, and commandments and training scholars as much as possible in those limited conditions. As a result of such constant attempts throughout the ages, hundreds of thousands of traditions in various scientific trends were published, most of which are recorded in tradition books. If the infallible Imams ('a) had more opportunity, the Islamic ummah benefitted from more Islamic sciences and teachings.

Holding the Caliphate Position

The second major duty of the Imams ('a) was incumbency of caliphate and managing the Islamic country's socio-political affairs, which was a duty of Prophet Muhammad's (s) too. The Messenger of Allah (s) had given necessary recommendations before and appointed Ali Ibn Abi Talib ('a) as his successor in Ghadir Khum. Imam Ali ('a) was ready for accepting the caliphate position, but people's acceptance and desirable conditions were necessary for realization of it too.

Unfortunately, a group of ambitious people ignored Prophet Muhammad's (s) recommendation regarding Muslims' caliphate, misused ignorance of the masses, and created a deviation in the course of caliphate, opposing the Prophet's (s) want. In such conditions, Imam Ali ('a) could do nothing but patience. Twenty five years passed until the people awakened and took the oath of allegiance with Imam Ali ('a) as Muslims' caliph. Later, however, some people, who had accustomed to and benefitted from prejudice and injustice in previous governments, could not accept Imam Ali's ('a) just ruling. They opposed his government by setting up wars and adversities. After about five years, Imam Ali ('a) was martyred in worshipping mihrab. The caliphate then returned to a devious course under the Ummayid and the Abbasids dynasties for many years, with no grounds for caliphate of the other infallible Imams ('a). Each of the Imams ('a) considered the caliphate after Messenger of Allah (s) his lawful right and was prepared for taking the position. None of them, nevertheless, could reach caliphate because of Muslims' delinquency.

The Signs of Genuine Shi'ah

The term Shi'ah is attributed to someone who believes in successive Imamate and caliphate of Ali Ibn Abi Talib ('a) and eleven of his progeny after Prophet Muhammad (s) and loves them. Such a person is a Twelver Shi'ah. Of course, mere verbal affection does not suffice for being a real Shi'ah nor does it guarantee salvation in this world and the Hereafter. Basically, the belief without practice is merely a mental concept.

The lexical meaning of 'Shi'ah' is 'follower'. There is a kind of practical adherence embedded in its meaning too. The Shi'ah were called so because they followed the Messenger of Allah (s), Imam Ali ('a), and infallible Imams ('a) in speech, behavior, and ethics. Practice is a necessity for real belief. If there is no practice, one's belief is probably superficial. Real affection brings about attention and satisfaction of the beloved. Can someone be a real lover of infallible Imams ('a) but behave against their recommendations?

For a better recognition of real Shi'ahs one should refer to the statements of infallible Imams ('a). Some of the traditions in this regard are pointed out here:

Jabir has quoted from Imam Muhammad Baqir ('a), "O Jabir! Is it enough for a Shi'ah to say 'I love the Ahlul-Bayt'? By Allah, a Shi'ah should be pious and obedient to the Almighty. O Jabir! Our followers (Shi'ahs) are known with these characteristics; humility, obeisance in worshipping, trusteeship, frequency of zikr (Allah's remembrance), sawm (fasting), salat (prayer), goodness to one's parents, consideration of poor neighbors, debtors, and orphans, except that leaving such deeds is better. Our Shi'ahs were trustees among the people."

Jabir then asked, "O son of Messenger of Allah! We do not see such people in this time." Imam Baqir ('a) stated, "O Jabir! Do not go astray! Does it suffice to say 'I love Ali ('a) and accept his guardianship' but not to follow Ali ('a) in practice? If someone says, 'I love Messenger of Allah (s)', but he does not follow the Prophet's (s) conduct, this affection will be of no use to him, though the Messenger of Allah (s) is better than Ali ('a). Fear Allah and do good deeds! The Almighty is no one's relative. The most beloved and honorable of the servants are the most righteous and pious ones. O Jabir! By Allah that only piety approaches the servants to Allah. Distance from the Hell is not in our hands. No one has a hujjat (argument) against Allah. Anyone who obeys Allah is our friend. Anyone who disobeys Allah is our enemy. No one can get to our guardianship except with righteous deed and avoiding the sins."[161]

Imam Ja'far Sadiq ('a) told Fuzayl, "Say our greetings to our Shi'ahs and tell them, 'We can do nothing for you against Allah's will, except when you avoid sins.' So keep your tongues and hands from wrongdoing. Establish prayers and be patient. Surely Allah is with the patient."[162]

Imam Sadiq ('a) told Ibn Jundab, "Tell our Shi'ahs, 'Do not go astray! By Allah that you will not get to our guardianship except by avoiding the sins, attempting in worshipping, and helping your religious brothers. Anyone who oppresses the people is not our Shi'ah.'"[163]

Imam Sadiq ('a) stated, "O Shi'ah! Keep our face! Do not lose our face! Be kind to people, keep your tongues from sins, do not say useless or obscene words!"[164]

Imam Sadiq ('a) told Abu Usamah, "Attempt in piety, avoiding sins, patience in worshipping, truthful speech, returning the trusts, kind manner, and goodness to neighbors. Attract people to yourselves with your deeds not verbally! Gain our face! Perform long ruku' and sujud, because while you perform them Satan cries out, 'Woe be on me! This servant of Allah obeyed Him and performed sujud, but I but I did not and disobeyed Him.'"[165]

Imam Sadiq ('a) stated, "Watch out not to do something by which we (the Ahlul-Bayt) are reproached, because a bad child loses his father's face by wrongdoing. Be an honor for someone to who you are

---

[161] Kafi, Vol 2, p. 74.

[162] Mishkatul Anwar, p. 44.

[163] Tuhaful Uqul, p. 314.

[164] Mishkatul Anwar, p. 67.

[165] Kafi, Vol 2, p. 77.

attached!"¹⁶⁶

Imam Hassan Askari ('a) told the Shi'ahs, "I recommend you to observe piety in religion, endeavor for the Almighty Allah, be truthfulness, return the trusts to everyone –good or bad, perform long sujud, and do good to the neighbors."

The Messenger of Allah (s) was appointed to prophet hood for the same things. Pray in Muslims' mosques, escort their dead bodies, visit their patients, and fully pay their rights, because when one of you is pious, truthful, payer of trusts, and good-mannered, it is said about him, 'He is a Shi'ah.' Then we will be pleased."

Be pious and gain our face. This way you will bring affection for us and remove bad reputation from us. Surely, whatever goodness is said about us we deserve it and we are away from whatever badness that is said about us. We have rights in Allah's Book, in relation with Messenger of Allah (s), and due to purification by the Exalted Allah. No one can claim these positions, but a liar."

Remember Allah much! Do not forget death! Recite Quran much! Say benediction (salawat) to Prophet Muhammad (s)! Salawat on Messenger of Allah (s) has a tenfold reward. Follow these recommendations! I say farewell to you. Allah's blessings be on you!"¹⁶⁷

Imam Sadiq ('a) wrote in his letter to the Shi'ahs, "Observe the salat times, especially salatul wusta (The Noon Prayer). Pray for Allah's sake, as the Almighty has ordered the believers in His Book. Befriend poor Muslims, because anyone who belittles them has gone astray and irritated Allah. My grandfather, Muhammad (s) stated, 'The Exalted Allah has ordered me to like poor Muslims.' Beware that anyone who humiliates Muslims will be belittled by Allah so that the people will

---

¹⁶⁶ Ibid, p. 219.

¹⁶⁷ Tuhaful Uqul, p. 518.

hate him." [168]

Imam Sadiq ('a) stated, "O the Shi'ah of Muhammad's Ahlul-Bayt! Anyone who does not control his anger, behaves unkindly with his friends and companions, does not reconcile with friends, and does not disagree with enemies is not our Shi'ah. O the Shi'ah of Muhammad's (s) Household! Observe piety as much as you can. Wa la hawla wa la quwwata illa bi Allah (There is no power except from Allah)."[169]

The mentioned traditions and many other similar ones reveal some points:

1. The mere expression of Shi'ism and affection for the Prophet's (s) Ahlul-Bayt ('a) does not suffice for proving Shi'ism; rather performing religious duties and avoiding sins are the major indicators of Shi'ism.

2. Expression of affection for the Ahlul-Bayt ('a) does not bring about salvation from calamities in the Hereafter if it does not accompany performing obligatory deeds and avoiding unlawful ones.

3. The wilayat (guardianship) of the Ahlul-Bayt ('a) is not guaranteed but by observing religious duties and avoiding the sins.

4. Everyone who obeys Allah's orders is the friend of the Ahlul-Bayt ('a) and anyone who transgresses the Divine regulations is an enemy of the Ahlul-Bayt ('a), even if he expresses affection for them verbally.

5. Salvation, distance from the Hell, and gaining the Paradise in not in the hands of infallible Imams ('a); rather, humans go to the Hell or the Paradise based on their own deeds.

6. The infallible Imams ('a) have asked their followers to make people optimistic about the Ahlul-Bayt ('a) by their good manner and speech and do not lose their face by wrongdoing.

7. The honorable Messenger of Allah (s) and infallible Imams ('a) were men of practice themselves. They were committed to not only

---

[168] Tuhaful Uqul, p. 327.

[169] Ibid, p. 401.

doing the obligatory deeds and avoiding the unlawful ones, but also to doing the desirable and avoiding the undesirable deeds. They were prominent in observing good manner and conduct among the people of their ages and were away from vices.

The Muslims and the Shi'ah are obliged to follow these noble characters as their pattern. The salvation in this world and the Hereafter is only provided in this way. Next, the twelve Imams of the Shi'ah are introduced in brief.

The First Imam; Ali Ibn Abi Talib

Birth and Martyrdom

The first Imam of the Shi'ah, Imam Ali ('a), was born on thirteenth of Rajab, thirty years after 'ᵃmul Fil in Mecca, inside the Ka'bah.

His father was Abu Talib and his mother was Fatimah Binti 'Asad. His nicknames were Abu Turab, Abul Hassan, Abus Sibtayn, and Abur Riyhanatayn. His titles were Amiral Mu'minin, Sayyidul Muslimin, Imamul Muttaqin, and Sayyidul 'Awsiya'.[170]

He was hit by Ibn Muljam Muradi when performing the Morning Prayer on nineteenth of Ramadan and was martyred on Ramadan twenty first. His holy body was buried outside Kufah (now called Najaf).

Ali ('a) in Prophet Muhammad's (s) Age

A precise detailed review of Imam Ali's ('a) life requires authoring tens of volumes of books. The present book, however, can only point out the major events of his lifetime briefly.

---

[170] A'lamul Wura, Vol 11, pp 306-307; Al-Irshad, Vol 1, p. 5.

Imam Ali ('a) left his father's house at age six to live with Prophet Muhammad (s), with suggestion of the Prophet (s), who accepted the guardianship of Ali ('a). This way, Ali ('a) learnt much from Prophet Muhammad's (s) conduct and followed his teachings. He accompanied Prophet Muhammad (s) in his 'i'tikaf (seclusion for worship) in Hara' cave, observing the signs of revelation and prophethood.[171]

Ali ('a) was the first man to accept Islam and pray with the Prophet (s). He was nearly ten years old then.[172]

In difficulties of early prophet hood of Muhammad (s), Ali ('a) was always at his service and the best helper for him. In economic, social, and political embargo of the infidels against the Muslims in Shi'bi Abu Talib (Abu Talib valley), Ali ('a) was present.

When the infidels threatened Prophet Muhammad's (s) life and he was going to immigrate to Medina, Imam Ali ('a) slept in his bed to save his life on Laylatul Mabit (the night of staying). Then he got a mission from the Messenger of Allah (s) to finish the Prophet's (s) incomplete works and immigrate to Medina along with some ladies from the Prophet's (s) Household.[173]

The Messenger of Allah (s) signed a brotherhood contract with Ali ('a) in medina.[174]

In the second year after Hijra, Ali ('a) was honored to become Prophet Muhammad's (s) son-in-law, marrying Hadrat Fatimah (s), the best lady of the world.[175]

At that time, Imam Ali ('a) was a powerful brave young man ready for war and jihad. He participated in all the wars, battled bravely, and

---

[171] Manaqib 'ali Abi Talib, Vol 2, p. 205-206.

[172] Ibid, p. 7.

[173] Manaqib 'ali Abi Talib, Vol 2, pp. 68-78.

[174] Ibid, p. 210.

[175] Ibid, p. 207.

killed the enemies of Islam. He had a major role in victory of the Muslims, being far ahead of other battlers.[176]

During his prophetic mission, the Prophet of Islam (s) gave two important duties to Imam Ali ('a); first, writing and colleting the Quranic verses (ayat) and chapters (surahs), and second, learning and maintaining religious sciences, teachings, commandments, and rules revealed to Prophet Muhammad (s).

Ali ('a) accomplished these two responsibilities very well by Allah's support and under direct supervision of Prophet Muhammad (s).

Ali ('a) After Prophet Muhammad's Demise

Imam Ali ('a) was thirty three at the demise of prophet of Islam (s). The Messenger of Allah (s) had frequently announced Ali's ('a) Imamate and caliphate after himself during his lifetime. Therefore, after the Prophet's (s) demise, the caliphate position was transmitted to Imam Ali ('a); he was the Prophet's (s) successor and the people were obliged to prepare the conditions for his caliphate. Unfortunately, however, a group of ambitious people ignored Prophet Muhammad's (s) recommendations, abandoned Ali ('a) for illogical excuses, such as young age, and took the oath of allegiance with Abu Bakr. After Abu Bakr, 'Umar got the caliph and after him 'Uthman. The caliphate of the three of them lasted twenty four years and some months.

During this period, though Imam Ali ('a) knew caliphate as his legitimate right, he avoided any severe opposition or schismatic speech in order to safeguard Islam. Furthermore, he helped the government officials when necessary, giving them consultation and scientific-cultural assistance. He also attempted in propagating authentic Islamic sciences and teachings and training virtuous perfect Muslims.

In the year thirty five after hijrah, 'Uthman was killed during the

---

[176] Ibid, p. 94.

riot of a group of Muslims. The Muslims, afterward, enthusiastically and urgently took the oath of allegiance with Ali Ibn Abi Talib ('a), selecting him as the caliph and Imam.[177]

From then on, caliphate of the Muslims found its real course and it was hoped that previous losses and problems be compensated and the Prophet's (s) authentic goals be pursued under Imam Ali's ('a) leadership and by cooperation of Prophet Muhammad's (s) sincere companions. Nevertheless, this was not accomplished. Imam Ali's ('a) justice, opposition with prejudices, and following Prophet Muhammad's (s) tradition was not liked by a group of opportunists. Although these people were among the allegiants, they began opposition with Imam Ali ('a) from the beginning, facing the newly-established Alawite government with three devastating wars; Jamal, Siffiyn, and Nahrawan. Imam Ali ('a) could do nothing but defense against these civil wars and stop the seditions. This way, the realization of Divine Justice, Imam Ali ('a), found little opportunity to lead the government in the direction of genius Islamic purposes, such as justice, equality, fighting prejudices, removing social gap, and defending the oppressed poor people.

Finally, Imam Ali ('a) was martyred by one of hypocrite people when worshipping and the pretty call of equality was silenced forever. Reviewing these three devastating wars requires a wider opportunity. The readers interested in historical discussions can refer to Islamic history books.

---

[177] Tadhkiratul Khawas, p. 56.

Texts Proving His Imamate

As mentioned before, the reasons for Imamate are of two kinds. The first kinds of reasons are general reasons used for proving the Imamate of every infallible Imam, which are not mentioned again here.

The second kinds of reasons are the ones mentioned by each Imam for the Imam after him. In biography of infallible Imams ('a), including Imam Ali ('a), we cite only these reasons.

As pointed out in previous sections, the honorable Messenger of Allah (s) prepared the conditions for Imam Ali's ('a) Imamate during his prophetic mission. He frequently emphasized the virtues of Ali ('a), recommending his companions to follow Ali ('a) as caliph. Finally, Prophet Muhammad (s) officially appointed Ali ('a) to wilayat (guardian) of the Muslims during his hajjatul wida' (last hajj pilgrimage) in Ghadir Khum.

Some of the traditions about this issue were cited in previous sections, which are not repeated here. The eager readers can refer to those sections and other related books.

Virtues and Ethics

As testified by tradition and history books, Imam Ali ('a) was a perfect human and the realization of all ethical virtues in the best possible way and he was away from any vices and evilness.

His enemies avoided publishing of his virtues, vilifying and cursing him in sermons and from atop tribunes for many years. His friends could not talk about his virtues for the fear of the enemies, who killed everyone demonstrating Shi'ism. Nevertheless, the Sunni and Shi'ah books are replete with his virtues.

Muhammad Ibn Mansur Tusi quotes from 'Ahmad Ibn Hanbal, "The virtues cited for Ali Ibn Abi Talib ('a) has not been cited for any of Prophet Muhammad's (s) companions."[178]

Asbagh Ibn Nabatah says, "One day Dharar Ibn Dhamarah came to Mu'awiyat Ibn Abi Sufyan. Mu'awiyah told him, 'Describe Ali for me.' Dharar said, 'Do not ask me this!' 'You should describe him,' said Mu'awiyah again. Dharar said, 'May Allah bless Ali! When he was among us he was like one of us. When we went to him we felt ourselves close to him. When we asked him questions he answered. When we went to see him he accepted us with no doorkeeper. Though we visited him face to face, we did not dare talk to him out of awe. His smile was like a string of pearl.'"

Mu'awiyat said, 'Tell me more.' Dharar said, 'May Allah bless Ali! By Allah that he was awake most of the times and slept little. He recited the Quran day and night. He surrendered his heart to Allah and repented to Him with tears. No curtains were hung for him and no one prevented us from seeing him. He did not lean in meetings and it was not hard for him.'"

'O Mu'awiyat! I wish you saw Ali ('a) in dark nights; holding his beard, agonizing like a snake-bitten person, and saying, 'O world! You have attended to me. I do not need you and divorce you three times. Woe! Woe! (I fear) the far destination, little provision, and difficult path!'"

Asbagh Ibn Nabatah continues, "Then Mu'awiyah cried and said, 'That is enough. By Allah that Ali was so. May Allah bless Abul Hassan!'"[179]

Sa'id Ibn Kulthum says, 'I was with Imam Ja'far Sadiq ('a), when we talked about Amiral Mu'minin, Ali ('a). Imam Sadiq ('a) praised him much and stated, "By Allah that Ali Ibn Abi Talib ('a) did not eat a

---

[178] Al-Imam Ali Ibn Abi Talib, Vol 3, p. 63.

[179] Biharul Anwar, Vol 41, p. 14.

single unlawful morsel in his whole life. If he were to choose between two desirable things, he chose the one more religiously desired. No difficult situation happened to Prophet Muhammad (s), except that he asked help from Ali ('a), because he trusted Ali ('a). No one could act as the Prophet (s) but Ali ('a). Ali ('a) behaved as if he was between the Paradise and the Hell; he was always hopeful of the Paradise and fearful of the Hell. He bought and freed one thousand servants from his own property acquired by hard work during his lifetime. The sustenance of his family and him was olives, vinegar, and dates. His clothing was only from burlap.'"[180]

Ali's ('a) Knowledge

As pointed out before, Prophet Muhammad (s) had a mission from the Exalted Allah to teach religious sciences, teachings, commandments, and rules to Imam Ali ('a). Prophet Muhammad (s) accomplished this mission gradually during his prophet hood. Imam Ali ('a) recorded and learned all the sciences by Allah's support and under Prophet's (s) supervision. Moreover, with the Prophet's (s) recommendation, he recorded this knowledge collection in some books for the Imams after himself. For this reason, Imam Ali ('a) can be called 'treasurer of Prophetic sciences'.

The Messenger of Allah (s) had praised the scientific stance of Ali ('a) many times. He stated, "I am the city of science and Ali is its gate. Everyone who wants the sciences should enter the city gate."[181]

The companions of Messenger of Allah (s) confessed to Ali's ('a) knowledge, especially in judgment. Abu Harirah has quoted from

---

[180] Ibid, p. 110.

[181] Manaqib Kharazmi, p. 40; Al-Mustadrak Hakim Niyshaburi, Vol 3, p. 127.

'Umar Ibn Khattab, "In judgment, Ali ('a) is the most knowledgeable of us."[182]

Sa'id Ibn Musayyib has said, "'Umar always took refuge in Allah from any difficult problem in which Ali ('a) was not present."[183]

'Alqamah has quoted from Abdullah, "We always said that Ali ('a) is the most learned one in Medina in issues of judgment."[184]

Aban Ibn 'Ayash said, "I asked Hassan Basri about Ali ('a). He said, 'What do I say about Ali ('a)? He is the first one to accept Islam. His jurisprudence, knowledge, and virtues are obvious to everyone. He always cooperated with Prophet Muhammad (s). His brevity, piety, familiarity with judgment issues, and his relation with the Messenger of Allah (s) are undeniable.'"[185]

Ibn Abbas has said, "The science of Messenger of Allah (s) is from Allah's science and the science of Ali ('a) is from the science of Messenger of Allah (s) and my science is from Ali's ('a) science. The science of other companions and I in comparison to Ali's ('a) science is like a drop in comparison to seven seas."[186]

Ibn Abbas has also said, "When a trustworthy person quoted a verdict from Ali ('a) we did not transgress it."[187]

Adhinah Abdi has said, "I asked 'Umar, 'Where should I become muhrim (wear hajj garb) for performing 'Umrah (a kind of hajj pilgrimage)?' 'Umar answered, 'Ask Ali ('a)!'"[188]

Abu Hazim has said, "Someone went to Mu'awiyyah and asked him

---

[182] Tabaqat Ibn Sa'd, Vol 2, p. 339.
[183] Ibid.
[184] Ibid, p. 338.
[185] Sharh Nahjul Balaghah, Ibn Abil Hadid, Vol 4, p. 96.
[186] Yanabi'ul Mawaddah, p. 80.
[187] Tabaqat Ibn Sa'd, Vol 2, p. 348.
[188] Dhakha'irul Uqba, p. 79.

a question. Mu'awiyyah told him, 'Ask Ali ('a), because he is the most knowledgeable.' The questioner told Mu'awiyyah, 'Your answer is better than Ali's answer for me.' Mu'awiyah said, 'You told something bad. You dislike the speech of someone who has learned the sciences of Messenger of Allah (s). The Messenger of Allah (s) told Ali ('a), 'Your relation to me is like the relation of Aaron to Moses. The difference is that no prophet comes after me.' 'Umar referred to Ali ('a) for solving difficult problems, too.'"[189]

Ali's ('a) Worship

Imam Ali ('a) was one of the best worshippers of his time. His worship was excellent both in quantity –the amount of worship– and in quality –sincerity, full attendance, presence of heart, and observation of Allah.

Amiral Mu'minin ('a) stated, "Some people worship the Almighty Allah in hope of reward; this is the worship of merchants. Some worship Allah for fear of punishment; this is the worship of servants. Still some others worship the Exalted Allah for thanking Him; and this is the worship of the tolerant."[190]

He has also stated, "O Allah! I do not worship you for fear of punishment or in hope of reward; rather, I know You worthy of worshipping so I worship You."[191]

Someone told Imam Ali ('a), "Have you seen your Lord that you worship Him?" Imam Ali ('a) answered, "Woe be on you! I do not worship the Lord Who I have not seen." The questioner asked, "How have you seen Him?" Imam Ali ('a) replied, "Human eye cannot see

---

[189] Ibid.

[190] Biharul Anwar, Vol 41, p. 14.

[191] Ibid.

Allah, rather his heart can perceive Allah by real belief."[192]

Qushayri writes, "When the prayer time came Amiral Mu'minin's ('a) face discolored and his body shook. He was asked about the reason for this change of state. Imam Ali ('a) answered, 'It is the time for returning a trust, which the Almighty Allah presented to the Heavens and the Earth and the mountains, but they could not bear accepting it. The weak human, however, accepted that trust. I wonder if I could have returned the trust well.'"[193]

Imam Sajjad ('a) read the book in which Ali's worship was recorded. Then he put the book down and said, "Who can worship like Ali Ibn Abi Talib ('a)?"[194]

Ibn Abbas says, "Two camels were granted to Prophet Muhammad (s). He told his companions, 'I will give one of these camels to the one who performs a two- rak'ah (unit) prayer, with complete attention to Allah and without thinking of worldly affairs.' Only Ali Ibn Abi Talib ('a) answered this request. Then Prophet Muhammad (s) granted both camels to him."[195]

Habbah Arani says, "One night Nuwf and I were sleeping in Darul 'Imarah yard. We saw Imam Ali ('a) who had put his hand on the wall while walking and said like a heartsick person, 'Behold! In the creation of the heavens and the earth, and the alternation of night and day, there are indeed Signs for men of understanding...' [196] He repeated these Quranic verses, walking infatuatedly. Imam Ali ('a) told me, 'O Habbah! Are you awake?' I answered, 'Yes I am. You behave like this (out of Allah's fear). What should we do?' Imam Ali ('a) began

---

[192] Ibid, p. 16.

[193] Biharul Anwar, Vol 41, p. 17.

[194] Ibid.

[195] Ibid, p. 18.

[196] Surah 'ali 'Imran (3), 190-200.

weeping and said, 'O Habbah! The Almighty Allah is closer to you and I than our neck vessel; nothing hides us from Him.'"

Then Imam Ali ('a) told Nuwf, 'Are you awake?' Nuwf replied, 'O Amiral Mu'minin! I am awake. You made us cry tonight.' Imam ('a) stated, 'If you cry in darkness of night for fear of Allah, your eyes will be illuminated on the Last Day.

O Nuwf! Everyone who drips a tear from Allah's fear his sins will be forgiven. O Nuwf! Everyone who weeps from Allah's fear and his loving and disliking is for Allah's sake will have a high position. O Nuwf! Everyone whose affection is for Allah's sake will prefer nothing to that affection. Everyone whose hatred is for Allah's sake will not spend his hatred for his own sake. This way the real belief will be maintained and improved.'"

Then Imam Ali ('a) preached us and said at last, 'Fear Allah!" Then he said while leaving, "O Lord! I am wondering if you have ignored me or attended to me. I wish I knew how my stance is with these long sleeps and little thanking!'"

Habbah has said, "By Allah that he was in the same state until the dawn."[197]

Mu'awiyah once told Dharar Ibn Dhamarah, "Describe Ali for me." He said, "I saw Ali ('a) in some occasions worshipping in darkness of night. He had grasped his beard, agonizing like a snake-bitten person, weeping, and saying, 'O world! Go way from me! Do you come to me? It is not your time. Deceive others, not me! I do not need you. I divorce you three times. Your period is short, your value is little, and my desire for you is scarce. Alas, my provisions are little, the travel is long, the destination is great, and the path is difficult!'"[198]

---

[197] Biharul Anwar, Vol 41, p. 22.

[198] Biharul Anwar, Vol 40, p. 345.

Ali's ('a) Piety

Piety means no affection for or interest in worldly issues, such as property, positions, wives, and children. Imam Ali ('a) was one of the greatest pious men. Hassan Ibn Salih says, "In the circle of 'Umar Ibn Abdul Aziz, the pious people were discussed. Everyone introduced a pious person. 'Umar Ibn Abdul Aziz said, 'The most pious person in the world was Ali Ibn Abi Talib.'"[199]

Sufyan says, "Ali ('a) did not add a brick over another brick and did not make a shelter. His food came from Medina, too."[200]

Ibn Abbas says, "Ali Ibn Abi Talib ('a) bought a garment with three dirhams and wore it when he was caliph."[201]

'Asbagh says, "Ali ('a) went to the bazaar for buying cloths. He bought two pieces of clothes; one was three dirhams and the other two dirhams. He told his servant Qanbar, 'You wear the three-dirham garment and I wear the two-dirham one.' Qanbar said, 'The three-dirham one is more proper for you; you perform sermons for the people.' Imam ('a) stated, 'You are young and the more expensive garment is better for you. I am ashamed of Allah to wear a better cloth than you wear.'"[202]

Imam Sadiq ('a) said, "Amiral Mu'minin ('a) was the most similar person to the Prophet (s) in eating. He ate bread, vinegar, and olives and fed the people on bread and meat."[203]

Imam Ja'far Ibn Muhammad (s) stated, "Some food was brought to Imam Ali ('a) made with dates, raisins, and oil, but he refused to eat.

---

[199] Translation of Al-Imam Ali Ibn Abi Talib, Vol 3, p. 202.
[200] Translation of Al-Imam Ali Ibn Abi Talib, Vol 3, p. 188.
[201] Ibid, p. 191.
[202] Biharul Anwar, Vol 40, p. 324.
[203] Ibid, p. 330.

He was then told, 'Do you know this kind of food unlawful?' Imam Ali ('a) replied, 'No, it is not unlawful, but I fear that I may like it and get used to it.' Then he recited this verse,

'And on the Day that the Unbelievers will be placed before the Fire, (It will be said to them): Ye received your good things in the life of the world.'[204]"[205]

Ali ('a) and Dividing War Booties

The method of Imam Ali ('a) in dividing war booties was this way:

First, he believed that war booties belong to all the people, who were generally poor at that time. For the same reason, when there were booties or other property in Muslims treasury, Imam ('a) divided them among the people at once, or else he was not calm.

Second, Imam Ali ('a) divided the existing property equally among all the people, not preferring the rich over the poor. He believed distribution of treasury property should not cause social gap.

On the second day after people's oath with him, Imam Ali ('a) performed a sermon, part of which was:

You are Allah's servants and this property is for Allah too. I will divide it equally among you. No one is preferred to another. The pious servants will get the best reward from the Almighty Allah in the Hereafter. The Exalted Allah has not set the reward of His pious servants in this world; rather the good people will have the best remuneration from Allah.[206]

He also stated elsewhere, "No one is preferred to another in dividing

---

[204] Surah Al-'Ahqaf (46): 20.

[205] Al-Gharat, Vol 1, p. 90

[206] Biharul Anwar, Vol 32, pp. 17-18.

biytul mal (Muslims' treasury). The method of dividing is clear. It is the property of Allah and you are His servants. Allah's Book is among us; we believe in it and are surrendered to it. We are well aware of the Prophet's (s) method of dividing it, too. Anyone who is not happy with this method of dividing the biytul mal can do whatever he wants to. Everyone who obeys Allah and follows His rule is not afraid of anything."[207]

Majma' says, "Ali ('a) swept the biytul mal place every Friday. Then he performed two rak'ahs of prayer and said, 'Testify for me on the Last Day!'"[208]

He also stated, "The Messenger of Allah (s) never postponed dividing of the biytul mal property to the next day."[209]

Abu Salih Samman says, "One day, Imam Ali ('a) entered the biytul mal building and saw some property there. He said, 'I do not like to see any property here.' Then Imam ('a) ordered to divide it among the Muslims. And he swept the place and performed prayer there." [210]

Abu Hakim has quoted from his father that Imam Ali ('a) divided the treasury property three times in a year. Then some property was brought from Isfahan. He told the people, "Come to divide the property among you for the fourth time. I cannot be a treasurer." [211]

Some property was brought from Isfahan. Imam Ali ('a) divided all of it equally among the people and even divided a loaf of bread into seven pieces and gave it away. [212]

Abu Is'haq says, "Once two women were present when dividing the

---

[207] Ibid, p. 20.

[208] Al-Gharat, Vol 1, p. 46.

[209] Ibid, p. 47.

[210] Al-Imam Ali Ibn Abi Talib, Vol 3, p. 180.

[211] Ibid, p. 181.

[212] Al-Gharat, Vol 1, p. 51.

biytul mal; an Arab woman and a non-Arab one. Imam ('a) gave each of them twenty five dirhams and a bowl of food. The Arab woman told Imam Ali ('a), 'O Amiral Mu'minin! Do you equal me with this non-Arab woman?' Imam ('a) stated, 'I found no preference for the progeny of Ismail to the progeny of Isaac in dividing the biytul mal property.'"[213]

Sahl Ibn Hanif came to Imam Ali ('a) with his servant and said, "O Amiral Mu'minin! This has been my servant who I have freed; give his share from the biytul mal." Imam ('a) gave both Sahl and his servant three dinars.[214]

A group of Imam Ali's ('a) companions went to him and stated, "O Amiral Mu'minin! Give more of the biytul mal to Arab nobles, the Quraysh nobles, and those you fear of their opposition compared to the non-Arabs and freed servants." Imam Ali ('a) stated, "Do you recommend me to oppress some people for getting victory? By Allah, I will never do this. By Allah that if this was my own property and I wanted to divide it among the people, I observed equality, let alone the property is for the public."

After a while he said again, "Everyone who has a wealth should avoid corruption, because improper granting of property is extravagance. It will make him famous among the people, but little before the Almighty Allah. If someone spends some property improperly and for wrong people, Allah will deprive him of their gratitude and attract their affection to others. If some of them thank him apparently, it is merely false and flattery and for more benefit. If the granter needs the grantees one day, they will be his worst friends. Therefore, if the Exalted Allah grants a property to someone, he should use it in strengthening kinship ties, hosting guests, freeing the servants, and helping the debtors, poor

---

[213] Ibid, p. 70.

[214] Biharul Anwar, Vol 41, p. 117.

travelers and immigrants and be patient in bearing the hardships. Surely acquiring these good characteristics is getting virtues in this world and the Hereafter, too."[215]

Imam Ali ('a) complained about people's fleeing into Mu'awiyah when speaking with Maliki Ashtar. Malik told Imam Ali ('a), "O Amiral Mu'minin! We fought the people of Basrah and Kufah while we were united. But now people have disagreement, the intentions are weak, and justice is decreased. You want to behave justly and follow the truth. You retrieve the right of weak people from oppressor powerful ones and give no preference to the noble. A group of your companions are afraid of the truth, because your conduct includes them too. They are afraid of your just performance, because it includes them too. Mu'awiyah, however, does not conduct so. He grants property and positions to the noble ones. Most of the people incline to worldly wealth. Most of them do not like the truth, tend to dishonesty, and prefer this world to the Hereafter."

O Amiral Mu'minin! If you grant money to the people too, they will incline to you, become benevolent, and like you. May the Almighty Allah prepare the conditions for you, defeat your enemies, and undo their plots; surely He is aware of their intrigues."

After praising Allah, Imam Ali ('a) stated, "Regarding what you said about my justice, the Exalted Allah says in the Holy Quran,

> *'Whoever works righteousness benefits his own soul; whoever works evil, it is against his own soul: nor is thy Lord ever unjust (in the least) to His Servants.' I am fearful of delinquency in establishing justice."*[216]

---

[215] Al-Gharat, Vol 1, p. 75.

[216] Surah Fussilat (41): 46

Regarding what you said about people's going toward Mu'awiyah –because accepting the truth is hard for them– Allah knows well that they do not do so due to my oppression and for Mu'awiyah's justice. Rather their goal is obtaining the bliss of this transient world. The Exalted Allah will question them in the Hereafter if they have pursued worldly goals or conducted for Allah's sake.

"Concerning your speech about preference of the noble in dividing the biytul mal, I cannot give more than people's right to them from the public property. The Almighty Allah says,

'How oft, by God's will, Hath a small force vanquished a big one? God is with those who steadfastly persevere.'[217]

Prophet Muhammad (s) was appointed prophet when he was alone. Allah, however, changed his loneliness to honor and intensity later. If Allah wants to strengthen our guardianship, he will ease the hardships. I accept your words, if Allah is content with them. You are one of my most reliable and benevolent companions."

Strictness in Defending the Truth

One of the major characteristics of Imam Ali ('a) is his strictness in opposing oppression and defending the oppressed people's right. He believed that oppression cannot be resisted by leniency, rather by sternness.

He said in this regard, "Weak people are dear to me, so that I revive their rights and the powerful people are weak to me, so that I take

---
[217] Surah Al-Baqarah (2): 249.

back the right of weak people from them." [218]

Mughayrat Ibn Sha'bah went to see Imam Ali ('a) and told him, "It is obligatory for us to advise you. The officials appointed by 'Uthman are powerful in cities. If you dismiss them all together, a riot will break out, which cannot be suppressed easily. You'd better renew their missions for one year to foster your government. Then you can do whatever you want. One of these officials is Mu'awiyah who is very powerful and weighty in Sham." Imam Ali ('a) replied, "Do you guarantee that I will be alive to dismiss Mu'awiyah?" Mughayrah said, "No." Imam ('a) stated, "If I give the guardianship of two Muslims to Mu'awiyah on a dark night, will I not be reckoned in the Day of Judgment? I will never ask help from the misled people. I frequently told 'Uthman to dismiss these oppressor people. Now should I hire the same people?"[219]

He also stated, "By Allah that I will take back the rights of the oppressed people from the oppressor ones. I will restrain the oppressor people and force them to commit to the truth."[220]

Defending the oppressed deprived people was one of the major goals of Amiral Mu'minin ('a), which he never abandoned. He did not bear oppression even in unimportant events.

Imam Baqir ('a) stated, "One day Ali ('a) came home when it was so hot. A woman waiting for him said, 'O Amiral Mu'minini! My husband has oppressed me, violated my right, and swore to bite me. I fear him. Help me!' Imam Ali ('a) said, 'O servant of Allah! Waite until it becomes a little cool, then we will go to your house.' The woman said, 'My husband was very angry. If I return home late, he will get angrier.' Amiral Mu'minin ('a) thought for a while and said, 'By Allah

---

[218] Nahjul Balaghah, Sermon 37.

[219] Biharul Anwar, Vol 32, p. 386.

[220] Nahjul Balaghah, Sermon 136.

that I should get back the right of an oppressed one. Where is your house?' Then Imam Ali ('a) accompanied that woman to her house, stood beside the door, and said, 'Assalamu Alaykum!' A young man came out and Imam ('a) told him, 'Fear Allah! Why did you scare and expel your wife?' The young man who did not know Imam ('a) told him, 'It is not your business! By Allah that I will fire her!' Amiral Mu'minin ('a) told him, 'I enjoin you goodness and avoid from evilness. Do you threat your wife in my presence?' At this time, the passengers said hello to Amiral Mu'minin ('a). The young man knew the Imam ('a), feared, and said, 'O Amiral Mu'minin! Excuse me! I will surrender to my wife's wishes from now on.' Imam Ali ('a) sheathed his sword and told the woman, 'Go to your home! Do nothing that enrages your husband this much!'"[221]

Equality before the Law

Imam Ali ('a) considered all people equal before the law, even a Christian citizen and himself.

Sha'bi says, "Ali Ibn Abi Talib ('a) found his armor with a Christian man and went to a judge called Shurayh. Imam Ali ('a) told Shurayh, 'This is my armor. I have not sold it nor have I granted it.' Shurayh told the Christian man, 'What do you say?' He replied, 'The armor is mine, but I do not consider Amiral Mu'minin a liar.' Shurayh asked Imam Ali ('a), 'Do you have a witness for your claim?' 'No,' Imam Ali ('a) answered. Shurayh voted for the Christian man and against Imam Ali ('a). The Christian man took the armor and went. But then he returned and said, 'I testify that this kind of judgment is like the prophets' verdicts. Amiral Mu'minin brought me before a judge appointed by himself and

---

[221] Biharul Anwar, Vol 41, p. 57.

the judge voted against him. I testify that there I no deity but Allah and I testify that Muhammad (s) is His servant and messenger. O Amiral Mu'minin! This is your armor. When you went toward Siffiyn, I was moving behind your army. This armor dropped from atop your camel and I took it. This is yours; take it!'"

Amiral Mu'minin ('a) stated, "Now that you embraced Islam, I give the armor to you." Then Imam Ali ('a) rode the Christian man on his horse.

Sha'bi says, "Later on I was informed that this Christian man fought in Imam Ali's ('a) army when fighting Khawarij."[222]

Ja'dat Ibn Hubayrah went to Imam Ali ('a) and said, "Two persons are coming to you to judge among them; one of them likes you more than his life and property and the other one is your enemy and he kills you if he can. So judge for your fan!" Amiral Mu'minin ('a) pounded on Ja'dah's chest and said, "My verdict will be Allah's verdict and I should issue verdict based on the truth."[223]

The Second Imam; Hassan ibn 'Ali

Birth and Martyrdom

Imam Hassan ('a) was born on fifteenth of Ramadan in the third year after Hijrah in Medina. His father was Ali Ibn Abi Talib ('a) and his mother was Fatimah (s), Prophet Muhammad's (s) daughter. His nickname was Abu Muhammad and his most famous titles were Taqi, Tayyib, Zaki, Sayyid, Sibt, and Wali.

At the time of Imam Hassan's ('a) birth, the Messenger of Allah (s) told 'Asma' Binti Umays and Ummi Salamah, "When the child of Fatimah

---

[222] Al-Imam Ali Ibn Abi Talib, Vol 3, p. 196.

[223] Ibid, p. 200.

(s) was born, recite 'adhan in his right ear and 'iqamah in his left ear and stay there until I come."

When Prophet Muhammad (s) went to Fatimah's (s) house, he cut the infant's navel cord and poured his saliva into the infant's mouth. Then he said, 'Allahumma 'inni 'a'udhu bika minash Shaytanir rajim, "O Lord! I take refuge in You from the ousted Satan." Then Prophet Muhammad (s) stated, "Name him Hassan!" He then ordered to sacrifice a sheep for him as 'aqiqah and divide the meat among the poor.

This auspicious birth gladdened not only Prophet Muhammad (s), Imam Ali ('a), and Hadrat Fatimah (s), but also the prophet's household. Imam Hassan ('a) lived for seven years with his grandfather, the Messenger of Allah (s). He was appointed to Imamate after his father, Ali Ibn Abi Talib ('a), at the age thirty seven. His caliphate –after Imam Ali's ('a) martyrdom until his peace with Mu'awiyah– lasted six months and three days.

In the year forty one after Hijrah, Imam Hassan ('a) inevitably signed a peace contract with Mu'awiyah. Then he returned from Kufah to Medina. On twenty eighth of Safar in the year fifty A.H., he was martyred and his gravesite is in Baqi' cemetery in Medina.

It is recorded that Mu'awiyah sent one hundred thousand dirhams for Ju'dah, Imam Hassan's ('a) wife, to poison Imam ('a). Mu'awiyah had promised Ju'dah to marry her with his son, Yazid, and she poisoned Imam Hassan ('a).[224]

Texts Proving His Imamate

In many traditions, the honorable Messenger of Allah (s) has stipulated the Imamate of Hassan ('a) and Hussayn ('a). Ali Ibn Abi

---

[224] 'A'lamul Wura, Vol 1, p. 402-403; Manaqib 'ali Abi Talib, Vol 4, p. 33; Kashful Ghumma, Vol 2, pp. 140-144.

Talib ('a), too, chose his son, Hassan ('a) as the Imam and successor after himself, before his martyrdom.

The Messenger of Allah (s) stated about Hassan ('a) and Hussayn ('a), "My two sons will be Imams, whether they rise for occupying Imamate position or not."[225]

Imam Sadiq ('a) stated, "Prophet Muhammad (s) willed to Imam Ali ('a), and Imam Ali ('a) willed to Hassan ('a) and Hussayn ('a). Therefore, Imam Hassan ('a) had guardianship over Imam Hussayn ('a), too."[226]

Salim Ibn Qiys says, "I witnessed the will of Ali Ibn Abi Talib ('a) about succession of Imam Hassan ('a). Imam Ali ('a) took as witness Hussayn ('a), Prophet Muhammad (s), his entire Household, and the Shi'ah chiefs. Then he gave Imam Hassan ('a) his books and weapon and said, 'O my son! The Messenger of Allah (s) ordered me to appoint you as my successor and give you the books and weapon, just as he appointed me as his successor and gave me his books and weapon.'"[227]

Shahr Ibn Huwshab says, "When Ali Ibn Abi Talib ('a) wanted to go toward Kufah, he gave his books and weapon to Ummi Salamah. When Imam Hassan ('a) returned from Kufah to Medina, Ummi Salamah gave them to him."[228]

Muhammad Ibn Hanafiyah told Ali Ibn Hussayn ('a), "I know that Prophet Muhammad (s) appointed Ali Ibn Abi Talib ('a) as his successor and caliph and then Imam Hassan ('a) and then Imam Hussayn ('a)."[229]

Tariq Ibn Shahab says, "Amiral Mu'minin ('a) told Hassan ('a) and Hussayn ('a), 'You will be the Imams after me and the masters of youth of Paradise. You are infallible. May Allah guard you! May Allah curse

---

[225] 'Ithbatul Hudat, Vol 5, p. 134.

[226] Ibid, p. 126.

[227] Ibid, p. 126.

[228] 'Ithbatul Hudat, Vol 5, p. 122.

[229] 'Ithbatul Hudat, Vol 5, p. 123.

your enemies!'"²³⁰

Fazl Ibn Hassan Tabarsi has written in his book 'A'lamul Wura, "The Shi'ah have frequently narrated that Imam Ali ('a) had emphasized the Imamate of his son, Hassan ('a), among the Shi'ah, introducing him as the successor to himself."²³¹

In the morning of his martyrdom day, Imam Hassan ('a) performed a sermon. Then Abdullah Ibn Abbas stood up and said, "O people! This is the son of your prophet (s) and will be your successor and Imam. Take oath of allegiance with him." The people hurried to take allegiance with him.²³²

Abu 'Abdullah Jadali said, "I was present when Amiral Mu'minin ('a) willed to his son Hassan ('a)." Then he quoted Imam Ali's ('a) will.²³³

When Amiral Mu'minin ('a) was hit by the sword of Ibn Muljam and the people had gathered around his bed, he told them, "Go out, because I want to will." So everyone went out except some of the close Shi'ahs. Then Imam Ali ('a) praised the Exalted Allah and said, "I set Hassan and Hussayn ('a) as my successors. Obey them, because Prophet Muhammad (s) has stressed their Imamate."²³⁴

'Asbagh Ibn Nabatah says, "When Amiral Mu'minin ('a) was hit by Ibn Muljam, he called Hassan and Hussayn ('a) and said, 'I pass away tonight. Listen to me! O Hassan! You are my successor and the Imam after me. O Hussayn! You will be my successor too. Obey Hassan until he is alive. You will be the teller of truth and establisher of government after your brother.'"²³⁵

---

[230] Ibid, p. 133.

[231] Tadhkiratul Khawas, Vol 5, p. 133.

[232] 'Ithbatul Hudat, Vol 5, p. 134.

[233] Ibid, p. 137.

[234] Ibid, p. 138.

[235] 'Ithbatul Hudat, Vol 5, p. 140.

Worshipping

It is narrated from Kamalid Din Talhah, "Worshipping is of three kinds; physical, financial, and a combination of the two. Physical worship includes prayer, fasting, reciting the Quran, and various zikrs. Financial worship includes alms-giving, charity giving, and other forms of granting. Physical-financial worship includes hajj, jihad, and 'umurah."

Imam Hassan's worship was perfect in all the three forms. His endeavor in prayer, fasting, and the like is famous.

Regarding his alms-giving, it is narrated in Hilyatul 'Awliya' that Imam Hassan ('a) granted his whole wealth twice in his lifetime in Allah's path. He also divided his property with the poor three times, granting half his wealth to the poor altogether, including his own shoes.

Regarding the physical-financial worship, the author of Hilyatul 'Awliya' has narrated from Imam Hassan ('a), "I am ashamed of the Almighty Allah that I ride a horse in hajj pilgrimage, rather than walking toward Mecca." Therefore, he traveled from Medina to Mecca for hajj on foot twenty times, while he had quadruped.[236]

It is written, "Hassan Ibn Ali ('a) was the most similar one to the Messenger of Allah (s) regarding ethics, conduct, and nobility."[237]

Imam Sadiq ('a) has quoted from his father from Imam Sajjad ('a), "Hassan Ibn Ali ('a) was the best most pious of the people in his own age. In hajj pilgrimage, he traveled on foot and sometimes barefooted. He cried when he remembered death. When he remembered the grave, the Resurrection, the Hereafter, or passing sirat (the path to Paradise), he wept. When he remembered statement of human deeds before the Almighty Allah, he cried and fainted. When he stood for prayer, his

---

[236] Kashful Ghummah, Vol 2, p. 181.

[237] Ibid, p. 142.

body shook from Allah's fear. When he remembered the Hell and the Paradise he agonized like a snake-bitten. He requested the Paradise from the Exalted Allah and took refuge in Him from the Hell." [238]

When he reached the verse 'O You who believe!', he said, "Here I am! O Allah! Here I am!" He always remembered Allah. He was the most righteous and the most eloquent of the people.[239]

Imam Riza ('a) has narrated from his father and grandfathers ('a) that Imam Hassan ('a) cried before his demise. He was asked, "O son of Messenger of Allah! Do you cry out of Allah's fear while you had a lofty position before the Messenger of Allah (s), went to hajj barefooted twenty times, and divided your wealth with the poor three times?!" Imam Hassan ('a) stated, "My crying is for two things; for fear of the Resurrection and for distance of the friends."[240]

When Imam Hassan ('a) reached the mosque door, he raised his head and stated, "'Ilahi! Zayfuka bi babik! Ya Muhsin! Qad 'atakal musi', fatajawaz 'an qabihi ma 'indi bi jamili ma 'indaka, ya Karim!" (O Allah! Your guest has come to Your door! O Beneficent! Surely Your sinner servant has come to You, so forgive me my wrongdoing because of Your Righteousness, O generous!)[241]

When Imam Hassan ('a) ended his Morning Prayer, he did not talk to anyone until dawn.[242]

Generosity

Imam Sadiq ('a) stated, "A man came to 'Uthman Ibn 'Affan in the mosque and had a request. 'Uthman gave him five dirhams. That man

---

[238] Biharul Anwar, Vol 43, p. 331.

[239] Ibid.

[240] Ibid, p. 332.

[241] Ibid, p. 339.

[242] Ibid.

said, 'Introduce me to the people who can help me more.' 'Uthman showed him a corner of the mosque in which Hassan ('a), Hussayn ('a), and Abdullah Ibn Ja'far had sat. The man went there, said hello, and asked for help."

Imam Hassan ('a) stated, 'Asking request from the people is unlawful, except in case of blood money of a murdered person, a debt that is due to be paid, and extreme poorness. What is your request?' That man answered, 'It is one of these three cases.' Imam Hassan ('a) gave him fifty dirhams, Imam Hussayn ('a) gave him forty nine dirhams, and Abdulla"h Ibn Ja'far gave him forty eight dirhams."

'Uthman said, 'Who can be as generous as these youth? They have learned knowledge from their father and received wisdom and generosity.'"[243]

Sa'id Ibn Abdul 'Aziz says, "Hassan Ibn Ali ('a) saw a man who prayed and asked ten thousand dirhams from the Almighty Allah. So he went home and sent the praying man ten thousand dirhams." [244]

A man came to Imam Hassan ('a) and said, "By Allah, Who has granted you so many blessings without a mediator, save me from this oppressor enemy who does not respect the elderly nor does he have mercy on the children!" Imam Hassan ('a), who had leaned, sat up and asked, "Who is your enemy?" That man answered, "Poorness!"

Imam Hassan ('a) told his servant, "Bring me whatever money we have at home!" The servant brought five thousand dirhams. Imam Hassan ('a) said, "Give all the money to this man!" Then he added, "By Allah that whenever this enemy forced you, come to me for help!"

Ibn 'ayishah has narrated that a Shami[245] man saw Imam Hassan ('a) riding a horse. He began insulting, but Imam Hassan ('a) did not talk

---

[243] Biharul Anwar, Vol 43, p. 332.

[244] Ibid, p. 341.

[245] From Sham (now Syria).

until the man stopped swearing. Imam Hassan ('a) said hello to him and said, "O old gentleman! I think you are a stranger and have made a mistake about me. If you seek my forgiveness, I forgive you. If you ask something, I will give it to you. If you want to be guided, I will guide you. If you do not have an animal to ride, I will give you one. If you are hungry, I will give you food. If you do not have clothes, I will give you. If you are poor I will make you needless. If you are ousted, I will shelter you. If you bring your luggage to my house, I will be very glad to host you; my house is large and equipped."

The Shami man heard Imam's ('a) speech, and then he cried and said, "I testify that you are Allah's caliph on the earth. 'God knoweth best where (and how) to carry out His mission.'[246]

You and your father were the most hated people for me before. But now you are my most beloved ones."

Then that man took his luggage to Imam Hassan's ('a) house, stayed there, and became one of Imam's ('a) fans and companions.[247]

The Third Imam; Hussayn ibn ali

Birth and Martyrdom

Imam Hussayn ('a) was born on the third or fifth of Sha'ban in the fourth year A.H. in Medina. His father was Ali Ibn Abi Talib ('a) and his mother was Fatimah (s), Prophet Muhammad's (s) daughter. His nickname was Abu 'Abdullah and his most famous titles were Tayyib, Sayyid, Sibt, Wafi, and Mubarak.

At his birth time, Gabriel was revealed to the Messenger of Allah (s) for congratulating and brought Allah's message to the Prophet (s) to name the infant Hussayn. The Messenger of Allah (s) recited 'adhan

---

[246] Surah Al-'An'am (6)124: .

[247] Biharul Anwar, Vol 43, p. 344.

in his right ear and 'iqamah in his left ear. On the seventh day after Imam Hussayn's ('a) birth, two sheep were sacrificed for him and the meat was divided among the poor.

Imam Hussayn ('a) lived fifty six years and some days, according to some narrations. He lived six years and several months with Prophet Muhammad (s) before the Prophet's (s) demise, thirty years with his father, ten years with his brother Imam Hassan ('a) after his father's demise, and ten years after his brother's demise. He was martyred on the day of 'ashura (tenth of Muharram) in the year sixty one A.H. in Karbala and his holy body was buried in that land.[248]

Texts Proving His Imamate

For proving the Imamate of Imam Hussayn ('a) general reasons can be used that were pointed out before. Moreover, the Messenger of Allah (s) has stipulated the Imamate of Imam Hassan ('a) and Imam Hussayn ('a) in many traditions.

The Messenger of Allah (s) has stated, "My two sons are the Imams, either they rise for Imamate or not." [249]

Moreover, Imam Hassan ('a) introduced his brother, Imam Hussayn ('a), as his successor and the Imam before his demise.

Imam Sadiq ('a) has stated in a tradition, "Hassan Ibn Ali ('a) called his brother, Muhammad Ibn Hanafiyah, before his demise and said, 'Do you know that Hussayn Ibn Ali ('a) will be the Imam after my demise? The Almighty Allah wants it and the Messenger of Allah (s) has stipulated it. The Exalted Allah knows well that you –the Ahlul-Bayt– are His best servants. Allah selected Prophet Muhammad (s) as prophet. The Prophet (s) selected Ali ('a) as the Imam and my father Ali

---

[248] Biharul Anwar, Vol 44, pp. 200-201; Kashful Ghummah, Vol 2, pp. 216- 252; 'A'lamul Wura, Vol 1, p. 420, Matalibul Mas'ul, Vol 2, pp. 49, 51, 69, & 70.

[249] 'Ithbatul Huda, Vol 5, pp. 134-171.

('a) selected me as the Imam and I select Hussayn ('a) for the Imamate position.' Muhammad Ibn Hanafiyah stated, 'O my brother! You are the Imam and surely fulfill your duty.'"250

Ali Ibn Yunusi 'amili has written in his book Sirati Mustaqim: Amiral Mu'minin ('a) had stipulated the Imamate of his son, Hassan ('a), as he stipulated the Imamate of his son, Hussayn ('a). The Shi'ah narrators have narrated that Hassan ('a), before his demise, selected his brother Hussayn ('a) as the Imam, entrusted prophet hood authority and Imamate covenant to him, and informed the Shi'ah of his Imamate and succession after himself. This is an obvious issue with no obscurity.[251]

Mas'udi has written in 'Ithbatul Wasilah: When Imam Hassan ('a) got sick, his brother Abu Abdillah came to visit him. They talked for a while and then Imam Hassan ('a) set his brother Hussayn ('a) as his successor. He taught Hussayn ('a) Allah's Great Name and entrusted the legacy of the prophets (s) and Amiral Mu'minin's ('a) will to him.[252]

Muhammad Ibn Hanafiyah told Imam Sajjad ('a), "You know that the Messenger of Allah (s) entrusted the Imamate and leadership after himself to Amiral Mu'minin ('a) and then to Hassan ('a) and Hussayn ('a)."[253]

Imam Hussayn's ('a) Virtues

The Messenger of Allah (s) stated, "Hussayn is from me and I am from Hussayn. Everyone who likes Hussayn is loved by Allah. Hussayn is a sibt (son of daughter) of my sibts." [254]

---

[250] Ibid, p. 169, Biharul Anwar, Vol 44, p. 174.

[251] 'Ithbatul huda, Vol 5, p. 173.

[252] 'Ithbatul huda, Vol 5, p. 174.

[253] 'Ithbatul huda, Vol 5, p. 170.

[254] Biharul Anwar, Vol 43, p. 261.

Prophet Muhammad (s) also said, "Everyone who wants to see the most beloved person in the heavens and the earth should look at Hussayn."[255]

Hadhifah has narrated from the Messenger of Allah (s), "Allah has granted Hussayn a virtue that He has given to no one, except to Joseph, son of Jacob."[256]

Hadhifat Ibn Yaman says, "I saw the Messenger of Allah (s) holding Hussayn's hand and saying, 'O people! This is Hussayn Ibn Ali. Know him! By Allah that he will be in the Paradise, along with his friends and the friends of his friends.' He then continued, 'Hassan and Hussayn are the best people on the earth, after their father and I, and their mother is the best woman in the world.'"[257]

Prophet Muhammad (s) said, "Hassan and Hussayn are my two flowers on the earth."[258]

The Prophet (s) stated, "Hassan and Hussayn are masters of the youth of the Paradise and their father is more virtuous than them."[259]

Worship

Imam Hussayn ('a) was asked, "Why do you fear Allah so much?" Imam Hussayn ('a) answered, "No one is safe from hardships of the Hereafter except that he fears Allah in this world."[260]

Abdullah Ibn 'Ubayd says, "Imam Hussayn ('a) went to hajj pilgrimage on foot twenty times, while he had a horse to ride."[261]

---

[255] Ibid, p. 297.
[256] Ibid, Vol 43, p. 316.
[257] Ibid, p. 262.
[258] Biharul Anwar, Vol 43, p. 316.
[259] Ibid, p. 264.
[260] Biharul Anwar, Vol 44, p. 192.
[261] Biharul Anwar, Vol 44, p. 193.

Imam Sajjad ('a) was asked, "Why are your father's children so few?" Imam ('a) replied, "I am even wondered of my birth; my father performed a thousand rak'ahs of prayer a day."[262]

It is narrated that Hassan ('a) and Hussayn ('a) were going to hajj pilgrimage on foot. Everyone who passed them on horseback landed and continued the way on foot. Walking was difficult for some of the pilgrims. They told Sa'd Ibn Abi Waqqas, "Walking is hard for us, but we cannot ride while these two honorable persons walk." Sa'd Ibn Abi Waqqas related their speech to Imam Hassan ('a) and added, "I wish you rode your horses for the comfort of these weak pilgrims." Imam Hussayn ('a) said, "We do not ride, since we are obliged to walk to hajj pilgrimage. However, we run away from this path for the sake of other pilgrims." Then Imam Hassan ('a) and Imam Hussayn ('a) did so.[263]

Almsgiving

Imam Hussayn ('a) went to visit Usamat Ibn Ziyd who was sick and told Imam Hussayn ('a), "Woe! I am sad!" Imam Hussayn ('a) told him, "Why are you sad my brother?" Usamah said, "O son of Messenger of Allah (s)! I am in debt to the tune of sixty thousand dirhams. I am fearful of dying with this debt." Imam Hussayn ('a) said, "Do not be sad! I will pay your debt before your demise." And he did so.[264]

Shu'ayb Ibn Abdur Rahman says, "After Imam Hussayn ('a) was martyred, a mark was seen on his holy shoulder. Imam Sajjad ('a) was asked, 'What is this sign?' Imam ('a) answered, 'This mark is for the sac of food my father used to carry on his shoulder to feed the poor, the orphan, and the widowed.'"[265]

---

[262] Ibid, p. 196

[263] Ibid, Vol 43, p. 276.

[264] Biharul Anwar, Vol 44, p. 189.

[265] Biharul Anwar, Vol 44, p. 190.

It is narrated from Imam Hussayn ('a), "This speech of Prophet Muhammad (s) that 'The best deed after salat (prayer) is joyfulness of the believer's heart, provided it does not include committing a sin,' is proved for me. One day I saw a slave who was eating along with a dog. He ate a mouthful then threw a piece for the dog. I asked him the reason. The slave answered, 'O son of Messenger of Allah! I am very sad. I try to make this dog happy so that Allah will delight me. My master is a Jew from who I want to separate.' Imam Hussayn ('a) went to the slave's master and paid two hundred dirhams to buy the slave. The Jewish man said, 'I grant this slave to you. I grant a farm to him and pay you back your money.' Imam Hussayn ('a) said, 'I accept your granting, grant all of it to the slave and free him.' The Jewish man's wife who witnessed all these events said, 'I embrace Islam and forgive my dowry to my husband.' The Jewish man said, 'I embrace Islam too and grant my house to my wife.'"[266]

Anas says, "I was with Imam Hussayn ('a) when a female slave came and gave some flowers to Imam ('a). Imam Hussayn ('a) told the female slave, 'I free you in Allah's path.' I said, 'O son of Messenger of Allah (s)! She gave you worthless flowers. Why did you free her?' Imam Hussayn ('a) stated, 'Allah has trained us this way, 'When a (courteous) greeting is offered you, meet it with a greeting still more courteous, or (at least) of equal courtesy.'[267] Better than the flowers was freeing that slave that I did.'"[268]

> *A slave of Imam Hussayn ('a) committed something wrong and deserved to be punished. Imam ('a) ordered to punish him. The slave said, "O my master! 'Those who restrain anger.'" Imam*

---

[266] Ibid, p. 194.

[267] Surah Al-Nisa' (4): 86.

[268] Biharul Anwar, Vol 44, p. 195.

('a) said, "I pardon you." The slave said, "O my master! 'And those who pardon (all) men.'" Imam ('a) said, "I forgive you." The slave then said, "O my master! **For God loves those who do good.**"[269] Imam Hussayn ('a) stated, "I free you in Allah's path and will pay you twice what I had given you before."[270]

An Arab nomad went to Imam Hussayn ('a) and said, "O son of Messenger of Allah! I have accepted a full blood-money, but cannot pay it. I thought I can ask it from the most generous person and found such a person in Prophet's (s) Ahlul-Bayt." Imam Hussayn ('a) said, "I ask you three questions; if you answered one of them, I will give you one third of the money you need, if you answered two questions, I will pay two third of the property, and if you answered all three questions, I will give you all of it." The Arab man said, "O son of Messenger of Allah! Does a noble knowledgeable character like you ask questions from someone like me?!" Imam ('a) replied, "Yes. I heard my grandfather, the Messenger of Allah (s), who said, 'Everyone does goodness as much as his understanding.'" The Arab man said, "Ask me! I will answer if I know and I will learn from you if I do not know. And there is no power but from Allah." Then Imam Hussayn ('a) asked the nomad these questions and he answered:

- What is the best deed?
- Belief in Allah.
- What is the means for delivering from the calamities?
- Reliance on Allah.
- What is human adornment?
- Knowledge that accompanies patience.
- What if it does not exist?

---

[269] Surah 'ali 'Imran (3): 134.

[270] Biharul Anwar, Vol 44, p. 195.

- Property that accompanies humanity and equanimity.
- And if this does not exist too?
- Poorness along with patience.
- And if it does not exist?
- Then a thunder should come from the heaven and fire him!

Imam Hussayn ('a) laughed and granted the Arab man a thousand dinars. Moreover, Imam ('a) gave the nomad his ring, which cost two hundred dirhams and said, "Fulfill your debt with that money. Sell the ring and spend it for your life."

The Arab nomad took them and said, "God knoweth best where (and how) to carry out His mission." [271]

The 'Ashura Event

The events, which happened on the day of 'ashura (tenth of Muharram of the year 61 A.H.), are among the most tragic events in the history of Islam and even in the world history. On this day, Imam Hussayn ('a), son of Messenger of Allah (s), was killed in Karbala, along with some of his brothers, sons, cousins, close relatives, and friends, by someone who knew himself the caliph of Messenger of Allah (s). In spite of all the recommendations about him, Imam Hussayn ('a) was cruelly martyred by an army that considered itself Muslim and follower of his grandfather, the Messenger of Allah (s). The cruel massacre and inhumane arrests in Karbala blackened the history record. Reviewing this bitter event is necessary for recognizing Imam Hussayn ('a). It, however, requires a separate work and is not possible in the present book. We only discuss the purposes of Imam Hussayn ('a) in his bloody uprising.

The Purposes and Method of Imam Hussayn ('a)

For knowing Imam Hussayn's ('a) purposes in Karbala exactly, it is

---

[271] Surah Al-'An'am (6): 124.

better to refer to his own words. When leaving Medina, Imam ('a) wrote in his will to Muhammad Ibn Hanafiyah, "I do not exit Medina for evilness, oppression, or corruption. Surely I leave Medina for reforming the affairs of my grandfather's ummah. I want to enjoin good and forbid evil and follow the tradition of the Messenger of Allah (s) and my father, Ali Ibn Abi Talib."[272]

According to Imam Hussayn's ('a) speech, he had three main purposes; reforming the Muslims' affairs, enjoining good and forbidding evil, and revitalizing the norms of the Prophet and Imam Ali ('a).

It can be concluded that the main purpose of Imam Hussayn ('a) has been reforming the affairs of the ummah, who had forgotten the tradition of Prophet Muhammad (s) and gone astray in worshipping, social, ethical, political, and economic aspects. Imam Hussayn ('a) wanted to do this important job completely via enjoining good and forbidding evil.

As a result, Imam Hussayn's ('a) movement was for protest and for reform, which was done in the form of enjoining good and forbidding evil in various levels and steps, based on time and place requirements:

The first step; immigration from Medina: After Mu'awiyah's death, his son, Yazid, wrote to and ordered Walid, the governor of Medina, to take the oath of allegiance from Hussayn Ibn Ali ('a) and kill him if he refused to do so. However, Imam Hussayn ('a) did not consider Yazid's government legal and refused to recognize it. For showing his disagreement, Imam Hussayn ('a) left Medina for Mecca. This is considered a kind of forbidding evil.

The second step; staying in Mecca: Imam Hussayn ('a) was going to stay in Mecca and speak for Muslim pilgrims coming from various countries to hajj to show his opposition to the government in office, which is another type of enjoining good and forbidding evil. In

---

[272] Biharul Anwar, Vol 44, p. 329.

Mecca, however, two new events occurred that could affect Imam Hussayn's ('a) intention. The first event was that the Shi'ah of Kufah were informed of Imam's ('a) opposition to allegiance with Yazid and his moving to Mecca. They wrote so many letters to invite Imam Hussayn ('a) to Kufah. The second event was that Imam Hussayn ('a) was informed that Yazid has hired some people to assassinate Imam ('a) secretly.

The third step; moving toward Kufah. The two mentioned events changed the situation. On one hand, Imam Hussayn ('a) could not stay in Mecca. The reason was that killing him inside haram (sanctuary) in Mecca dishonored the sanctuary of Allah's House and had no benefit. On the other hand, the Shi'ah of Kufah had invited Imam ('a) and he had no reason for not accepting their invitation.

Therefore, Imam Hussayn ('a) felt duty-bound to move toward Kufah, which was the continuation of his protest movement. Of course, to be on the safe side, he sent Muslim Ibn 'Aqil along with a letter to Kufah in order that he observe the situation directly and report to Imam Hussayn ('a). After a while, Imam Hussayn ('a) received a letter from Muslim, saying, "A great number of Kufah people have took the oath of allegiance with me and are waiting for you."

Imam Hussayn ('a) felt that he should move toward Iraq, not only for continuing his protest, but also for establishing an Islamic government. The letters of Kufah Shi'ahs and that of Muslim showed that it would be possible without probable battles and with the support of many Shi'ahs. Therefore, Imam Hussayn ('a) could revitalize the tradition of his grandfather, Messenger of Allah (s), in an Islamic government and reform the Muslims' affairs, which is the best level of enjoining good and forbidding evil.

Meanwhile, if the Kufah Shi'ahs did not fulfill their promises or other problems arose, Imam Hussayn ('a) could do his new duty according to time and place conditions. In any case, he would not abandon his protest movement. Imam Hussayn ('a) changed his hajj pilgrimage to 'Umurah and went toward Kufah.

The fourth step; being informed of Muslim's martyrdom. Imam Hussayn ('a) heard the news of Muslim's martyrdom in Tha'labiyyah and faced new conditions to decide accordingly. The first measure was relating the event directly to his companions and taking their advice.

The sons of 'Aqil said, "We should avenge Muslim's murder or be killed in this way." Imam Hussayn ('a) stated, "Life has no value after the martyrdom of Hani and Muslim." Some of the companion said, "O son of Messenger of Allah (s)! By Allah that you are not like Muslim. When you enter Kufah, the Shi'ah who have invited you will surely rush to you and support you."

In such conditions, Imam Hussayn ('a) had two options; continuing his way to Kufah, or abandoning this way and going toward another city to fulfill his duty according to the new conditions there.

Imam Hussayn ('a) preferred the first option, because first, he was not disappointed of support of people of Kufah, as emphasized by his companions too. Second, he thought that if the Kufah people would not fulfill their promises, he could fulfill his duty in Kufah better than in other lands and continue his opposition movement. Therefore, he decided to continue his way toward Kufah.

At this phase, Imam Hussayn ('a) did something to help anyone of his companions who feared continuing this movement, but was ashamed to leave him. Imam ('a) told his friends, "As you have heard, Muslim is martyred and the conditions in Kufah have changed. I am going to Kufah anyway. However, I remove my oath of allegiance from you. Everyone who likes to leave me can go wherever he wants to."

A few of the people left the caravan of Imam Hussayn ('a) and it went toward Kufah.

The fifth step; facing the army of Hur: Imam Hussayn ('a) had planned to reach Kufah as soon as possible, but before reaching there, Hur and his army blocked their way. Imam Hussayn ('a) told Hur, "The people of Kufah have invited me there. If they have relented, I will return to Hijaz or another land."

Hur replied, "I know nothing of this invitation. I have a mission to seize you and take you to Ibn Ziyad to decide about you."

This changed the conditions again. Surrendering to Ibn Ziyad led to a humiliating allegiance or martyrdom, neither of which was accepted by Imam Hussayn ('a). Therefore, he changed his path and went another way to exit the blockage and move toward another destination.

The sixth step; reaching Karbala land. The caravan of Imam Hussayn ('a) was proceeding and the army of Hur watched it without resorting to force until they reached Karbala. Then Ibn Ziyad sent a letter to Hur and ordered him to stop the caravan of Imam Hussayn ('a). This new command created a new milieu. Imam Hussayn ('a) could not proceed to Kufah or any other place. Imam Hussayn ('a) faced another dilemma here; he could surrender to Ibn Ziyad's will to be able to live some more years with humiliation, or he could resist his enemies, preferring honorable defiance and martyrdom to humiliating life.

Imam Hussayn ('a) did not abandon pursuing his purpose in these harsh risky conditions. He chose holy courageous war until martyrdom to teach a practical lesson of liberalism, religiousness, justice-seeking, and resisting autocracy and oppression. This way he unsteadied the bases of the Umayyites illegal government. This was in fact the best level of enjoining good and forbidding evil.

Imam Hussayn's ('a) 'ashura is the school of liberty, religiousness, resistance against oppression, and defending the poor and the oppressed. This liberator school should always remain active and alive throughout history. Anytime and anywhere that oppression and autocracy exist and peaceful measures for opposing it does not suffice, the last resort will be revitalizing the lessons of 'ashura school. That is why the infallible Imams ('a) attended to and recommended holding mourning sessions for Imam Hussayn ('a) to encourage people to fight oppression. Crying for someone martyred in the way of combating oppression and defending the religion has so many rewards, as mentioned in various traditions.

The Fourth Imam; 'Ali ibn Hussayn

Birth and Martyrdom

According to some traditions, Imam Ali Ibn Hussayn ('a) was born on the fifteenth of Jamadul 'ula' in the year thirty one or thirty six A.H. in Medina.[273] His father was Hussayn Ibn Ali ('a) and his mother, based on some narrations, was Shahrbanu, daughter of Yazdgird (Iranian King).[274] His nicknames were Abul Hassan, Abul Qasim, Abu Muhammad, Abu Bakr, and his most famous titles were Ziynul 'abidin, Ziynus Salihin, and Sajjad.[275]

According to some traditions, he was martyred on twelfth of Muharram in the year ninety four A.H. in Medina and his holy body was buried in Baqi' cemetery.

Imam Ali Ibn Hussayn ('a) lived fifty seven years in this world. When he was two years old, his grandfather Ali Ibn Abi Talib ('a) was martyred. He then experienced the Imamate of his uncle, Imam Hassan ('a) for ten years. On 'ashura of the year sixty one A.H., when his father was martyred, Imam Ali Ibn Hussayn ('a) was twenty two. He lived thirty five years –his Imamate age– after his father.[276]

---

[273] Biharul Anwar, Vol 46, p. 14.

[274] Ibid, p. 13.

[275] Ibid, p. 4.

[276] Ibid, Vol 46, pp. 8 & 154.

Texts Proving His Imamate

In addition to general reasons for Imamate of the twelve infallible Imams ('a), certain specific reasons are pointed out for proving the Imamate of Ali Ibn Hussayn ('a), some of which are quoted here from his father, Imam Hussayn ('a).

Abu Bakr Hazrami has narrated from Imam Sadiq ('a), "When Hussayn Ibn Ali ('a) was going to travel to Iraq, he gave a book and a will to Ummi Salamah. When Ali Ibn Hussayn ('a) returned from Karbala to Medina, Ummi Salamah gave the trusts to him."[277]

Fuzayl Ibn Yasar has narrated from Imam Muhammad Baqir ('a), "When Imam Hussayn ('a) was going to Iraq, he gave a book, his will, and some other things to Ummi Salamah, Prophet Muhammad's (s) wife, and said, 'When my eldest son comes to you, give these to him.' After Imam Hussayn's ('a) martyrdom, his son Ali went to Ummi Salamah and took the trusts." [278]

Abul Jarud has quoted from Imam Muhammad Baqir ('a), "Imam Hussayn ('a) called his daughter, Fatimah, before his martyrdom and gave her a wrapped book and an open will. At that time, Ali Ibn Hussayn ('a) was very sick. Later, Fatimah gave him the book. By Allah that the book is now with us." Abul Jarud asked, "What is in this book?" Imam Baqir ('a) answered, "Whatever the people need exists in the book. By Allah that all Islamic commandments and limits (the Hudud) are in it, even the compensation fee for a scrape on the skin."[279]

---

[277] 'Ithbatul Hudat, Vol 5, p. 212.

[278] Ibid.

[279] Ibid, p. 213. There may appear a doubt here that needs to be clarified. This tradition cites that Imam Hussayn (a.s) gave his book and will to his daughter, Fatimah, while according to two previous traditions Imam Hussayn (a.s) had given the book and the will to Ummi Salamah. It can be explained that perhaps the books and wills have been numerous; therefore, Imam Hussayn (a.s) had given some of them to Ummi Salamah and some of them to his daughter, Fatimah.

Abdullah Ibn 'Atabah says, "I was with Hussayn Ibn Ali ('a) when Ali Ibn Hussayn ('a) came in. I asked Imam Hussayn ('a), 'If you pass away one day, who should we refer to?' Imam ('a) answered, 'Refer to this son of me. He will be the Imam and the father of Imams.'"[280]

Mas'udi has written in his book 'Ithbatul Wasilah, "In Karbala, Hussayn ('a) called Ali Ibn Hussayn ('a), who was sick, presented Allah's Great Name and the legacy of the prophets (s) to him, and informed him that the Prophet's books, sciences, and weapon are trusted to Ummi Salamah and she will give all of them to him."[281]

Sayyid Murtaza has written in 'Uyunul Murtaza, "The narrators have narrated that Hussayn Ibn Ali ('a) willed that Allah's Great Name and the prophet's (s) legacy be given to his son Ali Ibn Hussayn ('a). Then Imam Hussayn ('a) stated, 'He will be the Imam after me.'"[282]

Muhammad Ibn Muslim says, "I asked Imam Sadiq ('a), 'Where is the ring of Hussayn Ibn Ali ('a)? I have heard that it was removed from his finger in Karbala.' Imam ('a) replied, 'That is not true. Hussayn ('a) willed to his son, Ali Ibn Hussayn ('a), gave Ali his ring, and left the Imamate to Ali, just as the Messenger of Allah (s) did in case of Amiral Mu'minin ('a), Amiral Mu'minin ('a) did in case of his son Hassan, and Hassan did in case of his brother Hussayn. After Ali Ibn Hussayn ('a), Imam Hussayn's ('a) ring was given to my father and then to me. I wear it every Friday and perform prayers with it.'

I went to Imam Sadiq ('a) on Friday and found him performing prayers. When his prayer finished, he stretched his hand toward me. I saw a ring in his holy finger with the sign: 'There is no deity but Allah; preparation for meeting Allah.' Then Imam ('a) said, 'This is the ring

---

[280] 'Ithbatul Hudat, Vol 5, p. 215.

[281] 'Ithbatul Hudat, p. 216.

[282] Ibid.

of my grandfather, Hussayn Ibn Ali ('a).'" [283]

The author of Kashful Ghummah has argued for the Imamate of Ali Ibn Hussayn ('a) using some other reasons:

First, Imam Sajjad ('a) was the most virtuous most knowledgeable of the people in his own age after his father. Logically, when such a person exists, no other one can be the Imam.

Second, it is proved using logical reasons and the traditions that the existence of Imam is necessary in all ages; the earth will never be void of Allah's successor. The people who claimed to be the Imam in the age of Ali Ibn Hussayn ('a) had no true reason for their Imamate and their claims were invalid. Therefore, the Imamate of Ali Ibn Hussayn ('a) is proved, as there should be an Imam on the earth.

Third, there are some traditions from the Messenger of Allah (s) about the Imamate of Ali Ibn Hussayn ('a), such as the tradition Jabir has narrated from Prophet Muhammad (s), Imam Muhammad Baqir ('a) narrated from his father, from his grandfather, and from Fatimah (s), daughter of the Messenger of Allah (s). The names of the twelve Imams, including Imam Sajjad ('a), are recorded in this tradition.

As mentioned in the traditions, Amiral Mu'minin ('a) had declared the Imamate of Ali, son of Hussayn Ibn Ali ('a), when Hussayn Ibn Ali ('a) was alive.

Moreover, Hussayn Ibn Ali ('a) referred to the Imamate of his son, Ali, in his will before being martyred and gave the will to Ummi Salaamh to be given to his son, Ali, after himself. Imam Hussayn ('a) has considered asking for the will from Ummi Salamah as a sign of the real Imam.[284]

Jabir Ibn Abdullah 'Ansari told the Prophet (s), "O Messenger of Allah! Who will be the Imams from the progeny of Ali Ibn Abi Talib?" Prophet Muhammad (s) stated, "Hassan and Hussayn, masters of youth

---

[283] Biharul Anwar, Vol 46, p. 17.

[284] Kashful Ghummah, Vol 2, p. 265.

of the Paradise. Then master of the worshippers, Ali Ibn Hussayn and then Baqir; Muhammad Ibn Ali. O Jabir! You will be alive and see him, so say my hello to him! After him, Sadiq, Ja'far Ibn Muhammad, then Kazim, Musa Ibn Ja'far, then Riza, Ali Ibn Musa. After him, Taqi, Muhammad Ibn Ali, and then Naqi, Ali Ibn Muhammad. After him, Zaki, Hassan Ibn Ali, and then his son, Qa'im, Mahdi. He will fill the world with justice after being filled with injustice and oppression.

O Jabir! They will be my successors, progeny, and caliphs. Everyone who obeys them has obeyed me. And everyone who disobeys them has disobeyed me. Everyone who denies one or all of them has denied me. Allah keeps the earth from swallowing its residents because of the bliss of their existence."[285]

Virtues of Imam Sajjad ('a)

Ali Ibn Hussayn ('a) was the best most virtuous of the people of his own age, so he was called the adornment of the worshippers.

Imam Sadiq ('a) stated, "In the Hereafter, a caller will cry out, 'Where is Ziynul 'Abidin (the adornment of worshippers)?' It is as if I see Ali Ibn Hussayn, who has stood up and is walking among people's lines in the Hereafter."[286]

When Ali Ibn Hussayn ('a) was leaving the circle of 'Umar Ibn Abdul 'Aziz, 'Umar asked the audience, "Who is the noblest of the people?" The people said, "You." 'Umar said, "No, it is not me. It is the one who just left us."[287]

Husham Ibn Abdul Malik went to hajj pilgrimage before his caliphate. He was going to touch and kiss the Hajarul 'Aswad, but he could not because of the crowd. At that time, Ali Ibn Hussayn ('a) arrived there. The hajjis opened a way for him to Hajarul 'Aswad. The

---

[285] Kamalid Din wa Tamamun Ni'mah, Vol 1, p. 372.
[286] Biharul Anwar, Vol 46, p. 3.
[287] Ibid.

companions of Husham asked, "Who is this man?" "I do not know him," answered Husham. Farazdaq, the poet, heard Husham's speech and told him, "I know him well; he is Ali Ibn Hussayn ('a), Ziynul 'abidin." Then he composed a pretty poem for introducing Imam Sajjad ('a).[288]

Abu Hazim, Sufyan Ibn 'Ayinah and Zahri have narrated, "We did not see anyone better and more knowledgeable than Ali Ibn Hussayn ('a) among Hashemite."[289]

Worship and Vigil

After Ali Ibn Abi Talib ('a), Ali Ibn Hussayn ('a) was the most devout person in his age, thus he was called Ziynul Abidin.

Imam Sadiq ('a) said about Ali Ibn Hussayn ('a), "When the prayer time came, his body trembled, his face paled, and shivered like a palm tree.[290]

Imam Baqir ('a) stated, "When my father began praying he was quite still as the stem of a tree."[291]

Abu Hamzah Thumali says, "I saw Ali Ibn Hussayn ('a) whose cloak fell off his shoulder in prayer, but he did not move to put it in place until his prayer completed. I asked him the reason. Imam ('a) said, 'Do you know who I was standing before? Surely one's prayer is accepted as much as his heart attends to Allah.'"[292]

When Imam Sajjad ('a) rose for performing prayer his face paled, his body trembled, and his state changed. When he was asked for the reason, he said, "I am going to rise before a Great King."

---

[288] Kashful Ghummah, Vol 2, p. 291.

[289] Biharul Anwar, Vol 46, p. 97.

[290] Biharul Anwar, Vol 46, p. 55.

[291] Ibid, p. 64.

[292] Ibid, p. 66

When he began praying, he ignored everything and it was as if he heard no voice.²⁹³

Abdullah, the son of Imam Sajjad ('a) says, "My father prayed at nights until he got tired and crawled to his bed like children."²⁹⁴

If Ali Ibn Hussayn ('a) could not perform nawafil (recommended prayers) of the day, he performed them at night. He told his children, "Though the nawafil are not obligatory, I like you to continue every good thing you get used to." Imam Sajjad's ('a) son continues, "My father did not leave the Night Prayer at home or in travel."²⁹⁵

The father of Abu Hamzah Thumali says, "I saw Ali Ibn Hussayn ('a), who was performing prayer beside Ka'bah. He lasted his standing so much until he got tired and lent over his feet alternatively. I heard him saying, 'O my Master! Do you punish me while my heart is full of your love? By Your honor do not gather me together with the people who have long been Your enemy.'"

Zahri has quoted from Ali Ibn Hussayn ('a), "If all the people die in East and West of the world but the Quran accompany me, I will not be fearful at all." Zahri continues, "And when he reached the Quranic verse 'Master of the Day of Judgment', he repeated it to the extent that he was going to die."²⁹⁶

Imam Baqir ('a) stated, "Fatimah, the daughter of Ali Ibn Abi Talib, saw Ali Ibn Hussayn ('a), who was exhausted from worship. So she went to Jabir Ibn Abdullah 'Ansari and said, 'O companion of Messenger of Allah! We deserve being advised by you in case one of us exhausts himself out of intensive worship and harms his health. Now Ali Ibn Hussayn, who is the memory of his father, has callus on

---

²⁹³ Biharul Anwar, Vol 46, p. 80.

²⁹⁴ Ibid, p. 99.

²⁹⁵ Ibid, p. 98.

²⁹⁶ Biharul Anwar, Vol 46, p. 107.

his forehead, knees, and hands. Come and talk to him so that he puts himself less in trouble for worship.'"

Jabir went to Imam Sajjad ('a) and saw him in worship. Ali Ibn Hussayn ('a) rose for Jabir, greeted him, and seated him beside himself.

Jabir said, " 'O son of Messenger of Allah! Do you know that the Exalted Allah has created the Paradise for you and your lovers and the Hell for your enemies? Why do you take yourself into trouble in worship?'"

Ali Ibn Hussayn ('a) said in reply, " 'O companion of Messenger of Alalh! Don't you know that my grandfather, the Messenger of Allah (s) had no sin, but did not leave intensive worship until his holy feet inflated? And he said in answer to the advisors, 'Shouldn't I be a grateful servant?'"

When Jabir heard Imam Sajjad's ('a) speech, he said, " 'O son of Messenger of Allah! Watch for your health, since you are from a family (the Ahlul-Bayt) for whose sake the earth is away from calamities and the rain is descending.'"

Imam Sajjad ('a) stated, " 'O Jabir! I do not leave the tradition of my father and grandfathers until I meet them.'"[297]

Ali Ibn Hussayn ('a) went to hajj on foot and traversed the distance between Medina and Mecca in twenty days.[298]

Almsgiving

Imam Muhammad Baqir ('a) said, "My father divided all his property into two parts, giving half of it to the poor, twice in his lifetime."[299]

Ali Ibn Hussayn ('a) filled his sack with bread and other foods, divided it among the poor, and said, "Almsgiving extinguishes the

---

[297] Biharul Anwar, Vol 46, p. 60.

[298] Ibid, p. 76.

[299] Ibid, p. 90.

fire of Allah's wrath." [300]

'Umar Ibn Dinar says, "Ziyd Ibn Usamah cried before his death. Ali Ibn Hussayn ('a) who was present asked the reason for his weeping. 'Umar answered, 'I have fifteen thousand dinars debt and cannot afford to pay it. I am fearful of dying and being still a debtor.' Imam Sajjad ('a) stated, 'Do not be upset. I will pay your debt.'"[301]

Abdullah was at the point of death. His creditors had surrounded him and asked their money. He told them, "I have no money to pay you, but I will to one of my two cousins, Ali Ibn Hussayn or Abdullah Ibn Ja'far to pay your loan. You can choose anyone you like." The creditors said, "Abdullah Ibn Ja'far is wealthy. Ali Ibn Hussayn is not wealthy but he is truthful; we choose him."

Ali Ibn Hussayn ('a) was informed of the issue. He said, "I will pay your loan after cropping the crop." The creditors were satisfied, though Imam Sajjad ('a) had no crop. However, at harvest time, the Almighty Allah granted him some property to pay the loan he had accepted.[302]

Imam Muhammad Baqir ('a) said, "My father held a sack of dinar and food at dark nights. He knocked on the poor houses and divided the money and food among them, while he had hid his face. After his demise, the poor found out that the unidentified man has been Ali Ibn Hussayn ('a)."[303]

Zahri has said, "On a cold rainy night, I saw Ali Ibn Hussayn ('a), who was going with some wheat on his shoulder. I told him, 'O son of Messenger of Allah! What are you carrying?' Imam Sajjad ('a) replied, 'I am going to travel, so I am transferring my sustenance to a safe place.'

---

[300] Ibid, p. 100

[301] Ibid, p. 56.

[302] Biharul Anwar, Vol 46, p. 94.

[303] Biharul Anwar, Vol 46, p. 62.

I said, 'Let my servant help you!' But Imam ('a) did not accept. I said, 'Let me help you!' Imam Sajjad ('a) answered, 'I should carry it myself and take it to the destination. Go away and leave me alone!' After some days, I saw Imam ('a), who had not gone to travel yet. I told him, 'O son of Messenger of Allah! Have you not gone on travel yet?' Imam Sajjad ('a) told me, 'O Zahri! That travel was not like what you thought. I meant the travel to the Hereafter for which I should prepare myself. Preparedness for death is in two ways; avoiding the unlawful deeds and spending property in charity.'"[304]

When Medina was attacked by the army of Yazid, Ali Ibn Hussayn ('a) accepted the guardianship of four hundred families until the army of Muslim Ibn 'Aqabah left Medina.[305]

Modesty

Ali Ibn Hussayn ('a) was ridding his horse when he passed a group of lepers who were eating food. They invited Imam Sajjad ('a) to eat with them. Imam ('a) said, "I am fasting, otherwise I accepted your invitation." When Imam ('a) reached home, he ordered to prepare a good food for the lepers. Then he invited them to his home and they ate together.[306]

Remission

One of the companions of Imam Sajjad ('a) has narrated that a relative of Imam ('a) insulted and misnamed him in presence of some of the companions. Imam sajjad ('a), however, did not answer him. After a while, Imam ('a) told his companions, "You heard the insult of this man. Now I want to go and answer him. Come with me if you want." The companions accompanied Imam Sajjad ('a) to the insulter man's

---

[304] Ibid, p. 65.

[305] Ibid, p. 101.

[306] Ibid, p. 94.

house and heard Imam ('a) reciting this Quranic verse,

> *"Those who restrain anger, and pardon (all) men; for God loves those who do good."*[307]

When they arrived at the house of that man, he came out angrily and offensively, since he thought Ali Ibn Hussayn ('a) had come to treat him as he had done. Then Imam Sajjad ('a) told him, "O brother! You said some words about me. If what you said is true, I repent, but if it is false, May Allah forgive your sins." The man regretted his speech, kissed the forehead of Imam ('a), and said, "I said things which are not true about you and deserve myself."[308]

The female slave of Ali Ibn Hussayn ('a) poured water for him to perform ablution. Suddenly the pitcher fell down from her hand, hit Imam's ('a) head, and injured his face. Imam Sajjad ('a) raised his head and looked at the slave. She said, "The Almighty Allah states in Holy Quran, 'Those who restrain anger.'" Imam Sajjad ('a) said, "I restrained my anger." The female slave said again, 'and those who pardon (all) men.' Imam ('a) said, "May Allah forgive your sins." She said, 'for God loves those who do good.' Imam Sajjad ('a) told her, "I make you free; go wherever you want."[309]

Imam Sajjad ('a) had some guests and his servant brought kebab for the guests.

Suddenly the iron kebab skewer fell on a child's head. The servant was embarrassed when Imam Sajjad ('a) told him, "You did not do it intentionally and I make you free."[310]

---

[307] Surah 'ali Imran (3): 134.

[308] Biharul Anwar, Vol 46, p. 54.

[309] Ibid, p. 68.

[310] Biharul Anwar, Vol 46, p. 99.

A man insulted Imam Sajjad ('a), using abusive language. The companions of Imam ('a) wanted to attack the insulter, but Imam Sajjad ('a) prohibited them. Then he told the rude man, "What you do not know about me is more than what you said. Do you have a request so that I may help you?" Then Imam ('a) granted him a garment and a thousand dinars. That man got ashamed of his conduct after Imam's ('a) benevolent conduct and regretted. From then on, whenever that man saw Imam Sajjad ('a), he said, "I testify that you are a progeny of the Prophet (s)."[311]

Ali Ibn Hussayn ('a) went to his cousin's house at nights and helped him in disguise. Imam's cousin said, "May Allah bless you that you help me. Ali Ibn Hussayn does not help me; may Allah give him no Mercy!" Imam Sajjad ('a) heard his speech, bore it, and did not introduce himself. After Imam's ('a) demise, the helps stopped, so his cousin realized that the helper has been Imam ('a). Then he visited Imam Sajjad's ('a) grave and cried there.[312]

Ali Ibn Hussayn ('a) saw a group of people who were back biting him. He stopped and said, "If you tell the truth, may Allah forgive me. And if you lie, may He forgive you."[313]

The Fifth Imam; Muhammad BAqir

Birth and Martyrdom

Muhammad Ibn Ali ('a) was born on the third of Safar in the year fifty nine A.H. in Medina. His father was Ali Ibn Hussayn ('a) and his mother was Fatimah, Ummi Abdullah, the daughter of Imam Hassan

---

[311] Ibid.
[312] Ibid, p. 100.
[313] Ibid, p. 96.

('a). His nickname was Abu Ja'far and his titles were Baqirul Ulum, Shakir, and Hadi.[314]

He lived fifty seven years and was martyred on the seventh of Zi Hajjah in the year 114 A.H. in Medina and was buried in Baqi' cemetery.[315]

Texts Proving His Imamate

In addition to general reasons pointed out in previous chapters for proving the Imamate of the twelve Imams ('a), there are some explicit reasons for Imamate of Imam Muhammad Baqir ('a) in the speech of his father, Ali Ibn Hussayn ('a).

'Isma'il Ibn Muhammad Ibn Abdullah Ibn Ali Ibn Hussayn has quoted from Imam Baqir ('a), "Imam Ali Ibn Hussayn ('a) brought a chest to me before his demise and said, 'O Muhammad! Take this chest and keep it.' When Ali Ibn Hussayn ('a) passed away, his brothers came to Imam Baqir ('a) and asked for their legacy from that chest. Imam Baqir ('a) told them, 'You have no share of this chest. If you had, it was not given to me. The chest contains the weapon and the books of Messenger of Allah (s).'"[316]

'Isa Ibn Abdullah has quoted from his father from his grandfather that Imam Ali Ibn Hussayn ('a) attended to his children before his demise and told his son, Muhammad Ibn Ali, "O Muhammad! Take this chest to your home!" There was no money in that chest; rather, there were scientific books in it.[317]

The same tradition is narrated by Muhammad Ibn Abdul Jabbar.[318]

---

[314] Biharul Anwar, Vol 46, pp. 216, 217 & 222.

[315] Ibid, p. 217.

[316] 'Ithbatul Hudat, Vol 5, p. 261.

[317] Ibid, p. 262.

[318] 'Ithbatul Hudat, Vol 5, p. 262.

'Aban Ibn 'Uthman has narrated from Imam Sadiq ('a) that one day Jabir went to Imam Ali Ibn Hussayn ('a), when his son Muhammad was there. Jabir asked Imam ('a), "Who is he?" Imam Sajjad ('a) answered, "He is my son and the successor to me, Muhammad Baqir."[319]

'Uthman Ibn Uthman Ibn Khalid has quoted from his father, "When Ali Ibn Hussayn ('a) got sick, he called his sons, Muhammad, Hassan, 'Umar, Ziyd, and Hussayn. He introduced his son, Muhammad Ibn Ali, as his successor among them, gave him the title Baqir, and entrusted the affairs of his other sons to him."[320]

Malik Ibn 'A'yun Jahni has said that Ali Ibn Hussayn ('a) set his son, Muhammad Ibn Ali his successor and stated, "O my son! You will be my successor and caliph."[321]

Zahri says, "I told Ali Ibn Hussayn ('a), 'O son of Messenger of Allah! If your death comes, who we should refer to?' Imam Sajjad ('a) replied, 'Refer to my son Muhammad; he will be my caliph, the heir of my knowledge, and Baqirul 'Ulum. This is a covenant from the Messenger of Allah (s) to us.'"[322]

Abu Basir has narrated from Imam Baqir, Abu Ja'far ('a), "One of my father's recommendations to me in his will was that when he passed away only I should wash his body, because only an Imam should wash an Imam after his death."[323]

Sayyid Murtaza have said, "Before the demise of Ali Ibn Hussayn ('a), he called his son, Muhammad Baqir, and introduced Muhammad Baqir as his successor in presence of a group of the noble Shi'ahs, emphasizing his Imamate and presenting Allah's Great Name and the

---

[319] Ibid, p. 263

[320] Ibid, p. 264.

[321] Ibid.

[322] Ibid.

[323] 'Ithbatul Hudat, Vol 5, p. 264.

prophets' (s) legacy to him."³²⁴

Mas'udi has narrated the same tradition in his book 'Ithbatul Wasiyyah.³²⁵

Virtues

Like other infallible Imams ('a), Imam Muhammad Baqir ('a) was a perfect human and infallible from any vices or faults. This is not only the opinion of their friends, but also that of their enemies.

Shiykh Mufid has written about Imam Muhammad Baqir ('a): Imam Baqir, Abu Ja'far, Muhammad Ibn Ali Ibn Hussayn ('a) was selected from among his brothers to be the successor and caliph of his father, Ali Ibn Hussayn ('a). He was superior to his brothers in regard to knowledge, piety, and nobility.

He was more famous and honorable for the masses and the elites. None of the progeny of Hassan ('a) and Hussayn ('a) was as knowledgeable as he was in religious sciences, Prophet's (s) traditions, Quranic exegesis, and life conducts. The Prophet's (s) companions, the companions' friends, and great jurisprudents have narrated traditions from Imam Muhammad Baqir ('a). He was famous for knowledge and understanding and was eulogized in poems.³²⁶

Abul Fida' has written about Imam Muhammad Baqir ('a): Muhammad Ibn Ali Ibn Hussayn Abu Ja'far Baqir has been an honorable follower of the Prophet (s) and a selected person in terms of knowledge, conduct, nobility, and honor. The Imamiyah Shi'ahs know him one of their twelve Imams...He has narrated many traditions from the companions of Messenger of Allah (s) and many followers of the companions have narrated traditions from him. Some of the narrators

---

[324] 'Ithbatul Hudat, Vol 5, p. 265.

[325] Ibid.

[326] Al-'Irshad, p. 157.

from him include his son, Ja'far Sadiq, Hakam Ibn 'Atibah, Rabi'ahi, 'A'mash, Abu 'Is'haq Sabi'i, 'Awza'i, 'A'raj, Ibn Jurayh, 'Ata', 'Amr Ibn Dinar, and Zahri.

Sufyan Ibn 'Ayinah has narrated from Imam Ja'far Sadiq ('a), "My father narrated traditions for me, while he was the best one in Prophet Muhammad's (s) nation." 'Ajali has said about him, "He was one of the most trustworthy followers of Prophet's (s) companions in Medina." Muhammad Ibn Sa'd has said about Imam Baqir ('a), "He was trustworthy and narrated many traditions."[327]

Furthermore, Abul Fida' has written about Imam Muhammad Baqir ('a), Abu Ja'far Muhammad Ibn Ali Ibn Hussayn Ibn Ali Ibn Abi Talib was son of Ziynul 'abidin and grandson of Hussayn, who was martyred in Karbala. He was called Baqir, because he split knowledge and deducted the rules. He was a humble patient person from the Prophet's (s) family. He was lofty and famous. He was aware of the dangers. He wept a lot (from Allah's fear) and avoided enmity and controversy. [328]

Ahmad Ibn Hajar Hiythami has written about Imam Muhammad Baqir ('a): Abu Ja'far Muhammad Baqir ('a) was the heir of knowledge, worship, and piety of Ali Ibn Hussayn ('a). He was called Baqir, because he discovered sciences. He gained treasures of teachings, commandments, and wisdom, which are only denied by blind-minded and deviant people. He was thus the splitter and distributer of knowledge. His heart was illuminated, his conduct was purified, his soul was clean, and his essence was good. He spent his lifetime in Allah's obedience. His mystical conduct and tradition cannot be described. He has many speeches about mystical conduct and teachings, which require a detailed discussion.[329]

---

[327] Al-Bidayah wan Nahayah, Vol 9, p. 338.

[328] Ibid, p. 339.

[329] Al-Sawa'iqul Muharraqah, p. 201.

Knowledge

Imam Muhammad Baqir ('a) was one of the greatest jurisprudents and scholars of his own age. The Messenger of Allah (s) had declared his scientific stance before.

Jabir Ibn Abdullah Ansari has narrated from Prophet Muhammad (s) who told him, "O Jabir! You will visit one of my progeny from the generation of Hussayn, whose name is my name. He will discover sciences and explain facts. When you meet him, say my hello to him." Jabir was alive until he met Imam Muhammad Baqir ('a) and said Prophet Muhammad's (s) greetings to him.[330]

Many great scholars have praised his scientific stance, including the following: Ibn Barqi has called him a learned jurisprudent among Medina jurisprudents and one of the followers of Prophet Muhammad's (s) companions.[331]

Abdullah Ibn 'Atayi Makki says, "The scholars showed a kind of humility before Muhammad Ibn Ali Ibn Hussayn that showed for no one else. I saw Hakam Ibn 'Atibah, who was so learned and honorable, that behaved like a child before his teacher when facing Muhammad Ibn Ali."[332]

When Jabir Ibn Yazid Ju'fi narrated a tradition from Imam Muhammad Baqir ('a), he said, "The successor of the 'awliya' and the heir of sciences of the prophets (s), Muhammad Ibn Ali Ibn Hussayn, told me..."[333]

Ibn Abil Hadid writes, "Muhammad Ibn Ali Ibn Hussayn was the greatest jurisprudent in Hijaz. The people learned jurisprudence from him and his son, Ja'far. He was titled Baqirul 'Ulum. When he was

---

[330] Al-Fusulul Muhimmah, p. 193.

[331] Tahdhibut Tahdhib, Vol 9, p. 350

[332] Biharul Anwar, Vol 46, p. 286; Al-'Irshad, p. 160.

[333] Ibid.

not yet born, the Messenger of Allah (s) gave him this title, gave good tidings of visiting him to Jabir Ibn Abdullah Ansari, and told Jabir, 'Say my greetings to him.'"[334]

Shiykh Mufid writes, "Some traditions are narrated from Imam Abu Ja'far ('a) about the beginning of creation of world, the history of Prophets (s), wars, conducts, traditions, and hajj rituals from Prophet Muhammad (s), as well as Quran exegesis by general and specific narrators. He had debates with some of the dissidents and deviant opinion makers. People have narrated various sciences from him."[335]

The best witness for proving scientific stance of Imam Baqir ('a) is the many traditions issued by him in belief, kalam, philosophy, jurisprudence, ethics, history, social issues, exegesis, etc. Narrators have narrated and recorded them in tradition books.

The traditions attributed to Imam Baqir ('a) are very numerous. After his son, Imam Sadiq ('a), he has the greatest number of traditions compared to other infallible Imams ('a).

Imam Baqir ('a) trained notable and knowledgeable students during his lifetime, who are narrators of his traditions, some of which are: Abu Hamzah Thumali, Thabit Ibn Dinar, Qasim Ibn Muhammad Ibn Abi Bakr, Ali Ibn Rafi', Zahhak Ibn Muzahim Khurasani, Hamid Ibn Musa Kufi, Abul Fazl Sadir Ibn Hakim Ibn Sahib Siyrafi, Abdullah Barqi, Yahya Ibn Ummi Tawil Mut'imi, Hakim Ibn Jubayr, Farazdaq, Furat Ibn Ahnaf, Ayyub Ibn Hassan, Abu Muhammad Qurayshi Sudi Kufi, Tawus Ibn Kisan Hamidani, Aban Ibn Taghlab Ibn Riyah, Qiys Ibn Ramanah, Abu Khalid Kabuli, Sa'id Ibn Musayyib Makhzumi, Umar Ibn Ali Ibn Hussayn, and his brother, Abdullah, and Jabir Ibn Muhammad Ibn Abi Bakr.[336]

---

[334] Sharh Nahjul Balaghah, Ibn Abil hadid, Vol 15, p. 227.

[335] Al-'Irshad, p. 163.

[336] Siriyi Rasulullah wa Ahli Baytih, Vol 2, p. 228.

'Asad Hiydar has introduced Imam Baqir's ('a) students and the narrators of his traditions as follows: 'Umar Ibn Dinar Hajami, Abdur Rahman Ibn Umar 'Awza'i, Abdul Malik Ibn Abdul 'Aziz, Qurat Ibn Khalid Sadusi, Muhammad Ibn Munkadir, Yahya Ibn Kathir, Abu Bakr Muhammad Ibn Muslim Ibn 'Ubayd Zahri, Abu Uthman Rabi'at Ibn Abdur Rahman, Abu Muhammad Suliyman Ibn Mihran 'Asadi, Abu Muhammad Abdullah Ibn Abi Bakr Ansari, Ziyd Ibn Ali Ibn Hussayn, Musa Ibn Salim Abu Jahzam, Musa Ibn Abi 'isa Hanat, Abul Mughayrah Qasim Ibn Fazl, Qasim Ibn Muhammad Ibn Abi Bakr Tiymi, Muhammad Ibn Suwqah, Hajjaj Ibn 'Artah, entitled Kharbuz Kufi, Aban Ibn Taghlab, Barid ibn Mu'awiyah 'Ajali, Abu Hamzah Thumali, Thabit ibn Dinar, Jabir Ibn Yazid Ju'fi, Muhammad Ibn Muslim Ibn Riyah, Hamran Ibn 'A'yun Shiybani, Zararat Ibn 'A'yun Shiybani, Abdul Malik Ibn 'A'yun Shiybani.

Worship

Like his father, Imam Ziynul 'abidin ('a), Imam Muhammad Baqir ('a) was the best person of his age in remembrance of Allah, supplication and prayer, and fearing the Almighty Allah.

Imam Sadiq ('a) stated, "My father frequently remembered Allah. While walking, eating, and even talking with the people, he did not forget Allah's remembrance (zikr). He always uttered *La illaha illa Allah* (There is no deity but Allah.) Sometimes he gathered us and ordered to be in Allah's remembrance until the dawn and told the people who could recite the Quean to recite it."[337]

Imam Sadiq ('a) also said, "My father wept when supplicating in the middle of night and called the Exalted Allah, 'You ordered me, but I did not obey. You prohibited me, but I did not avoid. So I am Your

---

[337] Biharul Anwar, Vol 46, p. 297.

servant before You and I have no excuse.'"[338]

'Aflah, Imam Baqir's ('a) servant says, "I had gone to hajj with Imam Baqir ('a). When we entered Masjidul Haram, he looked at the Ka'bah and wept loudly. I told him, 'May my parents be sacrificed for you! People are looking at you. I wish you wept more quietly!' Imam ('a) said, 'Woe be on you! Why should not I weep? Perhaps the Almighty Allah has Mercy on me and saves me in the Hereafter.' Then he performed tawaf (circumambulation) and then prayed before the standing place of Abraham. When he raised his head after sajdah, the earth was wet beneath his forehead."[339]

Jabir Ju'fi says, "Imam Muhammad Ibn Ali ('a) told me, 'O Jabir! I am worried and upset.' I said, 'Why are you upset and worried?' Imam ('a) answered, 'O Jabir! When the religion is deeply placed in one's heart, it engages him with Allah and separates from anything other than the Almighty. O Jabir! This world is not as worthy as a horse you ride, a cloth you wear, or a wife you meet in privacy. O Jabir! The believers do not trust the world and do not consider themselves away from death and the Hereafter. What they hear in the world does not distract them from Allah's remembrance. The luxuries of the world do not distract them from seeing Allah's light; they will be bestowed with the reward of the good-doers. The pious people have the least expenses and are the best helpers for you. If you forget, they remind you of Allah. If you remember Allah, they help you. Their tongues utter the truth about Allah. They establish Allah's orders. Their affection is purely for Allah; their hearts are full of His love. In obeying their real Owner, they fear the world. And they consider such conduct as their duty.

The pious see the world like a transient house that should be left

---

[338] Kashful Ghummah, Vol 2, p. 330.

[339] Kashful Ghummah, Vol 2, p. 329.

soon, or like a property that is earned in dream, but does not exist in reality. Attempt in maintaining Allah's religion and wisdom!'"[340]

Imam Sadiq ('a) stated, "Every night I prepared my father's sleeping place and waited for him to come and sleep, so that I could go to sleep too. One night I waited for him long, but he did not come. I went to look for him and found him in the mosque, while everyone else was asleep. I saw him in sajdah and heard him wailing, 'O Allah! Glory be to You! You are my Lord really; I go to sajdah for You, while I am Your servant. O Allah! Surely my deeds are little; so You increase them. O Allah! Save me from Your Punishment the Day You resurrect Your servants. Forgive me; surely You are the Relenting, the Merciful.'"[341]

Imam Sadiq ('a) stated, "When my father was upset about something, he gathered the women and the children. He prayed and they said, 'Amen!'"[342]

'Aban Ibn Miymun Qaddah says, "Imam Abu Ja'far ('a) told me to recite the Quran. I asked him where I should recite. Imam ('a) told me to recite the ninth surah. When I wanted to find the ninth surah, Imam ('a) told me to recite surah Yunus. I recited until I reached the verse,

"To those who do right is a goodly (reward)- Yea, more (than in measure)! No darkness nor shame shall cover their faces![343]

Imam Baqir ('a) said, 'That is enough. The Messenger of Allah (s) said,

---

[340] Ibid, p. 333.

[341] Biharul Anwar, Vol 46, p. 301.

[342] Ibid, p. 297.

[343] Surah Yunus (10): 26.

'I wonder why I recite Quran and my hair does not become gray.' "[344]

Almsgiving

Although Imam Muhammad Baqir ('a) was not wealthy and his life expense was great, he granted the poor alms as much as he could.

Imam Sadiq ('a) stated, "My father had less property than his relatives had and more expenses than they had, but he gave one dinar as charity every Friday. My father then said, 'Alms-giving on Fridays is better than on other days.'"[345]

Hassan Ibn Kathir says, "I told Imam Baqir ('a) about my financial need and my friends' indifference about it. Imam Baqir ('a) said, 'How bad are the friends who attend to us when we are wealthy, but leave us in need.' Then he ordered his servant to give me a bag of seven hundred dinars and said, 'Spend this money and let me know whenever it finished.'"[346]

'Umar Ibn Dinar and 'Ubiydullah Ibn 'Ubayd have said, "Whenever we went to Imam Baqir, he gave us clothes and money and told us, 'I had prepared these for you before.'"[347]

Suliyman Ibn Qaram said, "Imam Abu Ja'far, Muhammad Ibn Ali, granted us five or six hundred and even sometimes one thousand dirhams and he never got tired of giving alms to the requesters and brothers."[348]

Salma, the female slave of Imam Muhammad Baqir ('a), said, "Everyone who came to visit Imam Baqir ('a) was fed and received clothes and money. Once I asked Imam ('a) to help the requesters less,

---

[344] Biharul Anwar, Vol 46, p. 302.

[345] Ibid, Vol 46, p. 294.

[346] Biharul Anwar, Vol 46, p. 287.

[347] Ibid, p. 288.

[348] Ibid.

but Imam ('a) stated, 'The best goodness in the world is charity to one's Muslim brothers.'"[349]

Imam Sadiq ('a) stated, "I was with my father when he divided eighty thousand dinars among the poor in Medina."[350]

All this happened while Imam Muhammad Baqir ('a) worked hard in the hot weather of Medina to make a living for himself and his family.

Muhammad Ibn Munkadir said, "I did not think Ali Ibn Hussayn ('a) would have a successor just like himself, until I saw his son, Muhammad Ibn Ali ('a). I was going to preach him, but he preached me instead." He was asked, "How did he preach you?" Muhammad Ibn Munkadir answered, "I had gone to the outskirt of Medina on a hot time of the day when I saw Muhammad Ibn Ali ('a) –who was a corpulent man– leaning over his two servants. I thought, 'It is a wonder that a nobleman from Quraysh has come out in hot weather for worldly desires. I am going to preach him.' I went toward him and greeted him. He greeted me sweating and panting. I told him, 'A Quraysh nobleman has come out for worldly reasons in this hot hour? How would you answer Allah's reckoning if your death comes in such state?' Muhammad Ibn Ali ('a) left his servants' shoulders and said, 'By Allah that if my death comes in this state, I will die obedient to the Almighty. I am going to work so that I am not dependent upon you and others. I should fear that my death comes while committing sins.'"

Muhammad Ibn Munkadir said, "May Allah bless you! I was going to preach you, but you preached me instead!"[351]

The Sixth Imam; Ja'far Sadiq

---

[349] Kashful Ghummah, Vol 2, p. 330.

[350] Biharul Anwar, Vol 46, p. 302.

[351] Biharul Anwar, Vol 46, p. 287.

Birth and Martyrdom

Imam Ja'far Sadiq ('a) was born on the seventeenth of Rabi'ul Awwal in the year eighty three A.H. in Medina. His father was Imam Muhammad Baqir ('a) and his mother was Fatimah, Ummi Farwah, the daughter of Qasim Ibn Muhamamd. His nicknames were Abu 'Abdillah, Abu 'Isma'il, and Abu Musa and his titles were Sadiq, Fazil, Tahir, Qa'im, Kafil, Munji, and Sabir.

He lived sixty five years and was martyred on the twenty fifth of Shawwal in the year 148 A.H. in Medina and was buried in Baqi' cemetery.

He lived twenty years with his grandfather, Imam Sajjad ('a), and nineteen years with his father, Imam Muhammad Baqir ('a), and his Imamate lasted thirty four years.[352]

Personality of Imam Sadiq ('a)

Imam Sadiq ('a) was the greatest most famous character of his own age in terms of knowledge, jurisprudence, parentage, worship, spiritual state, and ethical virtues. Some of the scholars have testified to this.

Malik Ibn Anas, the jurisprudent of Medina, has said about Imam Sadiq ('a), "When I went to Ja'far Ibn Muhammad Sadiq, he respected me, brought me cushion (to lean), and said, 'O Malik! I like you.' I was happy of his conduct and thanked the Almighty Allah. He was in either of three states; fasting, praying, or remembering Allah. He was one of the greatest worshipper and pious men. He narrated many traditions and held useful meetings. Whenever he narrated from the Messenger of Allah (s), his face changed color, in a way that he could be hardly identified."

Once I accompanied him in hajj. When he wanted to recite talbiyah for 'ihram, his voice stopped in his throat and could not utter it. He

---

[352] Biharul Anwar, Vol 47, pp. 1-11.

nearly fell from atop his horse. I told him, 'O son of Messenger of Allah! You inevitably should recite talbiyah.' He told me, 'O Ibn 'amir! How can I dare say 'Here am I O Allah!' while I fear that the Exalted Allah may respond me, 'No to you, nor are you blissful!)'"[353]

Malik Ibn 'Anas has said, "By Allah that I saw no one superior to Ja'far Ibn Muhammad ('a) in terms of piety, knowledge, and worship."[354]

'Amr Ibn Abil Maqdam has said, "When I looked at Ja'far Ibn Muhammad ('a), I felt he was from the progeny of the prophets (s)."[355]

Ziyd Ibn Ali has said, "In every age there is someone from us, the Ahlul-Bayt, who is the hujjat (argument) of the Almighty Allah for the people. The hujjat of this age is Ja'far Ibn Muhammad, my brother's son. Everyone who follows him will not go astray and everyone who disobeys him will not be guided."[356]

'Isma'il Ibn Ali Ibn Abdullah Ibn Abbas has said, "One day I went to see Abu Ja'far Mansur. He wept until his beard was wet. He told me, 'You do not know what has happened to the Ahlul-Bayt!' I asked, 'O Amiral Mu'minin! What is that happening?' He answered, 'The master of the world; the remnant of the good people has passed away.' I asked, 'Who is he?' Abu Ja'far Mansur replied, 'Ja'far Ibn Muhammad.' I said, 'May Allah give you reward and long life in this calamity.' He said, 'Ja'far Ibn Muhammad was one of the people about who the Almighty Allah has stated, 'Then We have given the Book for inheritance to such of Our Servants as We have chosen.' [357] Ja'far Ibn Muhammad was

---

[353] Biharul Anwar, Vol 46, p. 287.

[354] Biharul Anwar, Vol 47, p. 20; Manaqib 'ali Abi Talib, Vol 4, p. 297; and Hilyatul 'Awliya', Vol 3, p. 193.

[355] Biharul Anwar, Vol 47, p. 29; Tahdhibut Tahdhib, Vol 2, p. 104; and Manaqib 'ali Abi Talib, Vol 4, p. 270.

[356] Manaqib 'ali Abi Talib, Vol 4, p. 299.

[357] Surah Fatir (35): 32.

one of those who was chosen by the Exalted Allah and was one of the pioneers of goodness."[358]

Ibn Haban has considered Ja'far Ibn Muhammad one of the trustworthy narrators of tradition, saying, "He was one of the noblemen of the Ahlul-Bayt in terms of jurisprudence and knowledge. His traditions are benefitted from."[359]

Shahristani writes about Imam Sadiq ('a), "He was very knowledgeable in science and religion and perfect in piety and wisdom. He avoided passions. He lived in Medina for a while; his friends from the Shi'ah benefitted from his knowledge. Then he moved to Iraq and stayed there for a while."[360]

Ahmad Ibn Hajar Hiythami has written, "The best son of Muhammad Baqir was Ja'far Sadiq; therefore, he became the successor to his father and the caliph after him. The people have narrated many traditions from him, which were spread in all regions. Great religious leaders, such as Yahya Ibn Sa'id, Ibn Jurayh, Malik, DuSufyani, Abu Hanifah, Shu'bah, Ayyub Sajistani have narrated tradition from him, too."[361]

Ibn Sabbagh Maliki has written, "Ja'far Sadiq was his father's caliph and successor after his father. He was superior to his brothers in terms of knowledge, intellect, and greatness. The people have narrated many scientific issues from him, which are distributed everywhere. The traditions narrated from him have not been narrated from any other relative of him."[362]

Muhammad Ibn Talhah Shafi'i writes, "Ja'far Ibn Muhammad Sadiq

---

[358] Tarikh Ya'qubi, Vol 2, p. 383.

[359] Tahdhibut Tahdhib, Vol 2, p. 104.

[360] Tarikh Ya'qubi, Vol 2, p. 383.

[361] Al-Sawa'iq Al-Muharriqah, p. 201.

[362] Al-Fusulul Muhimmah, p. 204.

was one of the noblemen of the Ahlul-Bayt. He was so knowledgeable. He worshipped and remembered Allah very much. He was very pious and recited Holy Quran much. He pondered in Quranic meanings, found trivial facts, and discovered amazing results. He spent his time in various kinds of worship, reckoning himself in this regard. Seeing him reminded the people of the Hereafter. Listening to his speech made the people pious. Following him brought about the Paradise. His illuminated face and his purified deeds showed that he was from the progeny of Prophet Muhammad (s)."

A group of religious leaders, such as Yahya Ibn Sa'id Ansari, Ibn Jurayh, Malik Ibn Anas, Thuri, Ibn Ayinah, Shu'bah, and Ayyub Sajistani have narrated traditions from him, considering it an honor for themselves."[363]

Shiykh Mufid has written about Imam Sadiq ('a), "Sadiq; Ja'far Ibn Muhammad Ibn Ali Ibn Hussayn ('a) was chosen among his brothers and appointed as his father's caliph and successor. He was superior to his brothers in terms of knowledge. He was the most famous and the most honorable of them for the public and the elites. His sciences were distributed in all regions. The great number of traditions narrated from him is not narrated from other members the Ahlul-Bayt. The tradition experts have counted four thousand trustworthy narrators for his traditions."[364]

Texts Proving His Imamate

As mentioned before, there are various reasons for proving the Imamate of the twelve infallible Imams ('a) that suffice for proving the Imamate of each. Moreover, there are specific reasons for proving the Imamate of each of the Imams ('a), namely the traditions from

---

[363] Matalibus Su'ul, Vol 2, p. 110.

[364] Al-Irshad, Vol 2, p. 179.

an Imam about the Imam after himself. The general reasons are not repeated here.

Abu Nazrah has said, "Imam Baqir ('a) called his son, Ja'far Sadiq, before his demise to devolve the Imamate to him. His brother, Ziyd Ibn Ali said, 'It was good if you did as Hassan ('a) did in case of Hussayn ('a).' Imam Baqir ('a) answered, 'The trusts cannot be compared via example. The imamate is an ancient promise, which has reached to us from Allah's hujjats.'"[365]

Abu Sabah Kanani has said, "Imam Abu Ja'far ('a) looked at his son, Abu Abdillah, and told me, 'Do you see him? He is one of the persons about who the Almighty Allah has stated, 'And We wished to be Gracious to those who were being depressed in the land, to make them leaders (in Faith) and make them heirs.'[366]"[367]

Jabir Ibn Yazid Ju'fi has said, "Imam Abu Ja'far, Muhammad Baqir, ('a) was asked about the Imam after himself. He patted his hand on the back of Abi Abdillah and said, 'By Allah that this son of me will be the Imam from Muhammad's (s) Ahlul-Bayt after me.'"

Ali Ibn Hakam has quoted from Tahir, Abu Ja'far's ('a) friend, who said, "I was with Imam Baqir ('a) when his son, Ja'far, came in. Imam ('a) told me, 'This is the best human on the earth.'"[368]

Abdul 'A'la has narrated from Imam Sadiq ('a), "My father said before his demise, 'Invite some people as witness!' I called four persons from Qurash, one of which was Nafi' (the master of Abdullah Ibn 'Umar). So my father told me, 'Write down: This is the legacy Jacob ('a) left to his sons, 'Oh my sons! God hath chosen the Faith for you; then

---

[365] Biharul Anwar, Vol 47, p. 12.

[366] Surah Al-Qasas (28): 5.

[367] Biharul Anwar, Vol 47, p. 13.

[368] Ibid.

die not except in the State of Submission (to Allah).'[369] Muhammad Ibn Ali wills to his son, Ja'far, to veil his body in the burd in which he prayed on Fridays, put his turban on his head, make his grave in the form of a square and four fingers higher than the ground, and put his old clothes off.' Then he told the witnesses, 'Go now! May Allah bless you!' I asked my father, 'Why did we call the witnesses?' My father answered, 'O my son! I feared that the people may overcome you and say that his father left no legacy for him. I wanted to leave a reason for you.'"[370]

Jabir Ibn Yazid Ju'fi has narrated that Imam Baqir ('a) was asked about the Qa'im after himself. Imam Baqir ('a) put his hand on Abi Abdillah's shoulder and said, "By Allah that this is the Qa'im of Muhammad's (s) Ahlul-Bayt."

Anbasah Ibn Mus'ab said, "When Imam Abu Ja'far ('a) passed away, I went to his son, Abu Abdillah, and told him the tradition of Jabir. He stated, 'Jabir is true; every Imam is the Qa'im after the previous Imam.'"[371]

Muhammad Ibn Muslim said, "I was with Imam Muhammad Baqir ('a) when his son, Ja'far, came in with grown hair and a stick in his hand. Imam Baqir ('a) hugged him close to his chest. Then he said, 'He will be your Imam after me. Follow him and benefit from his knowledge. By Allah that he is Sadiq, who is named by the Messenger of Allah (s). The Almighty Allah will help all his Shi'ahs in this world and the Hereafter. His enemies are cursed by all the prophets (s).' Then Ja'far ('a) laughed and his face got red. Imam Baqir ('a) told me, 'Ask my son whatever you want.' So I asked him, 'O son of Messenger of Allah!

---

[369] Surah Al-Baqarah (2):132.

[370] Biharul Anwar, Vol 47, p. 14; Al-Fusulul Muhimmah, p. 204; Al-Irshad, Vol 2, p. 181.

[371] Biharul Anwar, Vol 47, p. 15; Al-Irshad, Vol 2, p. 180.

Where does laughing emerge from?' Ja'far Sadiq ('a) replied, 'Wisdom emerges from the heart, sadness from the liver, breath comes from the lungs, and laugh from the lien.' Then I stood up and kissed his head."[372]

Hammam Ibn Nafi' said, "Imam Abu Ja'far ('a) once told his companions, 'When you did not find me, follow him, he will be the Imam and the caliph after me.' And he pointed to Abi Abdillah, Imam Sadiq ('a)."[373]

Husham Ibn Salim has narrated from Imam Sadiq ('a), "My father told me before his demise, 'O Ja'far! I recommend you about my companions.' I asked him, 'O father! By Allah that I will train them in a way that they will not need anyone in gaining knowledge and acquiring sustenance.'"[374]

Surat Ibn Kalib said, "One day, Ziyd Ibn Ali told me, 'How did you understand that your master (Ja'far) is the Imam?' I answered, 'Because we have gone to Imam Muhammad Baqir ('a) before. When we asked him a question, he said, 'The Messenger of Allah (s) said and the Almighty Allah said in His Book...' and then he answered our question. When your brother, Muhammad Baqir, passed away, we came to you, the progeny of Prophet Muhammad (s), for acquiring knowledge. You answered some questions, but could not answer some of them. After that we went to Ja'far, your brother's son, who answered all our questions, just like his father.' Ziyd Ibn Ali smiled and said, 'By Allah that this is because Ja'far has the books of Ali Ibn Abi Talib.'"[375]

'Amr Ibn Abil Miqdam said, "I saw Imam Sadiq ('a) on the day of 'Arafah in pilgrims' staying place. He said with a loud voice, 'O people!

---

[372] Biharul Anwar, Vol 47, p. 15.

[373] Biharul Anwar, Vol 47, p. 15; Al-Irshad, Vol 2, p. 180.

[374] Biharul Anwar, Vol 47, p. 12; Al-Irshad, Vol 2, p. 180.

[375] Biharul Anwar, Vol 47, p. 36; Manaqib 'ali Abi Talib, Vol 4, p. 272.

The Messenger of Allah (s) was the Imam. After him, Ali Ibn Abi Talib was the Imam. Then Hassan and then Hussayn Ibn Ali were the Imams. After Hussayn, Ali Ibn Hussayn and then Muhammad Ibn Ali were the Imams. After him, etc.' He repeated this speech for the people in front of him, the ones behind him, those on his right, and the people on his left three times for each group. When I went to Mina, I asked the exegesis of the word 'etc.' from Arab literary men. They said that it means 'I; so ask me.' I asked it from other people and all of them interpreted it in the same way." [376]

Abdul Ghaffar Ibn Qasim said, "I told Imam Baqir ('a), 'O son of Messenger of Allah! If something bad happened to you, who we should refer to after you?' Imam Baqir ('a) replied, 'Refer to Ja'far. He is my best son, the father of Imams, and trustworthy in speech and action.'"[377]

Shiykh Mufid, arguing the reasons for Imamate of Imam Sadiq ('a), has written, "Logically, it is proved that the Imam should be the most knowledgeable of the people. Imam Ja'far Sadiq ('a) was so; his knowledge, piety, and deeds were superior to those of his brothers, cousins, and other people in his own age."[378]

Knowledge

One of the major duties of infallible Imams ('a) was publishing original Islamic sciences, teachings, ethics, and jurisprudence they had acquired from the Messenger of Allah (s). All the infallible Imams ('a) were fully prepared to fulfill this great responsibility. Unfortunately, however, they often faced limitations. The oppressor rulers of their times, in addition to illegal seizing of the caliphate, did not allow distribution of religious sciences and teachings, which the people really

---

[376] Biharul Anwar, Vol 47, p. 58.

[377] Ithbatul Hudat, Vol 5, p. 328.

[378] Biharul Anwar, Vol 47, p. 58.

needed. The followers of infallible Imams ('a) did not dare refer to them for gaining knowledge and they usually hid their real belief. Especially in the time of Umayyad caliphs, a milieu of dread and strangulation existed among the Islamic Ummah and propaganda against Ali Ibn Abi Talib ('a) and his progeny was very much. In the times of Imam Baqir ('a) and Imam Sadiq ('a), nevertheless, some changes took place in the society atmosphere. The strangulation atmosphere was removed to some extent. The people found out about the oppressions that took place against the Prophet's (s) Ahlul-Bayt and felt the need to original religious sciences that were deposited with infallible Imams ('a).

The Umayyid government was gradually weakening and it had to reduce the limitations created previously. So was early Abbaside government, because their government had not been strengthened and they had to give more freedom to the Household of Prophet Muhammad (s).

For the reasons mentioned as well as other reasons, Imam Baqir ('a) and Imam Sadiq ('a) benefitted from the transient situation for publicizing original sciences, teachings, and jurisprudence of prophet hood. Imam Sadiq ('a) trained many students, teaching thousands of traditions in various skills, instances of which are present in tradition books. Most of the traditions in such books are narrated from these two honorable Imams ('a).

We read in Manaqib, "The scientific issues quoted from Imam Sadiq ('a) are not quoted from anyone else. Some of the tradition narrators have recorded the names of narrators from Imam Sadiq ('a), which are nearly four thousand."[379]

The book Hilyatul 'Awliya' by Abu Na'im cites, "great religious scholars and leaders, such as Malik Ibn Anas, Shu'bat Ibn Al-Hajjaj, Sufyan Thuri, Ibn Jurayh, Abdullah Ibn Amr, Ruh Ibn Qasim, Sufyan

---

[379] Manaqib 'ali Abi Talib, Vol 4, p. 268.

'Ayinah, Sulayman Ibn Balal, 'Isma'il Ibn Ja'far, Hatam Ibn 'Isma'il, Abdul Aziz Ibn Mukhtar, Wahab Ibn Khalid, and Ibrahim Ibn Tahhan have narrated traditions from Ja'far Ibn Muhamamd."

Muslim has narrated traditions from Imam Sadiq ('a) in his book Sahih and deducted commandments based on them.[380]

Other authors have said that Malik, Shafi'i, Hassan, Salih, Abu Ayyub Sajistani, 'Amr Ibn Dinar, and Ahmad Ibn Hanbal have also narrated traditions from ja'far Ibn Muhammad.

Malik Ibn Anas has said, "No one is ever heard to be superior to Ja'far Sadiq ('a) in terms of knowledge, piety, and worshipping."[381]

Imam Sadiq ('a) stated, "I know everything that is in the heavens and the earth, in the Paradise and the Hell, and in the past and the future, using the Quran." Then he opened his hands toward the sky and said, "That is why the Almighty Allah has stated in Quran, '(The Book) explaining all things.'[382]"[383]

Salih Ibn 'Aswad has said, "I heard from Ja'far Ibn Muhammad, 'Ask me whatever you want before I pass away, because no one can narrate traditions for you like me after myself.'"[384]

'Isma'il Ibn Jabir has quoted from Imam Sadiq ('a), "The Exalted Allah sent Prophet Muhammad (s) as the prophet and will send no other prophet after him. He revealed a book to Muhammad (s) and will not reveal any other books after it. In that book, Allah set some deeds halal (lawful) and some haram (unlawful). The halal and haram deeds will remain so forever. The news of the people in the past, in the future, and in the present time exist in this heavenly Book." Then

---

[380] Surah Al-Nahl (16): 89.

[381] Ibid.

[382] Surah Al-Nahl (16): 89.

[383] Ibid, p. 270.

[384] Biharul Anwar, Vol 47, p. 33.

Imam Sadiq ('a) pointed to his own chest and said, "We do know all these facts." [385]

Imam Sadiq ('a) said, "Our sciences are four types; the past records, the written ones, what is inspired to our hearts, and what is whispered in our ears. The Books of Jafr Ahmar, Jafr Abyaz, Mus'haf Fatimah, and Jami'ah are with us. Whatever the people need is recorded in them." [386]

Ibn Abil Hadid writes, "The companions of Abu Hanifah, such as Abu Yusuf, Muhammad, etc. learned jurisprudence from Abu Hanifah. Shafi'i was the student of Muhammad Ibn Hassan, who had learned jurisprudence from Abu Hanifah. Ahmad Ibn Hanbal has learned his jurisprudence from Shafi'i, so his jurisprudence is from Abu Hanifah. Abu Hanifah has acquired his jurisprudence from Ja'far Ibn Muhammad ('a)."[387]

Mas'udi has written, "Abu Abdillah, Ja'far Ibn Muhammad ('a) had teaching sessions for the masses and the elites. People came to his sessions from around the Islamic land to ask him about halal, haram, Quranic exegesis and explanation, and judicial commandments. No one exited Ja'far Ibn Muhammad's ('a) sessions except that he was content with the reply he had received."[388]

Worship

Imam Sadiq ('a), like his father and grandfathers, was the best person of his own age in terms of humility before Allah, remembrance of Allah, supplications, and prayers.

It is narrated that Imam Sadiq ('a) was reciting Holy Quran while

---

[385] Ibid, p. 35.

[386] Biharul Anwar, Vol 47, p. 26.

[387] Explanation of Nahjul Balaghah, Vol 1, p. 18.

[388] 'Ithbatul Wasiyyah, p. 156.

performing prayer when he fainted. When he awakened, he was asked about the reason for that state. Imam Sadiq ('a) stated, "I repeated some Quranic verses so much that it was as if I heard them from Gabriel or the Almighty Allah."[389]

'Aban Ibn Taghlab has said, "I went to Imam Sadiq ('a) while he was performing prayers. I counted his zikrs in ruku' and sajdah; he glorified the Exalted Allah for sixty times."[390]

Hamzah Ibn Hamran and Hassan Ibn Ziyad said, "We went to Imam Sadiq ('a) and found him performing the Afternoon Prayer with a group of other people. He repeated the phrase subhana rabbiya al-azeemi wa-bihamdih 'Glory be to my Great Lord and I praise Him.' thirty three or thirty four times in ruku' and sajdah."[391]

Yahya Ibn 'Ala' has said, "Imam Sadiq ('a) was very sick and in bed on the twenty third night of Ramadan. He ordered to take him to the mosque of Messenger of Allah (s) and he worshipped until the dawn."[392]

Ibn Taghlab has said, "While traveling from Medina to Mecca I was with Imam Sadiq ('a). When he reached the haram, he landed, performed ghusl, held his shoes, and entered the haram barefooted."[393]

Hafz Ibn Bakhtari has quoted from Imam Sadiq ('a), "I was very serious in worship as a youth. My father, Imam Baqir ('a) said, 'O my son! Do not take yourself into trouble in worship, because when Allah likes His servant He accepts his little worship, too.'"[394]

Mu'awiyat Ibn Wahab has said, "Imam Sadiq ('a) and I were going

---

[389] Biharul Anwar, Vol 47, p. 58.

[390] Ithbatul Wasiyyah, p. 156.

[391] Ibid.

[392] Ibid, p. 53.

[393] Biharul Anwar, Vol 47, p. 54.

[394] Ibid, p. 55.

toward Medina bazaar on a donkey. When we reached near the bazaar, Imam ('a) landed from the donkey and performed a long sajdah. Then I asked him, 'Why did you landed and performed sajdah?' Imam Sadiq ('a) answered, 'I remembered one of the blessings of the Almighty Allah, so I performed sajdah to thank Him.' I asked again, 'Did you do it near the bazaar that the people are coming and going?' Imam ('a) replied, 'No one saw me.'"[395]

Malik Ibn 'Anas has said, "I had relations with Ja'far Ibn Muhammad ('a) for some time. I always saw him in one of three states; performing prayer, fasting, or reciting Holy Quran. When narrating traditions, he was always with wudu (ablution)."[396]

Malik Ibn 'Anas has also said, "In a hajj pilgrimage, I was with Imam Sadiq ('a). He stopped his horse in Miqat to become muhrim. However, he could not say labbayk and his voice stopped in his throat. He nearly fell off his horse. I told Imam Sadiq ('a), 'O son of Messenger of Allah (s)! Why don't you say labbayk?' Imam ('a) answered, 'How can I say labbayk, while the Almighty Allah may reply, 'No, nor are you blissful!'"[397]

Seeking Halal (Lawful) Sustenance

Although Imam Sadiq ('a) had many scientific engagements, spending most of his time in publishing religious sciences and teachings and training students, he attempted for making a living in his spare time.

'Abdul 'A'la has said, "On a hot day, I saw Imam Sadiq ('a) in a route leading to Medina. I told him, 'O son of Messenger of Allah (s)! May I sacrifice for you! You have taken yourself into trouble in such a hot day, while you have a high stance before Allah and a relation with

---

[395] Ibid, p. 21.

[396] Tahdhibut Tahdhib 2/104; Manaqib 'ali Abi Talib, Vol 4, p. 297.

[397] Manaqib 'ali Abi Talib, Vol 4, p. 297.

Prophet Muhammad (s)?' Imam ('a) said, 'I have come out of my house not to be dependent upon you and others.'"[398]

'Isma'il Ibn Jabir has said, "I saw Imam Sadiq ('a) in his farm, wearing a burlap cloth and watering the farm with a shovel."[399]

Abu 'Umar Shiybani has said, "I saw Imam Sadiq ('a) in his farm, wearing a harsh garment and working with a shovel while he was sweating. I told him, 'Let me help you! He answered, 'I like to work in hot weather for making halal sustenance.'[400]"

Shu'ayb has said, "I hired some workers to work in the farm of Imam Sadiq ('a). They had to continue working until the evening. When they finished, Imam Sadiq ('a) said, 'Pay their wage before their sweat is dried.'"[401]

Muhamamd Ibn 'Adhafar has narrated, "Imam Sadiq ('a) gave my father a thousand and seven hundred dinars to merchandise for him. Then Imam ('a) said, 'Profiting is good, but it is not my purpose. My purpose is that the Almighty Allah sees me while I am benefitting from his blessings.' My father said, 'I merchandised with that money and gained one hundred dinars profit. I told Imam ('a) about the profit. Imam ('a) said, 'Add it to the capital!' ' After some time, my father died. Imam Sadiq ('a) wrote to me, 'May Allah grant you good health! I have a trust of a thousand and eight hundred dinars with your father. Give the money to 'Umar Ibn Yazid!' I searched in my father's records and found that he had written down, 'Abu Musa has trusted a thousand and eight hundred dinars with me; Abdullah Ibn Sanan and 'Umar Ibn Yazid know this too.'"[402]

---

[398] [398] Biharul Anwar, Vol 47, p. 55.

[399] Ibid, p. 56.

[400] Ibid, p. 57.

[401] Ibid.

[402] Biharul Anwar, Vol 47, p. 56.

Almsgiving

Like his father and grandfathers, Imam Sadiq ('a) helped the poor and the debtor as much as he could, though he did not have much property.

Husham Ibn Salim has said in this regard, "Imam Sadiq ('a) used to hold a sack of bread, meat, and money in the middle of night and divide the content of the sack among the poor of Medina. The poor did not know him and realized his identity only after his demise."[403]

Mu'alli Ibn Khanis has said, "On a rainy night, I saw Imam Sadiq ('a), who was going toward Bani Sa'idah sunshade. I was following him from distance. Suddenly, his sack fell off his shoulder. Imam ('a) said, 'In the Name of Allah; O Allah! Return it to me!' I approached Imam Sadiq ('a) and greeted him. Imam ('a) greeted me and told me, 'O Mu'alli! Try to find what is fallen on the ground for me!' I searched the ground in darkness. I found some loaves of bread and a sack. Then I told Imam Sadiq ('a), 'Let me carry it for you!' Imam ('a) answered, 'I am more deserved to carry it, but you accompany me.' We went until we reached Bani Sa'idah sunshade. A group of the poor had slept there. Imam ('a) left one or two loaves of bread for each of them. When returning I asked Imam Sadiq ('a), 'O son of Messenger of Allah! Have they recognized the truth?' Imam Sadiq ('a) replied, 'If they had recognized the truth, I divided all my property equally among them, even the salt.'"[404]

Harun Ibn 'isa has said, "Imam Sadiq ('a) told his son, Muhammad, 'How much money is left with you?' Muhammad answered, 'Forty dinars.' Imam ('a) said, 'Divide it among the poor.' Muhammad told his father, 'Then we will have nothing for ourselves.' Imam Sadiq ('a) said, 'Give it as charity and the Almighty Allah will return it to us.

---

[403] Ibid, p. 38.

[404] Biharul Anwar, Vol 47, p. 20.

Don't you know that charity is the key to sustenance?' Muhammad obeyed his father's order and gave away the existing money. Soon four thousand dinars was sent fors Imam Sadiq ('a). Then Imam ('a) told his son, 'We gave away forty dinars in Allah's path; the Almighty Allah sent back four thousand dinars for us.'"[405]

Hiyaj Ibn Bastam has said, "Sometimes Imam Sadiq ('a) gave whatever he had to the poor as charity, then nothing was even left for his family."[406]

Mufazzal Ibn Qiys has said, "I went to Imam Sadiq ('a), told him about my problems, and asked him to pray for me. Imam Sadiq ('a) told his female slave, 'Bring the bag Abu Ja'far has sent for us!' She brought that bag. Imam ('a) told me, 'There is four hundred dinars in this bag; spent it for solving your problems!' I said, 'O son of Messenger of Allah! I did not mean to get money from you. I only wanted you to pray for me.' Imam Sadiq ('a) stated, 'Of course I will pray for you. And you should not tell all your problems to other people, because they will humble you.'"[407]

A poor man asked help from Imam Sadiq ('a). Imam ('a) told his slave, 'How much money is with you?' He answered, 'Four hundred dirhams.' Imam Sadiq ('a) told him, 'Give the money to this poor man!' The salve did so. The poor man took the money, thanked, and went. Imam Sadiq ('a) told his slave, 'Go and bring the poor man here!' The slave asked, 'You granted him what he wanted. Why should I bring him back?' Imam ('a) stated, 'The Messenger of Allah (s) said that the best charity is the one that makes the poor needless, but we did not do so.' Then Imam Sadiq ('a) gave his ring to the poor man and said, 'This ring costs ten thousand dirhams. Whenever you needed money,

---

[405] Biharul Anwar, Vol 47, p. 38.

[406] Ibid, p. 23; Tadhkiratul Khawas, p. 342.

[407] Biharul Anwar, Vol 47, p. 34.

sell it and spend it for your life.'⁴⁰⁸

'Umar Ibn Yazid has said, "A man expressed his problem and asked help from Imam Sadiq ('a). Imam ('a) told him, 'I have nothing to help you now. Wait until I receive some goods; I will sell them and give you the money, insha'allah!' That man told Imam Sadiq ('a), 'Promise me!' Imam ('a) said, 'How can I promise about something that is not certain?'"⁴⁰⁹

Walid Ibn Sabih has said, "A man went to Imam Sadiq ('a) and said, 'Mu'alli Ibn Khanis had borrowed a sum of money from me and violated (not paid) my right.' Imam Sadiq ('a) stated, 'His killer has violated your right. If Mu'alli were alive now, he would pay your money back.' Then Imam ('a) told me, 'Pay Mu'alli's debt! I want his soul to rest in peace, though he is in peace now.'"⁴¹⁰

Abu Hanifah, the hajjis' camel driver has said, "My brother-in-law and I were quarreling over legacy, when Mufazzal passed us. He stopped and said, 'Come to my house!' At his home, we compromised on four hundred dirhams and he paid it to us himself, saying, 'This is not my money, but that of Imam Sadiq ('a). He has ordered me to make peace among his companions with his money, whenever they have monetary disputes.'"⁴¹¹

Fazl Ibn Abi Qurrah has said, "Imam Sadiq ('a) gave some bags of money to a person and told him to take them to the houses of two of Imam's ('a) relatives, telling them that the money is sent from Iraq. That person did as Imam Sadiq ('a) had ordered him. Imam's ('a) relative took the money and said, 'May Allah reward you! May Allah punish Ja'far who is heedless to us!' Imam's ('a) envoy returned and related

---

⁴⁰⁸ Biharul Anwar, Vol 47, p. 61.

⁴⁰⁹ Ibid, p. 58.

⁴¹⁰ Ibid, p. 337.

⁴¹¹ Biharul Anwar, Vol 47, p. 57; Manaqib 'ali Abi Talib, Vol 4, p. 295.

the relatives' speech. Imam Sadiq ('a) performed sajdah and said, 'O Lord! Make me humble before the sons of my father!'"[412]

A narrator says, "I told Imam Sadiq ('a), 'O son of Messenger of Allah (s)! I have heard you want to do something special about the products of 'Iyn Ziyad garden?' Imam Sadiq ('a) replied, 'Yes. I have ordered to make a break in the garden wall after the fruits are ripe, so that everyone can enter and eat the fruits. Also we are going to prepare ten large bowls of fruit every day, each enough for ten people. Then we will invite the people to come in and eat ten at a time. Some dates will also be given to everyone. Moreover, we will send some dates for all garden neighbors who cannot come, including the elderly, children, women, or the sick. When I pay the wages of workers, farmers, lawyers, and others from the fruits, I will carry the rest of it to Medina. Some I will give to poor families two or three times as they need. Finally, four hundred dinars will remain for myself, while the whole garden costs four thousand dinars.'"[413]

Equanimity

Abu Ja'far Nazari has said, "Imam Sadiq ('a) gave a thousand dinars to his servant, Musadif, and told him, 'Go to Egypt and merchandise with this money, because my family has largened.' Musadif bought some goods with that money and traveled to Egypt along with the merchants. When they reached near a city in Egypt, a group of people welcomed them outside the city. The merchants asked about their goods and they were told that the goods were rare in the city. So the merchants promised each other to sell their goods twice the price they had bought. They did so and returned to Medina with the profit they had earned. Musadif came to Imam Sadiq ('a) with two bags of money,

---

[412] Biharul Anwar, Vol 47, p. 60.

[413] Ibid, p. 51.

each containing a thousand dinars. He told Imam ('a), 'One bag is the capital and the other is the profit.' Imam ('a) said, 'This is a good profit. How did you earn it?' Musadif related the story to Imam Sadiq ('a). Imam Sadiq ('a) stated, 'Glory be to Allah! How did you make such a promise?' Then he took one of the bags and said, 'This is my original money and I do not need a profit earned in this way. O Musadif! Fighting with a sword is easier than earning halal sustenance.'"[414]

Mu'tab has said, "Imam Sadiq ('a) told me, 'The goods have got expensive in Medina. How much food do we have?' I said, 'As much as the food for some months.' Imam ('a) told me, 'Take them to bazaar and sell them!' I said, 'But necessary goods are expensive in Medina.' Imam Sadiq ('a) told me, 'Sell them and buy our food day by day like other people.' Then he added, 'The food of my family should be of wheat and barley. Allah knows that I can afford making food with pure wheat, but I like the Almighty Allah to see that I am moderate in my family life.'"[415]

Recommendation to Making Happy

Imam Sadiq ('a) not only did good and solved the problems of people, but also recommended others to do so.

A man told Imam Sadiq ('a), "The government of Najashi that rules Ahwaz and Fars has obliged me to pay a tax, but I cannot afford it. Najashi is a sincere lover of you; recommend him about me." Imam Sadiq ('a) wrote in a letter, "In the Name of Allah, the Beneficent, the Merciful. Behave leniently towards your brother; may Allah be lenient with you too!" So the man took the letter and went to his own city. He visited Najashi, gave him the letter, and said, "Imam Sadiq ('a) has sent you this letter." Najashi took the letter, kissed it, and said, "What

---
[414] Biharul Anwar, Vol 47, p. 59.
[415] Ibid.

is your request?" The man answered, "I cannot pay the tax that is due on me." Najashi asked, "How much is that?" "Ten thousand dirhams," the man replied. Najashi called his ascribe and told him, "Pay the debt of this man from my own property!" He ordered not to take the tax of next year from the man. Then Najashi told the man, "Did I make you happy?" "Yes," the man answered. So Najashi ordered to give him a horse, a slave, a female slave, and some clothes, asking him the same question every time. The man repeated the same answer every time. Then Najashi said, "Give this carpet on which I received the letter of my master, Imam Sadiq ('a), to this man too." And he told the man, "Come to me whenever you have a request!"

The man took the property and went. He went to Imam Sadiq ('a) after a while and told him about what Najashi had done. Imam Sadiq ('a) became very happy. That man asked Imam ('a), "O son of Messenger of Allah (s)! Did you become happy of his conduct?" Imam ('a) replied, "By Allah yes! Allah and His Messenger (s) became happy too."[416]

Muhammad Ibn Bashar owed a thousand dinars to Shahab, but he could not pay it to Shahab. Muhammad went to see Imam Sadiq ('a), asking him to talk to Shahab to take his money back after hajj time. Imam Sadiq ('a) called Shahab and told him, "You know Muhammad and his relation with us. He owes a thousand dinars to you. He has not spent it for food or lusts, rather other people owe him money. I like you to grant him this money and become happy of him. Maybe you think that the Almighty Allah grants Muhammad's good deeds to you in return for the money you grant him." Shahab said, "I think so." Imam Sadiq ('a) stated, "The Exalted Allah is just; He does not take the reward of His servant's worship on cold nights, fasting on hot days, and tawaf of His house to give it to another one. It is not true. Allah's Mercy is great and He blesses His servant." Shahab said, "O son of

---

[416] Biharul Anwar, Vol 47, p. 370.

Messenger of Allah! I forgave him!"[417]

Patience in Calamity

Qutaybah has said, "I went to Imam Sadiq's ('a) house to visit his sick child. I found him very sad and asked about his sick child. Imam ('a) said, '(S)he is in the same state.' After a while, Imam ('a) entered the house. He soon returned, with red face and happiness. I thought his child was better and asked about him. Imam ('a) said, '(S)he passed away.' I told Imam Sadiq ('a), 'When your child was sick, you were sad. How is it you are not sad anymore now that (s)he has passed away?' Imam ('a) answered, 'We, the Ahlul-Bayt, are this way; we are sad before happening a calamity, but become happy with Allah's will after it.'"[418]

Sufyan Thuri went to see Imam Sadiq ('a) and found him embarrassed. He asked Imam Sadiq ('a) the reason and Imam ('a) replied, "I had prohibited my family from going atop the roof. When I entered the house, I saw a female slave, ascending the ladder with one of my children on his shoulder. When she saw me, she trembled with fear. The child fell on the ground and died. Now I am not sad of my child's death, but I am upset that it happened because of the slave's fear of me." Then Imam Sadiq ('a) told the female slave, "I make you free in Allah's path. You have no sin." And he repeated his speech again.[419]

'Ala' Ibn Kamil said, "I was with Imam Sadiq ('a). Suddenly crying was heard from inside the home. Imam Sadiq ('a) said, inna lillahi wa-inna ilayhi raju'oon "Surely we belong to Allah and we will return to Him." Then he sat and continued his speech. When he finished, he said, "We are interested in the health of ourselves and our family

---

[417] Biharul Anwar, Vol 47, p. 364.

[418] Biharul Anwar, Vol 47, p. 49.

[419] Ibid, p. 24; Manaqib 'ali Abi Talib, Vol 4, p. 296.

members and our property, but when Allah's destine comes we'd better like what Allah likes."[420]

The Seventh Imam; Musa Kazim

Birth and Martyrdom

Imam Musa Ibn Ja'far ('a) was born on the seventh of Safar in the year 128 A.H. in a village called Abwa' between Mecca and Medina. His father was Imam Ja'far Sadiq ('a) and his mother was Hamidah. His nicknames were Abul Hassan, Abu 'Ibrahim, Abu Ali, and Abu 'Isma'i and his titles were 'Abd Salih, Nafs Zakiyyah, Ziynul Mujahidin, Sabir, Amin, Zahid, and Salih. His most famous title is Kazim.

Imam Musa Kazim ('a) was martyred in the prison of Sandi Ibn Shahak in Baghdad on twenty fifth of Rajab in the year 183 A.H. He was buried in Quraysh tomb (Kazimiyn city). He was fifty five then. Imam Kazim ('a) lived twenty years with his father and his Imamate lasted thirty five years.[421]

Imam Kazim ('a) did not make much trouble for the incumbent caliphs, due to unprepared conditions. He spent his time in worshipping, working for making a living, publishing religious sciences and teachings, guiding the people, and training students and hadith narrators. He was, in fact, considered a famous scholar and jurisprudent. Nevertheless, the caliphs in office feared his scientific stance and social popularity. They always watched Imam Kazim ('a), his companions, and his students, hindering their activities in various

---

[420] Biharul Anwar, Vol 47, p. 49.

[421] Al-'Irshad, Vol 2, p. 215; Biharul Anwar, Vol 48, pp. 1, 6 & 7; Matalibul Mas'ul, Vol 2, p. 120; Al-Fusulul Muhimmah, p. 214; Manaqib 'ali Abi Talib, Vol 4, p. 348; Kashful Ghummah, Vol 3, pp 1-9.

ways. Imam Kazim ('a) was called from Medina to Baghdad several times and was inquired. Once they were going to kill Imam ('a), but they were dissuaded because of some considerations and Imam Kazim ('a) returned to medina.

Finally, because of enmity of some of his relatives, Harunur Rashid, the Abbaside caliph, called Imam Kazim ('a) from Medina to Baghdad. Imam Kazim ('a) was in prisons of Basrah and Baghdad for long. His last prison was Sandi Shahak prison –a very hideous prison– in Baghdad.

At last, Sandi Ibn Shahak poisoned Imam Kazim ('a) by the order of Harunur Rashid. Imam Kazim ('a) was martyred some days later and his holy body was buried in Quraysh tomb, near Baghdad.[422]

Texts Proving His Imamate

As mentioned before, the reasons for Imamate are of two kinds; the general reasons used for proving the Imamate of any of twelve infallible Imams, and the specific reasons or explicit traditions from each of the Imams about the next Imam. The first type of reasons has been discussed in detail before. Here only the traditions from Imam Sadiq ('a) about Imamate of his son, Imam Kazim ('a), are cited.

Shiykh Mufid has written, "Mufazzal Ibn 'Umar Ju'fi, Ma'adh Ibn Kathir, Abdur Rahman Ibn Hajjaj, Fiyz Ibn Mukhtar, Ya'qub Siraj, Suliyman Ibn Khalid, Safwan Ibn Jamal, and many more are close trustworthy companions of Imam Sadiq ('a) who have narrated traditions about Imamate of Abul Hassan Musa ('a)."

'Is'haq and Ali, Imam Sadiq's ('a) pious scholar sons, are among narrators of traditions about Imamate of their brother, Musa Ibn Ja'far ('a).

Mufazzal Ibn 'Umar has said, "I was with Imam Sadiq ('a) when Abu

---

[422] Al-'Irshad, Vol 2, pp. 237-243.

'Ibrahim Musa ('a), who was a child, came in. Imam Sadiq ('a) told me, 'I recommend you about my son's Imamate. Recommend his Imamate to any of reliable companions.'"[423]

Ma'adh Ibn Kathir has said, "I told Imam Sadiq ('a), 'I ask the Almighty Allah to grant you an honorable child to remain after your death, just as He granted you, with this high stance, to your father.' Imam Sadiq ('a) stated, 'The Exalted Allah has granted me such a child.' I asked, 'Who is he?' Imam ('a) pointed to 'Abd Salih, who was sleeping, and said, 'The one who is asleep.'"[424]

Abdur Rahman Ibn Hajjaj has said, "I entered a house in which Ja'far Ibn Muhammad ('a) was praying and Musa Ibn Ja'far ('a) was sitting on his right, saying Amen. I asked, 'You know that I am a sincere lover of you. Tell me who will be the Imam after you?' Imam Sadiq ('a) answered, 'O Abdur Rahman! My son, Musa, wore the armor of Messenger of Allah (s) and it fitted him.' So I said, 'I found out the truth now and need no other reason.'"[425]

Fiyz Ibn Mukhtar has said, "I told Imam Sadiq ('a), 'Take my hand and save me from the Hell! Who will be my master after you?' At that time, Abu 'Ibrahim, who was a child, came in. Imam Sadiq ('a) replied, 'He will be your master; follow him!'"[426]

Mansur Ibn Hazim has said, "I told Imam Sadiq ('a), 'May my parents be sacrificed for you! The death is a truth and everyone will die. If it happens to you, who will be the Imam after you?' Imam Sadiq ('a) put his hand on Abul Hassan's shoulder and said, 'He will be your master.' Then Abul Hassan was only five and Abdullah Ibn Ja'far was

---

[423] Al-'Irshad, Vol 2, p. 216; Kashful Ghummah, Vol 3, p. 9.

[424] Al-'Irshad, Vol 2, p. 217; Kashful Ghummah, Vol 3, p. 9.

[425] Al-'Irshad, Vol 2, p. 216; Kashful Ghummah, Vol 3, p. 9.

[426] Al-'Irshad, Vol 2, p. 217; Al-Fusulul Muhimmah, p. 213; Kashful Ghummah, Vol 3, p. 10.

also there."[427]

'Isa Ibn Abdullah has said, "I told Imam Sadiq ('a), 'If, Allah forbids, something bad happens to you, who should we follow?' Imam Sadiq ('a) pointed to his son, Musa, and said, 'Follow him!' I asked again, 'If something bad happens to Musa, who should we follow?' Imam Sadiq ('a) replied, 'Follow his son!' I asked, 'If something happens to him, while he has an elder brother and a little child, who should we follow?' Imam Sadiq ('a) answered, 'Follow his son, and this will continue forever.'"[428]

Tahir Ibn Muhammad has said, "I saw Imam Sadiq ('a), who was preaching his son, Abdullah, saying, 'Why are you not like your brother? By Allah that I see a light in his face.' Abdullah told his father, 'Don't we have the same father?' Imam Sadiq ('a) stated, 'He is from my essence and you are my son.'"[429]

Ya'qub Sarraj has said, "I went to see Imam Sadiq ('a), who was standing beside the cradle of Abul Hassan, talking to him quietly for a long time. I waited until his talking finished. Then I approached Imam ('a). He told me, 'Go to your master and greet him.' I approached the child and said hello. He said hello eloquently and said, 'Change your newborn daughter's name; Allah dislikes such a name.' My daughter was born some time ago and I had named her Humiyra'. Imam Sadiq ('a) told me, 'Obey my son's order!' So I changed my daughter's name."[430]

Safwan Jammal has said, "I asked Imam Sadiq ('a), 'Who is the Muslim's guardian?' Imam Sadiq ('a) answered, 'He is someone who

---

[427] Al-'Irshad, Vol 2, p. 218; Al-Fusulul Muhimmah, p. 214; Kashful Ghummah, Vol 3, p. 10.

[428] Al-'Irshad, Vol 2, p. 218; Al-Fusulul Muhimmah, p. 214; Kashful Ghummah, Vol 3, p. 10.

[429] Al-'Irshad, Vol 2, p. 218; Kashful Ghummah, Vol 3, p. 10.

[430] Al-'Irshad, Vol 2, p. 219; 'Ithbatul Wasiyyah, p. 162; Kashful Ghummah, Vol 3, p. 11.

avoids useless works.' Then Abul Hassan came in with a little lamb in his arms, saying to it, 'Perform sajdah for Allah!' Imam Sadiq ('a) hugged him and said, 'May my parents be sacrificed for you that do not do useless works.'"[431]

'Is'haq Ibn Ja'far has said, "One day, I was with my father (Imam Sadiq ('a)). Ali Ibn 'Umar Ibn Ali told him, 'Who will the people and I restore to after you?' Imam Sadiq ('a) said, 'The one wearing two pieces of yellow cloth and has two crimps of hair that is coming now.' Soon the door opened and Abu Ibrahim Musa entered, who was a child then wearing two pieces of yellow cloth."[432]

Muhammad Ibn Walid has said, "I heard from Ali Ibn Ja'far Ibn Muhammad Sadiq ('a), 'I heard from my father, Ja'far Ibn Muhammad ('a), addressing some of his close companions, 'I recommend you follow my son, Musa, because he is my best son. He will be the caliph and guardian of the people after me.' '"[433]

In conclusion, Shiykh Mufid has written, "Ali Ibn Ja'far loved his brother, Musa, very much, followed him, and learned religious commandments from him. Ali asked Musa many questions and narrated his answers to others."[434]

Nasr Ibn Qabus has said, "I went to see Imam Sadiq ('a) and asked him, 'Who will be the Imam after you?' Imam ('a) answered, 'My son, Abul Hassan Musa Ibn Ja'far will be the Imam after me.'"[435]

Suliyman Ibn Khalid said, "One day, we were with Imam Sadiq ('a). He called his son, Abul Hassan, and told us, 'Refer to him after me! By

---

[431] Al-'Irshad, Vol 2, p. 218; Kashful Ghummah, Vol 3, p. 10.

[432] Ibid.

[433] Al-'Irshad, Vol 2, p. 220.

[434] Ibid.

[435] 'Ithbatul Wasiyyah, p. 162.

Allah that he will be your guardian.'"[436]

Dawud Ibn Kathir has said, "I told Imam Sadiq ('a), 'May I sacrifice for you! If something happens to you, who should I refer to?' Imam ('a) answered, 'refer to my son, Musa.' After Imam Sadiq's ('a) demise, I never doubted about the Imamate of Musa."[437]

Muhammad Ibn Sanan and Abu Ali Zarrad have narrated from 'Ibrahim Karkhi, "I was with Imam Sadiq ('a) when Abul Hassan, Musa Ibn Ja'far, who was a child, came in. I stood up, kissed his face, and then sat down. Then Imam Sadiq ('a) said, 'He will be your guardian after me.'"[438]

The above-mentioned were few examples of many traditions about Imamate of Imam Musa Ibn Ja'far ('a). Moreover, many miracles have been cited from him, which cannot be pointed out in this brief work.

Virtues

Imam Kazim ('a), like his fathers, was a perfect human in terms of all good characteristics and the best person of his own age. Many of the scholars have admired his great character.

Ibn Sabbagh Maliki has written, "Musa Kazim was a great honorable Imam. He was a unique scholar. He spent his nights in prayers and worship and his days in fasting. He forgave the sinners a lot, thus he was called Kazim. The people of Iraq know him as Babul Hawa'ij (the answer to all requests)."[439]

'Ahmad Ibn Hajar Hiythami has written, "Musa Kazim was the holder of his father's legacy in regard to knowledge, understanding, and virtues. He was so tolerant that he was called Kazim. He is

---

[436] Ibid.

[437] Biharul Anwar, Vol 48, p. 14.

[438] Ibid, p. 15.

[439] Al-Fusulul Muhimmah, p. 213.

entitled Babul Hawa'ij by Iraqi people. He was the most pious, the most generous person of his own age."[440]

Ibn Sabbagh Maliki has written, "Musa Kazim was the most pious, most knowledgeable, most generous, and most forgiver person of his own age. He identified the poor of Medina and regularly sent money for them, while they did not know the sender. After his demise, the poor understood that the help has been from him."[441]

Ibn Hajar 'Asqalani has written about Imam Kazim ('a), "His virtues are numerous."[442]

Khatib Baghdadi has narrated from Abdur Rahman Ibn Salih 'Azadi, "When Harunur Rashid had gone to hajj, he went to the shrine of Messenger of Allah (s), along with a group of nobles from Quraysh and other Arab tribes. Musa Ibn Ja'far ('a) accompanied them too. When Harun reached the holy shrine, he said, 'Greetings to you, o Messenger of Allah! O my cousin!' He wanted to boast about his relationship with the Prophet (s). Then Musa Ibn Ja'far approached the grave and said, 'Greetings to you, o my father!' Hearing this, Harun's face changed color and said, 'O Abul Hassan! The real honor is about what you said.'"[443]

Ibn Shahr ashub has written, "Musa Ibn Ja'far was superior to the people of his own age in terms of jurisprudence and memorization of Quran. He recited the Holy Quran with a good voice. He wept while reciting it and the listeners wept too. His stance was above other people. His generosity was more than others. His speech was more eloquent than that of others. His heart was braver than others' hearts. He was honored by having the guardianship of the people. He

---

[440] Al-Sawa'iqul Muharriqah, p. 203.

[441] Al-Fusulul Muhimmah, p. 219.

[442] Al-Sawa'iqul Muharriqah, p. 203.

[443] Tarikh Baghdad, Vol 13, p. 31.

received the legacy of prophet hood. He was appointed to caliphate position."⁴⁴⁴

Shiykh Mufid has written, "Imam Abul Hassan Musa ('a) was the most pious, the best jurisprudent, the most generous, and the most forgiver of the people in his own age."⁴⁴⁵

Ali Ibn Abil Fat'h 'Arbali has narrated from Kamalid Din, "Musa Ibn Ja'far ('a) was a great honorable Imam. He attempted in worshipping Allah much. His virtues were obvious and his worship was famous. He was careful in performing the obligatory deeds. He spent his nights in sajdah and qiyam. He was fasting and giving charity on days. He was so tolerant that he was entitled Kazim. He did good to the people who did bad to him. He was entitled Abd Salih because of his much worship. He is called Babul Hawa'ij in Iraq. His miracles are numerous, which show his stance before the Almighty Allah."⁴⁴⁶

Ma'mun has said, "I told my father Rashid, 'O Amiral Mu'minin! Who was the man you honored so much, stood up when he came in, sat him in your own place, and ordered us to hold his horse stirrup when leaving?' My father answered, 'He was people's Imam, Allah's hujjat for his servants, and Allah's caliph.' I asked, 'O Amiral Muminin! Don't you have these qualities?' He answered, 'I am the superficial caliph, who has taken the place by force. But he is the real Imam. By Allah that he is more deserved than anyone elses in occupying the Prophet's (s) position. By Allah that if you quarrel with me about caliphate, I will behead you too. Surely sovereignty is helpless.'"⁴⁴⁷

Knowledge

---

⁴⁴⁴ Manaqib 'ali Abi Talib, Vol 4, p. 348.

⁴⁴⁵ Al-'Irshad, Vol 2, p. 231.

⁴⁴⁶ Manaqib 'ali Abi Talib, Vol 4, p. 348.

⁴⁴⁷ Biharul Anwar, Vol 48, p. 131.

It was proved in previous sections that a thorough knowledge of all religious issues is a necessary condition for Imamate. All the infallible Imams ('a) possessed this quality. So was Imam Kazim ('a). His knowledge and jurisprudence was famous in his own age. Everyone recognized his scientific position as the jurisprudent of the people.

Ibn Sabbagh Maliki has written, "Musa Kazim was the most pious, most knowledgeable, most generous, and most forgiving person of his own age."[448]

Ma'mun has said, "I asked my father, Rashid, 'Who was the man you honored so much?' He answered, 'He was Musa Ibn Ja'far; the heir of sciences of the prophets (s). If you seek true knowledge, it is with him.'"[449]

For more information on scientific stance of Imam Kazim ('a), you can refer to traditions narrated from him in tradition books, as well as his debates with incumbent caliphs, the Sunni scholars, and others.

A researcher called Mr. Atarudi has collected Imam Kazim's ('a) traditions about belief, teachings, kalam, jurisprudence, exegesis, ethics, supplications, history, debates, and even hygiene, benefits of fruits and vegetables in a book and published it. The narrators of Imam Kazim's ('a) traditions, which exceed six hundred and thirty eight persons, are reviewed in this book.[450]

Worship

Like his father and grandfathers, Imam Kazim ('a), was the most pious person of his own age. He frequently remembered and worshipped Allah, prayed, recited Quran and was humble before the Lord of the worlds. Because of his deep understanding of monotheism

---

[448] Al-Fusulul Muhimmah, p. 219.

[449] Manaqib 'ali Abi Talib, Vol 4, p. 335.

[450] Musnad Al-Imam Al-Kazim (a.s) in three volumes.

and Allah's Power and Greatness, he did everything even making a living for Allah's sake. Some instances of his worship are cited here, as narrated in history and tradition books.

Hassan Ibn Muhammad Ibn Yahya 'Alawi has narrated from his grandfather, "Musa Ibn Ja'far attempted so much in worship that he was entitled Abd Salih (the righteous servant)."

Some of Imam Kazim's ('a) companions have narrated that one night Imam ('a) entered the mosque of Messenger of Allah (s). He had a long sajdah early at night, saying, "Great sins are with me, good forgiving is with You! O Lord of pardon and Piety!" And Imam ('a) repeated the same supplication in his sajdah until the dawn.[451]

Yahya Ibn Hassan has said, "Musa Ibn Ja'far was called Abd Salih because of his resolution in worship."[452]

Ibn Sabbagh has written, "Musa Ibn Ja'far was the most pious, the most learned, the most generous, and the most tolerant person of his own age."[453]

Ibn Hajar has written, "Musa Kazim was the most pious, the most learned, and the most generous person of his age."[5]

Ibn Juwzi Hanafi has written, "Musa Kazim was called Abd Salih because of determination in worship and the Night Prayer."[454]

Shiykh Mufid has written, "Abul Hassan Musa ('a) was the most learned jurisprudent, the most pious, the most generous, and the most tolerant one in his own age. It is narrated that he linked the Night Prayer to the Morning Prayer, and then he performed supplications until the sunrise. He then performed sajdah and recited zikr until

---

[451] Tarikh Baghdad, Vol 13, p. 27.

[452] Tahdhibut Tahdhib, Vol 10, p. 340.

[453] Al-Fusulul Muhimmah, p. 219.

    5 Al-Sawa'iqul Muharriqah, p. 203.

[454] Tadhkiratul Khawas, p. 348.

noon. He repeated this prayer a lot, 'O Allah! I ask You comfort at the time of death and forgiveness at the time of Reckoning.' Another prayer of Imam Musa Kazim ('a) is, 'My sins are great, so how good is Your forgiveness!' He wept so much from Allah's fear that his holy beard got wet."[455]

The sister of Sandi Ibn Shahak who was a guard in Imam Kazim's ('a) prison, says about him, "In prison, Musa Ibn Ja'far had this daily routine; he began praying and supplication after performing the Evening Prayer until the midnight, when he performed the night prayer and lasted it until the morning adhan. Afterwards, he performed the Morning Prayer and was engaged in prayer and supplication until the sunrise. Then he rested until the sun rose in the sky. Afterwards, he brushed his teeth, ate a meal, and slept a little until before the noon. At noon, he got up, performed wudu, and performed the Noon Prayer. Then he performed nafilah prayer until the time for Afternoon Prayer. After performing the Afternoon Prayer, he sat in the direction of qiblah and remembered Allah until the sunset. After the Evening Prayer, he performed nafilah prayers until the Night Prayer. He did the same every day." Seeing Imam Musa Kazim ('a) in this state, she said, "The people who misbehave such a pious servant of Allah will be losers."[456]

Ahmad Ibn Abdullah has narrated from his father, "One day, I went to see Fazl Ibn Rabi' who was on the roof of his house. He told me, 'Look at that house through that window! What do you see?' I said, 'I see a garment on the ground.' He said, 'Look more carefully!' I said again, 'It is as if a man is performing sajdah.' He asked me, 'Do you know him? He is Musa Ibn Ja'far. I watch him day and night and find him only in this state. After performing the Morning Prayer, he

---

[455] Al-'Irshad, Vol 2, p. 231.

[456] Tarikh Baghdad, Vol 13, p. 31.

recites supplications until the sunrise. Then he performs sajdah until before the noon. He has hired someone to inform him of prayer times. When he is informed of the prayer time, he finishes the sajdah and begins praying without performing ablution again. After performing the Night Prayer, he breaks his fast, performs ablution, and performs a sajdah again. He performs prayers from the midnight until the dawn. '" Some observers have heard him say in his supplications, 'O Allah! I ask You to give me spare time for Your worship, and if You do it, I will praise you.'[457]

Ibrahim Ibn Abil Bilad said, "Imam Abul Hassan said, 'I say astaghfirullah (I seek Allah's forgiveness) five thousand times a day.'"[458]

Almsgiving

Shiykh Mufid has written, "Musa Ibn Ja'far ('a) observed the ties of kinship. He watched the poor in Medina, sending money, wheat, and dates for them, while they did not know the sender."[459]

Muhammad Ibn Abdullah Bikri has said, "I went to Medina to borrow money, but I found no one who could lend me. I thought to myself that I'd better go to Imam Kazim ('a). I went to see him in his farm outside Medina. He sat beside me, along with his servant, who had a colorful bowl of cooked meat. Imam ('a) and I ate the meat. Then he asked about my request. When I talked about my need, he went and brought a bag. First, he told his servant to leave and then gave me the bag of three hundred dinars. Then he left me, too. I got the money, rode my horse, and returned home."[460]

'Isa Ibn Muhammad, a ninety-year-old man said, "I had built a farm

---

[457] Manaqib 'ali Abi Talib, Vol 4, p. 343.

[458] Biharul Anwar, Vol 48, p. 119.

[459] Al-'Irshad, Vol 2, p. 231; Al-Fusulul Muhimmah, p. 219.

[460] Al-'Irshad, Vol 2, p. 232; Tarikh Baghdad, Vol 13, p. 28.

beside Ummi 'Izam shaft and grew watermelon, cucumbers, and gourd. When the harvest was near, suddenly grasshoppers attacked the farm and destroyed it. I had spent a hundred and twenty dinars plus the work of two camels for my farm. I had sat down, thinking of the loss when Musa Ibn Ja'far ('a) came to me and greeted me. I told him the story. He said, 'How much have you spent?' I said, 'A hundred and twenty dinars, plus the work of two camels.' Imam ('a) told his agent, 'Give a hundred and fifty dinars to Abil Ghiyth!' Then he added, 'Thirty dinars is your profit.' I told Imam ('a), 'O son of Messenger of Allah! Pray for me so that Allah will increase my profit.' So Imam ('a) prayed for me."[461]

Some of the scholars have said, "The grant of Musa Ibn Ja'far was always two hundred to three hundred dinars, in a way that his gift bags of money were famous."[462]

Mansur asked Imam Musa Kazim ('a) to stay at home so that Mansur could visit him on Nuruz. Imam ('a) answered, "I searched in documents of my grandfather, the messenger of Allah (s), but found nothing about Nuruz. It is a Persian tradition, ignored in Islam. I do not want to revitalize it." Mansur told Imam ('a), "Holding Nuruz ceremony is good as a policy of the army. I ask you by Allah to accept it." Imam ('a) accepted and stayed at home. The army commanders and leaders visited Imam Kazim ('a), congratulated him, and presented gifts. Mansur's servant supervised the gifts. After the session, an old man came to Imam ('a) and said, "O son of Fatimah, daughter of Messenger of Allah (s)! I am a poor man. I had nothing to bring as gift for you. But my grandfather composed three lines of poem in calamity of your grandfather, Imam Hussayn ('a). I present it to you." Then the old man recited the poem. Imam Musa Ib Ja'far ('a) told him,

---

[461] Tarikh Baghdad, Vol 13, p. 29; Kashful Ghummah, Vol 3, p. 7.

[462] Kashful Ghummah, Vol 3, p. 19.

"I accept your gift." Then Imam ('a) told Mansur's servant, "Go to your master, report the list of gifts to him, and ask what we should do with them." The servant went to Mansur, then returned and told Imam ('a), "My master said that he grants all the gifts to you and you can spend them as you wish." Musa ibn Ja'far ('a) told that old man, "I grant all this property to you."[463]

It is narrated that one of progeny of 'Umar Ibn Khattab lived in Medina. He always teased Imam Kazim ('a) and cursed Ali Ibn Abi Talib ('a). Some of Imam's ('a) companions told him, "Let us kill this man!" Imam Kazim ('a) severely prohibited them. One day, Imam ('a) asked about that man and he was told, "He is working in his farm."

Imam Musa Kazim ('a) rode his donkey and went toward the man's farm. The man wondered of Imam's ('a) coming. Imam Kazim ('a) sat, smiled, and asked, "How much have you spent for your farm?"

- One hundred dinars.
- How much profit do you expect?
- I cannot foretell.
- How much you hope to benefit?
- I hope to have two hundred dinars.

Imam Kazim ('a) granted him three hundred dinars and said, "The farm is for you too." The man raised and kissed the forehead of Imam Kazim ('a).

Musa Ibn Ja'far ('a) returned to Medina. Another day, Imam ('a) went to the mosque and saw that man there. He told Musa Ibn Ja'far ('a), "God knoweth best where (and how) to carry out His mission." [464] The man's friends opposed his new behavior toward Imam Kazim ('a). He argued with them and lauded Musa Ibn Ja'far ('a). From then on, he always praised Imam Kazim ('a).

---

[463] Manaqib 'ali Abi Talib, Vol 4, p. 344.

[464] Surah Al-'An'am (6): 124.

Imam Musa Kazim ('a) told his companions who had proposed to kill that man, "Was your suggestion better or my conduct for reforming this man?"[465]

Mu'tab has said, "When the fruits became ripe, Imam Musa Ibn Ja'far ('a) told us, 'Sell the fruits in the bazaar and buy our needs every day, just like other Muslims.'"[466]

The Eighth Imam; 'Ali ibn Musa Riza

Birth and Martyrdom

Ali Ibn Musa ('a) was born on eleventh of Zil Qa'dah in the year 148 A.H., according to some narrations. His father was Musa Ibn Ja'far ('a) and his mother was 'Ummul Banin or Najmah. His name was Ali, his nickname was Abul Hassan, and his titles were Riza, Sabir, Razi, Wafi, Zaki, and Wali. His most famous title was Riza. He was martyred on the last day of Safar in the year 203 A.H. in Sanabad village of Tus and was buried there.

He lived 55 years, 35 years of which was simultaneous with his father. Imam Riza's ('a) Imamate lasted about twenty years.[467]

Texts Proving His Imamate

As mentioned earlier in this book, the reasons for Imamate are of two kinds; the general reasons used for proving the Imamate of any of twelve infallible Imams, and the specific reasons or explicit traditions from each of the Imams about the next imam. In this part,

---

[465] Tarikh Baghdad, Vol 13, p. 28; Al-'Irshad, Vol 2, p. 233.

[466] Biharul Anwar, Vol 48, p. 117.

[467] Al-'Irshad, Vol 2, p. 247; Biharul Anwar, Vol 49, pp. 2, 3 & 29; Al-Fusulul Muhimmah, p. 226; Kafi, Vol 1, p. 486; Tarikh Ya'qubi, Vol 2, p. 453.

the traditions about Imamate of Imam Riza ('a) are cited.

Shiykh Mufid has written, "Some trustworthy, pious, and scholar narrators have narrated traditions about Imamate of Imam Riza ('a) from his father Imam Musa Kazim ('a), including Dawud Ibn Kathir Ruqqi, Muhammad Ibn Is'haq Ibn Ammar, Ali Ibn Yaqtin, Na'im Qabusi, Hussayn Ibn Mukhtar, Ziyad Ibn Marwan, Makhzumi, Dawud Ibn Suliyman, Nasr Ibn Qabus, Dawud Ibn Zarbi, Yazid Ibn Salit, and Muhammad Ibn Sanan."[468]

Dawud Ruqqi said, "I told Imam Kazim ('a), 'May I sacrifice for you! Take my hand and save me from the Hell. Who will be our guardian after you?' Imam ('a) pointed to his son, Abul Hassan, and said, 'He will be your guardian after me.'"[469]

Muhammad Ibn Is'haq Ibn 'Ammar has said, "I told Imam Kazim ('a), 'Do you introduce someone to me to learn my religious issues from him?' Imam ('a) answered, 'My son, Ali. Surely my father took me to the shrine of Messenger of Allah (s) and said, 'O my son! The Almighty Allah stated, 'I will create a vicegerent on earth.'[470] If Allah promises, He will surely fulfill his promise.'"[471]

Hussayn Ibn Na'im Sahhaf has said, "Husham Ibn Hakam, Ali Ibn Yaqtin, and I were in Baghdad. Ali Ibn Yaqtin said, 'I was with Abd Salih, Imam Kazim ('a) and he told me, 'O Ali Ibn Yaqtin! He is Ali, my best son. I granted him my nickname (or my books).' ' Hearing this, Husham said, 'O Ali Ibn Yaqtin! How do you say this?' Ali Ibn Yaqtin answered, 'I say it as I heard it.' So Husham said, 'Surely Imamate will be for him after his father, Musa Ibn Ja'far ('a).'"[472]

---

[468] Al-'Irshad, Vol 2, p. 247.

[469] Al-'Irshad, p. 248; Al-Fusulul Muhimmah, p. 225.

[470] Surah Al-Baqarah (2): 30.

[471] Al-'Irshad, Vol 2, p. 248.

[472] Ibid, p. 249.

Na'im Qabusi has said, "Abul Hassan Musa ('a) said, 'My son, Ali, is the greatest, most honorable, and most beloved of my sons. He and I read the jafr, while no one can read it except the Prophet (s) or his successors.'"[473]

Hussayn Ibn Mukhtar has said, "When Imam Musa Kazim ('a) was in prison, he sent us letters, saying that my eldest son should do this thing and that thing and that person cannot harm him, until I meet you or I pass away."[474]

Ziyad Ibn Marwan Qandi has said, "I went to see Abu Ibrahim Musa ('a), when his son Abul Hassan was also there. Imam Musa Kazim said, 'O Ziyad! He is my son; his writing is my writing, his speech is my speech, and his messenger is my messenger. Whatever he says is what I say.'"[475]

Makhzumi –whose mother is a progeny of Ja'far Ibn Abi Talib– has said, "Once Abul Hassan Musa ('a) gathered us and said, 'Do you know why I have gathered you here?' We answered, 'No.' Imam ('a) said, 'Witness that my son is my successor, vicegerent, and caliph. Everyone who has a request from me, ask it from him. He will fulfill my promises. Anyone who should visit me should have his written recommendation.'"[476]

Dawud Ibn Suliyman has said, "I told Imam Abu Ibrahim ('a), 'I fear that an accident happens and I cannot visit you. Tell me who will be the Imam after you?' Imam ('a) answered, 'My son Abul Hassan ('a).'"[477]

Nasr Ibn Qabus has said, "I told Abu Ibrahim ('a), 'I asked your father about the Imam after him and he introduced you as the next Imam.

---

[473] Ibid.

[474] Ibid, p. 249.

[475] Al-'Irshad, p. 250; Al-Fusulul Muhimmah, p. 226.

[476] Ibid.

[477] Al-'Irshad, Vol 2, p. 251.

When your father passed away, the people were scattered in search of his successor, but my companions and I accepted your Imamate. Now tell me who will be the Imam after you?' Imam ('a) answered, 'My son, Ali.'"[478]

Dawud Ibn Zarbi has said, "I took some property for Imam Abu Ibrahim ('a). He accepted some of it, but rejected some. I asked him, 'Why did you reject some of it?' He answered, 'The guardian after me will demand it from you.' After Imam Kazim's ('a) demise, Imam Riza ('a) sent someone to me and demanded the remaining property, so I presented it to him."[479]

Yazid Ibn Salit has said in a long tradition, "Imam Abu Ibrahim ('a) told me in the year he passed away, 'I will be arrested and imprisoned this year. So the Imamate will be for my son, Ali, who has the same name as Ali Ibn Abi Talib ('a) and Ali Ibn Hussayn ('a). He has the legacy of knowledge, patience, piety, remembrance, and religion from the first Ali, and having calamities and patience from the second Ali.'"[480]

Muhammad Ibn 'Isma'il Ibn Fazl Hashimi has said, "I went to see Abul Hassan Musa Ibn Ja'far ('a), who was very sick. I told him, 'If, Allah forbids, an incident happens to you, who should we refer to?' Imam ('a) stated, 'To my son, Ali. His writing is my writing. He will be my successor and caliph.'"[481]

'Abdullah Ibn Marhum has said, "I got out of Basrah and went toward Medina. In my way, I met Imam Abu Ibrahim Musa ('a), who was going toward Basrah. He gave me some letters and said, 'Take these to Medina and give them to my son, Ali. Surely, he will be my successor

---

[478] Ibid.

[479] Ibid.

[480] Al-'Irshad, Vol 2, p. 252.

[481] Kashful Ghummah, Vol 3, p. 88.

and vicegerent and is my best son.'"[482]

Muhammad Ibn Ziyd Hashimi has said, "Now the Shi'ah are obliged to follow Ali Ibn Musa ('a) as the Imam." He was asked about the reason. He answered, "Because Abul Hassan Ibn Ja'far ('a) defined Ali Ibn Musa ('a) as his successor."[483]

Hiydar Ibn Ayyub has said, "I was in Quba, Medina. Muhammad Ibn Ziyd Ibn Ali came there but he was late. I said, 'May I sacrifice for you! Why did you come late?' He answered, 'Abu Ibrahim had called me along with some of the progeny of Ali ('a) and Fatimah (s), who were seventeen people. Then he told us, 'Witness that I define my son, Ali, as my successor in my lifetime and after my death. Surely his rule will be allowed.' By Allah that after Musa ib Ja'far ('a), the Shi'ah will select his son, Ali ('a), as the Imam.' I said, 'May Allah prolong the life of Musa Ibn Ja'far ('a)! How do you say this?' Muhammad Ibn Ziyd said, 'O Hiydar! When Musa Ibn Ja'far ('a) defined Ali ('a) as his successor, he devolved Imamate to him.'" Ali Ibn Hakam says, "Nevertheless, Hiydar died while he was doubtful about Imamate of Ali Ibn Musa ('a)."[484]

Abdur Rahman Ibn Hajjaj has said, "Abul Hassan Musa ('a) willed to his son, Ali ('a), wrote a letter to him, and took sixty of the elites in Medina as witness."[485]

Hassan Ibn Ali Ibn Khazzaz has said, "We were going to Mecca for pilgrimage. Ali Ibn Abu Hamzah was with us, carrying his own property and goods. We told him, 'Where do you take this property?' He answered, 'This is the property of Abd Salih, who has ordered me to give it to his son, Ali ('a). He has defined Ali ('a) as his successor.'"[486]

---

[482] Biharul Anwar, Vol 49, p. 15.

[483] Ibid, p. 16.

[484] Biharul Anwar, Vol 49, p. 16.

[485] Ibid, p. 17.

[486] Ibid.

Ja'far Ibn Khalaf has said, "I heard from Abul Hassan Musa Ibn Ja'far ('a), 'A blissful person is someone who sees his successor before his death. The Almighty Allah has introduced my son, Ali ('a), Riza, as my successor.'"[487]

Musa Ibn Bakr has said, "I was with Imam Abu Ibrahim ('a), who said, 'Ja'far Sadiq ('a) stated, 'A blissful person is the one who sees his successor before his death.' ' Then he pointed to his son, Ali ('a), and said, 'The Exalted Allah has introduced him as my successor.'"[488]

Ibn Fizal has said, "I heard from Ali Ibn Ja'far ('a), 'I was with my brother, Musa Ibn Ja'far ('a). By Allah he was Allah's caliph after his father. His son, Ali ('a) came in. Musa Ibn Ja'far ('a) told me, 'O Ali Ibn Ja'far! He is your guardian. His relation to me is like my relation to my father. May Allah keep you steady in your religion.' So I cried and thought to myself that my brother Musa is informing me of his death. Then he said, 'O Ali! Allah's destine will happen. The Messenger of Allah (s), Amiral Mu'minin ('a), Fatimah (s), Hassan ('a), and Hussayn ('a) will be my patterns.' Musa Ibn Ja'far ('a) said this three days before he was summoned by Harunur Rashid for the second time.'"[489]

There are other traditions about the Imamate of Ali Ibn Musa Al-Riza ('a), which are not cited here for the sake of briefness. Moreover, many miracles of Imam Riza ('a) are recorded in tradition books, which can prove his Imamate.

Virtues and Social Personality

Like his father, Imam Riza ('a) possessed all human virtues, being a notable character among the people of his age. Shiykh Mufid has written, "After Musa Ibn Ja'far ('a), his son Ali Ibn Musa Al-Riza ('a)

---

[487] Ibid, p. 18.

[488] Ibid, p. 26.

[489] Biharul Anwar, Vol 49, p. 26.

became the Imam, because he was superior to all his brothers and relatives. His knowledge, tolerance, piety, and jurisprudence were clear to everyone. The masses and the elites acknowledged his virtues and perfection. His father had stipulated his Imamate."[490]

He has also written, "Ali Ibn Musa Al-Riza ('a) was the best, wisest, greatest, and most knowledgeable of his brothers."[491] 'Ibrahim Ibn Abbas has said, "I never saw Imam Riza ('a) speak harshly, stop someone's talking, or reject someone who has a request. I never saw him stretch his foot or lean when others are present or misname his servants. He never laughed loud, rather he smiled. When he ate he invited all his servants and even the doorman and ate with them. His sleeping was little and his wakefulness was much. He was awake most of the nights until the dawn. He fasted much. He never forgot to fast three days in month. He said, 'Three days of fasting every month has the thawab of fasting all days.' His alms-giving was hidden at dark nights. Anyone who thinks there is someone better than Ali Ibn Musa ('a) is not right."[492]

Ibn Sabbagh Maliki has written, "If one attends to the character of Ali Ibn Musa ('a) it becomes clear that he has the legacy of his grandfathers, Ali Ibn Abi Talib ('a) and Ali Ibn Hussayn ('a). He had a lofty stance and a strong belief. His fans were so many and his arguments were so clear that the incumbent caliph, Ma'mun, placed him near himself in government. Ma'mun devolved the government after himself to Ali Ibn Musa ('a) and married his daughter to Ali Ibn Musa ('a). Ali Ibn Musa ('a) had great virtues and excellent attributes. His honorable

---

[490] Al-'Irshad, Vol 2, p. 247.

[491] Ibid, p. 244.

[492] Biharul Anwar, Vol 49, p. 90; Manaqib 'ali Abi Talib, Vol 4, p. 389.

soul was like the Hashemite and his essence was like the prophets."[493]

Ziyad Ibn Marwan has said, "I was with Imam Musa Kazim ('a) and Abil Hassan Riza was present. Imam ('a) told me, 'This is my son Ali. His writing is my writing and his speech is my speech and his envoy is my envoy. Everything he says is true.'"[494]

Ma'mun, the Abbasside caliph, wrote a letter to Ali Ibn Musa ('a) to devolve vice regency to him. In a part of that letter he wrote: "From the beginning of my caliphate I have always tried to find the best person for my vice regency. I found no one more deserved than Abul Hassan Ali Ibn Musa Al-Riza, since his knowledge, piety, and virtues were more than other people. He has denied the world and its lovers, preferring the Hereafter to this world. I am sure of it and everyone knows it. Hence, I appoint him to vice regency." [495]

Abus Salt has said, "Ma'mun told Ali Ibn Musa ('a), 'O son of Messenger of Allah! Since your virtues, knowledge, piety, and devotion to Allah were proved to me, I know you more deserved for caliphate than me.'"[496]

Knowledge

As it was mentioned in previous sections and proved by logical reasons and traditions, one of the major conditions of the Imam knows all religious issues. His major duty is maintaining, publishing, and enforcing religious commandments and rules. Basically, the philosophy of Imamate is fulfilling this important duty. All the Imams have done it and Imam Riza ('a) did it in his own time.

---

[493] Al-Fusulul Muhimmah, p. 225; Matalibus Su'ul, Vol 2, p. 128; Kashful Ghummah, Vol 3, p. 49.

[494] Al-Fusulul Muhimmah, p. 226.

[495] Tadhkiratul Khawas, p. 353.

[496] Biharul Anwar, Vol 49, p. 129; Manaqib 'ali Abi Talib, Vol 4, p. 392.

During his twenty years of Imamate, Imam Riza ('a) attempted for publishing religious commandments and training scholar sincere students. Because of the attempts of Imam Riza ('a) and his sincere students and narrators many traditions were publicized, which are cited in tradition books. There are traditions from Imam Riza ('a) in all religious issues, including monotheism, theology, Allah's attributes, creation of the world and its philosophy, Allah's Justice, force and option, destiny, prophet hood and its philosophy, infallibility, Imam's knowledge, Imam's conditions, philosophy of Imamate, ethical virtues and vices, various sins and their punishment, and different jurisprudential issues.

The tradition books contain some traditions in above-mentioned topics and many other subjects from Imam Riza ('a). Moreover, Imam Riza had debates and scientific discussions with incumbent rulers, scholars, and priests of other religions that are exactly recorded in history and tradition books. An accurate study of Imam Riza's ('a) traditions and debates shows his real scientific stance.[497]

Imam Riza ('a) trained sincere scholar students in his fruitful life. They have pursued Imam's ('a) purposes, defending the religion and publishing its sciences and teachings. Ahmad Ibn Muhammad Ibn Abi Nasr Baznati, Muhammad Ibn Fazl Kufi, Abdullah Ibn Jundab Bajli, 'Isma'il Ibn Ahwas Ash'ari, Ahmad Ibn and Muhammad Ash'ari are some of the notable and trustworthy students of Imam Riza ('a).

Hassan Ibn Ali Khazzaz, Muhammad Ibn Suliyman Diylami, Ali Ibn Hakam Anbari, Abdullah Ibn Mubarak Nahawandi, Hamad Ibn Uthman Bab, Sa'd Ibn Sa'd, Hassan Ibn Sa'id Ahwazi, Muhammad Ibn Faraj Rakhji, Khalaf Basri, Muhammad Ibn Sanan, Bikr Ibn

---

[497] All the traditions from Imam Riza (a.s) in various fields are recorded in a book entitled Musnad Al-Imam Al-Riza (a.s). This book also mentions the names of narrators of hi traditions and his students, who exceed 312 people.

Muhammad Azdi, Ibrahim Ibn Muhammad Hamidani, Muhammad Ibn Ahmad Ibn Qiys, and Is'haq Ibn Muhammad Hasibi were some of close companions of Imam Riza ('a).[498]

Abus Salt has said, "I saw no one more knowledgeable than Ali Ibn Musa Al-Riza ('a). Every scholar who saw him testified to his great knowledge. Ma'mun invited scholars of other religions, jurisprudents, and lecturers to his circles to debate with Imam Riza ('a). Imam Riza ('a) overcame all of them in discussion and they confessed to his knowledge ability and their own imperfection."

Ali Ibn Musa Al-Riza ('a) said, "I sat inside the shrine of Messenger of Allah (s), while many scholars of Medina were present. When they could not find the answer to a problem, they asked me and I answered all their problems."

Muhammad Ibn Is'haq Ibn Musa Ibn Ja'far has narrated from his father that Imam Musa Ibn Ja'far ('a) told his children, "Your brother, Ali Ibn Musa, is 'alim 'ali Muhammad (Scholar of Household of Muhammad (s)). Ask him religious questions and record his answers. Surely I frequently heard from Abu Ja'far, "alim 'ali Muhammad is one of your progeny. I wish I could see him. He has the same name as Amiral Mu'minin, Ali ('a).'"[499]

Raja' Ibn Abi Zahhak, who accompanied Imam Riza ('a) from Medina to Tus, says, "In every city we entered, the people came to Imam Riza ('a) for learning religious issues and asked him questions. Imam ('a) replied their questions with a tradition he narrated from his father from his grandfathers from Imam Ali ('a) from the Messenger of Allah (s)." Ma'mun says, "Yes, Ibn Zahhak! He was the best person on the earth and the most knowledgeable most pious of the people."[500]

---

[498] Manaqib 'ali Abi Talib, Vol 4, p. 397.

[499] Biharul Anwar, Vol 49, p. 100.

[500] Ibid, p. 95.

'Ibrahim Ibn Abil Abbas has said, "I never saw Imam Riza ('a) unable to answer a question. I saw no one more scholar than him. Ma'mun asked him questions about various issues and he answered them all. All his answers came from the Quran. He recited the whole Quran every three days. He said, 'I can recite the Quran completely in less than three days, but I ponder about every verse and the time and place of its revelation when reciting. Therefore, it takes three days to read it thoroughly.'"[501]

Worship

Like his father and grandfathers, Imam Riza ('a) was diligent in worship. He performed obligatory prayers early at their times with complete attendance and humility. He was accurate in performing Nafilah prayers too, never leaving vigilance and performing night prayer. He constantly engaged in reciting supplications and the Quran. Instances of his sincere worship are cited below.

Raja' Ibn Abi Zahhak said, "Ma'mun assigned me a mission to bring Ali Ibn Musa Al-Riza ('a) from Medina to Tus. Ma'mun had ordered me to pass Basrah, Ahwaz, and Fars, and not to pass Qum in our way. I was ordered to watch Ali Ibn Musa ('a) until we got Marw. By Allah I saw no one more pious, in Allah's remembrance, and fearful of Allah than him."

After performing the Morning Prayer, he sat in his praying place and recited the zikrs: subhanallah, Alhamdulillah, allahu-akbar, la-ilaha-illallah (Glory be to Allah, Praise be to Allah, Allah is Great, There is no deity but Allah) and salawat to Prophet Muhammad (s) until the sunrise. Then he performed sajdah and continued it until the sun arose in the sky."

Then he preached the people and narrated traditions for them until

---

[501] Ibid, p. 95.

before the noon. He then performed wudu and went to his prayer place again."

After the noon adhan, he performed six rak'ahs of nafilah prayer. In the first rak'ah, he recited Suratul Hamd and Suratul Kafirun. In the second rak'ah, he recited Al-Hamd and Al-'Ikhlas. In the other four rak'ahs, he recited Al-Hamd and Al-'Ikhlas. After each two-rak'ahs he recited salam and recited qunut before the ruku' of the second rak'ah. Then he recited adhan and performed two rak'ahs of nafilah. Then he recited iqamah and performed the Noon Prayer. After the Noon Prayer, he said the zikrs: subhanallah, Alhamdulillah, allahu-akbar, la-ilaha-illallah for a while. Afterwards, he performed sajdah shukr and recited shukran-lillah (Thanks to Allah) one hundred times. He then performed six rak'ahs of nafilah prayer with Al-Hamd and Al-'Ikhlas, each two rak'ahs with a salam, and performed the qunut before ruku'. Then he recited the adhan and performed two rak'ahs of nafilah with qunut in the second rak'ah. He then recited the iqamah and performed the Afternoon Prayer. After that he said subhanallah, Alhamdulillah, allahu-akbar, la-ilaha-illallah again. Then he performed sajdah and said alhamdulillah (Praise be to Allah) one hundred times. After the sunset, he performed wudu again, recited adhan and iqamah, and performed three rak'ahs of Evening Prayer with qunut before the ruku'. After the prayer, he engaged in reciting subhanallah, Alhamdulillah, allahu-akbar, la-ilaha-illallah again and then performed sajdah shukr."

When his sajdah finished, he raised and without talking to anyone he performed four rak'ahs of nafilah each two rak'ahs with one salam. He recited qunut in the second rak'ah. In the first rak'ah he recited Al-Hamd and Al-'Ikhlas Surahs and in the second rak'ah he recited Al-Hamd and Al-Kafirun Surahs. After finishing the prayer, he sat and recited supplications for a while and then he broke his fast."

After about one third of the night passed, he performed four rak'ahs of Night Prayer with qunut before the ruku'. After the Night

Prayer, he stayed in his prayer place and recited the zikrs subhanallah, Alhamdulillah, allahu-akbar, la-ilaha-illallah for a while. Then he performed sajdah shukr and went to have a rest."

In the last one third of the night, Imam Riza ('a) got up, brushed his teeth, and performed ablution for prayer, while he repeated the zikrs subhanallah, Alhamdulillah, allahu-akbar, la-ilaha-illallah. He performed eight rak'ahs of prayer, every two-unit of which with a salam. In the first rak'ah of each prayer, he recited the Surahs Al-Hamd and Al-'Ikhlas thirty times –he performed Ja'far Tayyar prayer four rak'ahs with two salams and recited the qunut before the ruku'. Ja'far Tayyar prayer was part of his night prayer. Then he performed the remaining two-rak'ahs of night prayer. In the first rak'ah he recited Al-Hamd and Al-Mulk Surahs and in the second rak'ah Al-Hamd and Al-'Insan."

Then Imam Riza ('a) performed shaf' prayer. He recited three times of Al-'Ikhlas after Al-Hamd surah in every rak'ah and recited the qunut in the second rak'ah. Then he rose and performed one rak'ah of watr prayer. After surah Al-Hamd, he recited Al-'Ikhlas three times, Al-Falaq, and Al-Nas surahs. He also recited the qunut before the ruku' in the second rak'ah. In this qunut, he recited this supplication: "O Allah! Bless Muhammad (s) and his progeny. O Allah! Guide us among those You have guided, cure us among those You have cured, love us among those You have loved, bless us in what You have granted us, save us from every badness You have destined for us. Surely You define destines but Your destine is not defined by anyone. The one You love will not be humble and the one You dislike will not be dear. You are Glorious and Lofty, o our Lord!" Then he recited, "I repent toward Allah and ask Him repentance" seventy times. After the salam, he sat and recited supplications for a while."

Before the dawn, he performed two rak'ahs of nafilah; in the first rak'ah, he recited Surahs Al-Hamd and Al-Kafirun, and in the second rak'ah, surahs Al-Hamd and Al-'Ikhlas. After the dawn, he recited 'adhan and 'iqamah and performed two rak'ahs of the Morning Prayer. After the salam, he sat and recited supplications until the sunrise. Then he performed sajdah shukr and remained in the same state until the sun rose in the sky."

In the first rak'ah of obligatory prayers, Imam Riza ('a) recited the surahs Al-Hamd and Al-Qadr and in the second rak'ah he recited Al-Hamd and Al-'Ikhlas. However, he recited surahs Al-Jumu'ah and Al-Munafiqin respectively in the first and second rak'ahs of the Morning, Noon, and Afternoon Prayers on Fridays."

In the Evening Prayer of Friday nights, he recited surahs Al-Hamd and Al-Jumu'ah in the first rak'ah and Al-Hamd and Al-'A'la in the second rak'ah."

In the Morning Prayer of Mondays and Tuesdays, he recited the surahs Al-Hamd and Al-'Insan in the first rak'ah and surahs Al-Hamd, Al-'Insan, and Al-Ghashiyah in the second rak'ah. He recited the surahs loud in the Evening, Night, midnight, shaf', watr, and Morning Prayers and quiet in the Noon and Afternoon Prayers. In the third and fourth rak'ahs of prayers, he recited three times of subhanallahi wal-hamdulillahi wala-ilaha-illallahu wallahu-akbar, instead of surah Al-Hamd."

The supplication of his qunut was this phrase, "O Lord! Forgive what we have done and have Mercy on us. Surely You are the most Honorable, the most Dear, and the most Generous."

"Everywhere he wanted to stay ten days or more, he was fasting in days. At the sunset he first performed his obligatory prayer and then broke his fast. During his travel he performed the obligatory four-rak'ah prayers with two rak'ahs, except the Evening Prayer that he performed with three rak'ahs. In travel or at home he did not abandon the nafilah of Evening and Night Prayers, the midnight prayer, shaf', watr, and Morning nafilah. But he did not perform

Noon and Afternoon nafilah prayers on travel. After short prayers, he repeated subhanallahi wal-hamdulillahi wala-ilaha-illallahu wallahu-akbar thirty times and said, 'This zikr compensates shortcomings of the prayer.'"

I never saw him perform zuha prayer in travel or at home. In travel he never fasted. At the beginning of every supplication, he recited salawat to Muhammad (s) and his Household. He repeated this zikr a lot. He recited the Holy Quran a lot at nights. When he reached a Quranic verse about the Hell or the Paradise, he wept. He sought the Paradise from Allah and sought refuge in Him from the Hell."

He recited bismillahirrahmanirrahim (In the Name of Allah, the All-Compassionate, the All-Merciful) aloud in all prayers. Every time he recited the verse "Say Allah is One." He quietly said, "Allah is One." After reciting this surah he said "He is our Lord" three times. When he recited surah Al-Kafirun, he said to himself, "O the disbelievers!" After finishing the surah he said three times, "My Lord is Allah and my religion is Islam."

When he recited the surah Al-Tin, he said, 'Yes, and I am a witness to this.' When he recited the surah Al-Qiyamah, he said, 'O Lord! You are Glorious! Yes.' When he recited the surah Al-Jumu'ah, after the word wattijarati (and bargain) in the verse: "Say: "The (blessing) from the Presence of God is better than any amusement or bargain! And God is the Best to provide (for all needs),"[502] he added the phrase "… for those who are pious," of course not as a part of the verse."

After reciting surah Al-Fatihah he said, "Praise be to Allah; Lord of the worlds."

When he recited the surah Al-'A'la, he quietly said, "Glorified is our Great Lord." When he recited the Quranic verse "O you who believe"

---

[502] Surah Al-Jumu'ah (62): 11.

he said quietly, 'Here I am! O Allah Here I am!'"[503]

'Ibrahim Ibn Abbas has said, "Imam Abul Hassan Riza ('a) slept little at nights and was vigilant a lot. Most of the nights, he was awake until the dawn and worshipped. He fasted most of the days. He fasted at least three days a month. He said, 'Three days of fasting a month is like fasting all one's life.'"[504]

Almsgiving

Beneficence, alms-giving to the poor, paying the debt of the debtors, feeding the believers, and helping everyone in need were examples of tradition of Prophet Muhammad (s) and the infallible Imams ('a). Imam Riza ('a) continued this conduct as much as possible.

'Is'haq Nubakhti has said, "A man came to Imam Riza ('a) and said, 'Grant me as much as your greatness.' Imam Riza ('a) answered, 'I cannot afford that much!' The man said again, 'So grant me as much as my greatness.' Imam Riza ('a) said, 'This amount is possible.' Then he ordered his servant to give two hundred dinars to that man."

Imam Riza ('a) gave away all his property as charity in Khurasan on the day of 'Arafah. Fazl Ibn Sahl told Imam Riza ('a), "This granting is not proper, but harmful." Imam Riza ('a) told him, "It is not harmful, rather quite useful. Do not consider something that is given in Allah's way and for reward harm!"[505]

Mu'ammar Ibn Khallad has said, "When Imam Riza ('a) ate food he placed a bowl beside him, pouring the best parts of food in it. Then he ordered to give it away to the poor. At the same time, he recited this verse, "and that ears (that should hear the tale and) retain its memory

---

[503] Biharul Anwar, Vol 49, p. 91.
[504] Biharul Anwar, Vol 49, p. 91; Al-Fusulul Muhimmah, p. 233.
[505] Biharul Anwar, Vol 49, p. 100.

should bear its (lessons) in remembrance."[506]

Then Imam Riza ('a) said, "The Almighty Allah knows that not everyone can free a slave, so He set the Paradise as the reward of feeding the people."[507]

Ghaffari has said, "A man from 'ali Abi Rafi' with a certain name had lent me some money. He asked it from me, but I could not pay it back. Therefore, I performed my Morning Prayer in the Prophet's (s) mosque. Then I went to meet Imam Riza ('a), who was in 'Urayz[508] then. When I reached there, I saw Imam Riza ('a) in his garment and cloak, riding a donkey. I got ashamed and said nothing. When he reached me, he looked at me. I said hello and said, 'One of your fans has lent me some money. Now he asks me the money and has brought me to ruin.' I thought that Imam Riza ('a) will recommend that person not ask his money from me. I did not mention the amount of my debt. Imam Riza ('a) told me, 'Stay here until I return.'"

I stayed there until the sunset, so I performed my prayer. I was fasting, so I got tired and wanted to return, when Imam Riza ('a) appeared with a group of other people. They asked him requests and he gave them alms. Then he entered his house and invited me too. I entered, sat beside Imam ('a), and talked about Ibn Musayyib, the governor of Medina. When I finished, Imam ('a) said, 'I think you are still fasting.' I said, 'Yes.' Imam Riza ('a) ordered to bring food for me and told his servant to sit and eat with me. Then he stated, 'Pick up this cushion and take whatever is beneath it.'"

I did as Imam ('a) had said and took some dinars. Imam Riza ('a) told four of his servants to accompany me to my house. I told him, 'The agents of Ibn Musayyib are guarding and I fear that they see me with

---

[506] Surah Al-Balad (90): 11.

[507] Biharul Anwar, Vol 49, p. 97.

[508] A village near Medina, whose lands were mostly for the infallible Imams (a.s).

your servants.' So Imam Riza ('a) confirmed it and told his servants to return whenever I told them. When I reached near my house, I told them to return."

Then I went into my house and lightened a lamp. I counted the money to find out that it was forty eight dinars, though my debt was only twenty eight dinars. One of the dinars was very shiny. I looked at it in the light and read this, 'Your debt is twenty eight dinars. The rest of the money is for you.' By Allah I was not sure how much my debt was."[509]

Yasir, the servant of Imam Riza ('a), has said, "When Imam Riza ('a) was in his privacy, he invited all his young and old servants and talked to them closely. When he sat to eat food, he called everyone to eat with him."[510]

The Ninth Imam; Muhammad Jawad

Birth and Martyrdom

Imam Muhammad Taqi ('a) was born on fifteenth or nineteenth of Ramadan in the year 190 A.H. in Medina. His name was Muhammad, his father was Ali Ibn Musa Al-Riza ('a), and his mother was called Sabikah or Khiyzaran.[511] His nickname was Abu Ja'far Al-Thani (the second), and his titles were Qani', Murtaza, Jawad, and Taqi.[512] He was seven years and eight months when his honorable father was martyred.

---

[509] Al-'Irshad, Vol 2, p. 255; Biharul Anwar, Vol 49, p. 97.

[510] Biharul Anwar, Vol 49, p. 164.

[511] Kafi, Vol 1, p. 492; Biharul Anwar, Vol 50, p. 2.

[512] Matalibus Su'ul, Vol 2, p. 140; Manaqib 'ali Abi Talib, Vol 4, p. 410.

His Imamate lasted seventeen years.[513]

Mu'tasam, the Abbaside caliph, called Imam Taqi ('a) and his wife, Ummul Fazl, the daughter of Ma'mun, to Baghdad. Imam ('a) went to Baghdad on twenty eighth of Muharram in the year 220 and was martyred in Zul Qa'dah in the same year in Baghdad. He was buried in Quraysh tomb beside the grave of his grandfather, Imam Musa Ibn Ja'far ('a). He was 25 years and some months then.[514]

Texts Proving His Imamate

Shiykh Mufid has written, "Some people have narrated traditions from Imam Abul Hassan Riza ('a) about the Imamate of his son, Abu Ja'far ('a), including Ali Ibn Ja'far Ibn Muhammad Sadiq, Safwan Ibn Yahya, Mu'ammar Ibn Khalad, Hussayn Ibn Yasar, Ibn Abi Nasr Baznati, Ibn Qiyama Wasiti, Hassan Ibn Jahm, Abu Yahya San'ani, Khiyrani, Yahya Ibn Habib Ziyarat…"[515]

Ali Ibn Ja'far Ibn Muhammad has said, "I took the hand of Abu Ja'far Muhammad Ibn Ali Al-Riza ('a) in my hand and told him, 'I testify that you are the Imam from Almighty Allah.' Imam Riza ('a) wept and said, 'O Uncle! Did you hear from my father that the Messenger of Allah (s) said, 'May my father sacrifice for the son of the best female slave, Nuwbiyah Tayyibah, from whose generation an Imam will be expelled from his home and take revenge of his father and uncle. He will have a long occultation, in a way that it will be said that he has died or gone to another land.' ' I said, 'May I sacrifice you! You are right.'"[516]

Safwan Ibn Yahya has said, 'I told Imam Riza ('a), 'Before the Almighty Allah granted you your son, Abu Ja'far, I came to you and

---

[513] Biharul Anwar, Vol 50, p. 12.

[514] Ibid, p. 1.

[515] Al-'Irshad, Vol 2, p. 274.

[516] Al-'Irshad, Vol 2, p. 275.

you said, 'The Almighty Allah will grant me a son soon.' Now Allah has granted you a son. If, Allah forbids, an event happens tos you, who should we refer to?' Imam Riza ('a) pointed to his son, Abu Ja'far, and said, 'Refer to him!' I said, 'May I sacrifice for you! How is it possible while he is only three years old?' Imam Riza ('a) replied, 'His little age does not contradict his Imamate. Prophet Jesus ('a) was Allah's Messenger too, while he was younger than three.' '[517]

Mu'ammar Ibn Khallad has said, 'I heard from Imam Riza ('a) some issues about the signs of Imamate. Then he continued, 'Why do you need these signs? I appoint my son, Abu Ja'far, as my successor and caliph after me.' Then he stated, 'We are a Household whose children are exactly like its elders.' '[518]

Hussayn Ibn Yasar has said, "Ibn Qiyama wrote in a letter to Abul Hassan Riza ('a), 'How can you be an Imam, while you have no son to be your successor?' Imam Abul Hassan ('a) wrote in reply, 'How do you know that I will have no son? By Allah that He will grant me a son in a few days and he will separate the truth from untruth.'"[519]

Ibn Abi Nasr Baznati has said, "One day, Ibn Najashi told me, 'Who will be the Imam after your master, Imam Riza ('a)? Ask it and tell me about the answer.' I went to Imam Riza ('a) and asked the question of Ibn Najashi. Imam ('a) answered, 'The Imam after me will be my son.' Then he continued, 'Who can talk about his son when he has no son?' Abu Ja'far ('a) was not born at that time, but he was born a few days after that."[520]

---

[517] Ibid, p. 276; Al-Fusulul Muhimmah, p. 247.

[518] Al-'Irshad, Vol 2, p. 277; Al-Fusulul Muhimmah, p. 247.

[519] Al-'Irshad, Vol 2, p. 277.

[520] Al-'Irshad, Vol 2, p. 277

Ibn Qiyama Wusta –who was a Waqifi⁵²¹– said, "I went to see Ali Ibn Musa Al-Riza ('a) and told him, 'Can two people be the Imams at the same time?' Imam Riza ('a) replied, 'No, except in case one of them is silent.' I asked again, 'Do we have a silent Imam now?' Imam ('a) answered, 'By Allah that He will grant me a son who will support the truth and its followers and will try to abolish the untruth.' At that time, Imam Riza ('a) had no son, but his son, Abu Ja'far, was born after one year."⁵²²

Hassan Ibn Jahm has said, "I was with Imam Abul Hassan ('a). He called his little son, sat him on my lap, and said, 'Take his garment off!' I did so. Then Imam ('a) told me, 'Look between his two shoulders!' I looked at it and saw something like a signet between his two shoulders. Then Imam Riza ('a) said, 'My father had the same sign.'"⁵²³

Abu Yahya San'ani has said, "I was with Abul Hassan Riza ('a) when his little son, Abu Ja'far, was brought. Imam Riza ('a) said, 'He is a great blessing for my Shi'ahs and no one has been born like him.⁵²⁴'"

Khiyrani has narrated from his father, "I was with Imam Riza ('a) in Khurasan. A man asked him, 'If something bad happened to you, who should we refer to?' Imam ('a) replied, 'To my son, Abu Ja'far.' That man wondered about Abu Ja'far's little age. So Imam Riza ('a) stated, 'The Exalted Allah appointed Prophet Jesus ('a) to prophet hood when he was younger than Abu Ja'far.'"⁵²⁵

Muhammad Ibn Abi 'Abbad –the ascribe of Imam Riza ('a)– has said, "Imam Riza ('a) always called his son, Muhammad, with his nickname,

---

⁵²¹ A person who believes in the Imamate of some of infallible Imams (a.s), not all of them.

⁵²² Ibid.

⁵²³ Ibid, p. 278.

⁵²⁴ Ibid, p. 279.

⁵²⁵ Ibid, p. 279.

Abu Ja'far. Imam Riza ('a) always treated his son so politely, while he was a child. Abu Ja'far's ('a) letters to his father, Imam Riza ('a), was written very eloquently and sent to Khurasan. I heard from Imam Riza ('a), 'Abu Ja'far is my successor and caliph.'"[526]

Musafir has said, "Abul Hassan Riza ('a) told me in Khurasan, 'Go to Abu Ja'far! He is your Imam and master.'"[527]

'Ibrahim Ibn Abi Mahmud has said, "I was with Imam Riza ('a) in Tus when a man said, 'If something happens to you, who should we refer to?' Imam Riza ('a) stated, 'To my son, Muhammad.' Perhaps the questioner considered the age of Abu Ja'far little. So Ali Ibn Musa Al-Riza ('a) said, 'The Almighty Allah appointed Jesus, son of Mary, to prophet hood, when he was younger than Abu Ja'far.'"[528]

Ibn Bazi' has said, "Abul Hassan Riza ('a) was asked, 'Is the Imamate position devolved to the Imam's uncles too?' Imam Riza ('a) answered, 'No.' He was asked again, 'Is it devolved to the Imam's brother?' 'No,' Imam ('a) answered. He was asked, 'Who is the Imamate devolved to?' Imam Riza ('a) answered, 'To my son.' At that time, Imam ('a) had no son."[529]

Virtues

As proved in previous sections, the Imam is a perfect human, possessing all humane virtues and void of any vices or imperfections. This is, in fact, one of the signs and necessities of infallibility.

After someone's Imamate is proved using certain reasons, his innate virtues are also proved. Therefore, knowledge, piety, worships, virtuousness, and being away from vices are necessities of every Imam

---

[526] Ibid; Al-Fusulul Muhimmah, p. 247.

[527] Ibid, p. 34.

[528] Ibid.

[529] Ibid, p. 35.

and there is no difference among the Imams in this regard. All of them are perfect humans with all virtues. Childhood, adolescence, youth, or old age does not affect these good qualities. If it is observed that less information has reached us from some of the Imams or fewer traditions are cited in history books about the worship or virtues of some of them, it does not mean that they have been less perfect than other Imams. Rather, socio-political situations, the length of their lives, and their time and place conditions have made such different accounts of their lives.

Though many traditions have been narrated from Imam Muhammad Taqi ('a) and recorded in tradition books, these traditions are less than those of his father and grandfathers. Not many traditions are cited about his worship, piety, alms-giving, and virtues.

The reason is twofold:

The first reason is the short life of Imam Muhammad Taqi ('a); unfortunately, he was only twenty five at his martyrdom. Therefore, he had less time and opportunity for publishing traditions.

The second reason is his young age at the time of Imamate. Imam Muhammad Taqi ('a) was appointed to Imamate at the age of seven years and some months. At this young age, his scientific stance and humane virtues was perfect enough. However, his stance was not obvious to most of the people, even the Shi'ahs. Naturally, less people came to him for learning religious sciences and teachings. So he was not attended to by the scholars much. It was so even after Imam Muhammad Taqi's puberty. Of course, his scientific and human stance became more obvious gradually and more people were attracted to him. But unfortunately, his early death came and the Muslims were deprived of his sciences and teachings. Nevertheless, some issues are remained from Imam Muhammad Taqi ('a) that can be useful for the enthusiasts.

Shiykh Mufid has written, "When the knowledge, wisdom, and

perfect mentality of Imam Abu Ja'far ('a) –in that young age– and his superiority over scholars of that time was proved for Ma'mun, he got Imam's ('a) enthusiast, married his daughter Ummul Fazl to Imam ('a), and sent her to Medina. Ma'mun always attempted in honoring and respecting Imam ('a)."[530]

Abul Faraj Abdur Rahman Ibn Juzi Hanafi has written, "Muhammad Ibn Ali Musa ('a) behaved like his father in terms of science, piety, and generosity. After the demise of his father, Ali Ibn Musa Al-Riza ('a), Ma'mun called Muhammad Ibn Ali from Medina to Baghdad, honored him, granted Muhammad Ibn Ali ('a) whatever he gave Imam Riza ('a), and married Imam Taqi ('a) to his daughter, Ummul Fazl.[531]

Rayyan Ibn Shabib has said that when Ma'mun wanted to marry his daughter, Ummul Fazl, to Abu Ja'far Muhammad Ibn Ali ('a), some of the Abbasside noblemen heard about it. They could hardly bear it. They feared that it led to Abu Ja'far's ('a) vice regency, as it had happened for Ali Ibn Musa Al-Riza ('a). Some of relatives of Ma'mun thought about this issue, went to see him, and said, "O Amiral Mu'minin! We beg you forget about marrying your daughter to the son of Riza, because we fear that the caliphate be taken from our family. You are well informed of our differences with the Hashemite and the conduct of previous caliphs with them. Because of what you did to Ali Ibn Musa Al-Riza ('a) and appointed him your vice regent, we faced great problems. The Almighty Allah helped us solve that problem. We beg you in the Name of Allah that you neglect this marriage, not to take us into trouble again."

Ma'mun answered, "You have caused the old controversy that exists between you and the progeny of Abu Talib. If you were fair enough, they were more deserved for caliphate than you."

---

[530] Al-'Irshad, Vol 2, p. 281.

[531] Tadhkiratul Khawas, p. 359.

"The previous caliphs cut ties of kinship with the progeny of Abu Talib. I take refuge in Allah and do not repeat what they did. By Allah I am not regretful of selecting Riza as my vice regent at all. I first suggested caliphate to him, but he rejected it. It was destined that he pass away before me and not reach caliphate position. I selected Abu Ja'far Muhammad Ibn Ali, because he is superior to all the scholars and the sage, with his little age. In fact, he is a wonder. I hope his wisdom becomes clear to the people, so that they know that my selection has been right."

The noble men said, "You know him a wonder, but he is still a youth and knows nothing of jurisprudence, sciences, and teachings. Let him learn jurisprudence and then do whatever you want."

Ma'mun said, "Woe to you! I know this young man better than you do. He is from a Household whose knowledge is inspired by the Almighty Allah. His father and grandfathers were always needless of other people in terms of religious sciences. You can test him if you wish."

They said, "O Amiral Mu'minin! It is a good suggestion. Set an appointment and one of our scholars tests him in your presence. If he answered correctly, we will have no objection to your decision."

Ma'mun said, "No problem. You can come for testing Abu Ja'far whenever you want."

The noble men went out and decided to invite Yahya Ibn Aktham –who was the head of the judges– for the testing session. They told him, "Prepare difficult questions to ask Ibn Al-Riza in the presence of Ma'mun, so that we will persuade Ma'mun." They even promised to give him expensive property.

On the promised day, the noble men went to Ma'mun along with Yahya Ibn Aktham. Ma'mun ordered to spread carpet on a part of the house and set two cushions. Then Abu Ja'far ('a), who was nineteen, entered and sat between the two cushions. Yahya Ibn Aktham also came in and sat in front of Abu Ja'far ('a). Other people stood around them according to their stance. Ma'mun sat near Abu Ja'far ('a).

Yahya Ibn Aktham asked Ma'mun, "O Amiral Mu'minin! Do you let me ask some questions from Abu Ja'far?" Ma'mun answered, "Ask permission from himself!" Yahya asked Abu Ja'far ('a) permission and then said, "What should a person who has hunted in the state of 'ihram do?"

Imam Abu Ja'far ('a) answered, "Has he hunted inside the haram (Masjidul Haram) or outside it? Has he been aware or ignorant? Has he hunted on purpose or unintentionally? Has he been a slave or free? Has he been a youngster or an adult? Has he hunted once or more than once? Has he hunted a bird or other animals? Has it been small or large? Has the hunter been relented or not? Has he hunted at night or day? Has he been muhrim in the hajj or in the 'umurah?"

Yahya Ibn Aktham got wondered of the questions and disability was quite obvious in his face, in a way that the audience understood it well. At that time, Ma'mun said, "I praise the Almighty Allah for this blessing." Then he looked at his household and relatives and said, "Did you see that what I said about Abu Ja'far is right?" Then he told Imam Abu ja'far ('a), "Now please answer these trivial jurisprudential questions, so that we will learn."

Imam Muhammad Taqi ('a) answered, "If a muhrim kills the prey, which is a large bird, outside the haram, he should pay a sheep as compensation. If he kills the prey inside the haram, he should pay two sheep. If the prey is a small bird outside the haram, the compensation is a lamb that is just weaned. If the same bird is killed inside the haram, the compensation is a lamb and the price of the small bird. If he has hunted a wild donkey, the compensation is a cow. If an ostrich is hunted, the compensation is zibh (Islamic slaughtering) of a camel. If the prey is a deer, the compensation is a sheep. If one of these animals is hunted inside the haram, the compensation is twofold and should be slaughtered beside the ka'bah. If the muhrim is in hajj, he should bring the animal to Mina and slaughter it there. The compensation of hunting is the same for an ignorant and an aware muhrim. However, intentional hunting in this state is a sin, while unintentional hunting is not a sin. The compensation of a free hunter should be paid by him, but the compensation of a slave hunter should be paid by his master. If the hunter is an adolescent, the compensation is not obligatory for him. If the muhrim person who has hunted repents, he will have no punishment in the Hereafter. But if he does not repent and resists on his deed, he will bear Allah's punishment."

At this time, Ma'mun said, "Excellent Abu Ja'far! May the Exalted Allah grant you reward. Now you ask Yahya a question, if you want."

Imam Abu Ja'far ('a) told Yahya Ibn Aktham, "Do you let me ask you a question?" Yahya answered, "Go on! If I know the answer I will say it. And if I do not know, I will learn it from you."

Imam Muhammad Taqi ('a) asked, "A man looked at a woman early at the morning and his look has been haram (unlawful). Later in the same day, looking at her became halal (lawful) for him. At noon, looking at the woman became haram again for that man, but in the afternoon, looking at her became haram for him again. After the sunset, she became haram for him again, but at night she became halal. In the midnight, the woman got haram for the man, but in the dawn she got halal for him once more. Who are the man and woman? How are the lawfulness and unlawfulness possible?" Yahya Ibn Aktham answered, "I do not know the answer. Please answer it yourself!"

Imam Muhammad Taqi ('a) said, "The mentioned woman is a female slave. Early in the morning a stranger man looks at him and this look is haram. Later in the day, the stranger man buys the female slave from her master, thus looking at her becomes halal. At noon, the man frees the female slave, so looking at her becomes haram for him. In the evening, the man marries the female slave, so looking at her becomes halal. After the sunset, he divorces her in the form of zihar. Therefore, looking at her becomes haram again. At night, he pays the compensation for zihar and the woman becomes halal for him again. In the midnight, he divorces her and she becomes haram for him. In the dawn, the man returns to the woman again and marries her, so she becomes halal for him again."

At this point, Ma'mun told the audience, "Which of you can answer jurisprudential problems this way?" They answered, "Neither of us can do so." Ma'mun said again, "This knowledge and scientific perfection is a characteristic of the Ahlul-Bayt of the Prophet (s) and young age is not a hindrance to this quality." When the virtues and knowledge of Imam Jawad ('a) became clear for the audience, Ma'mun married his daughter Ummul Fazl to Imam ('a). The marriage sermon was recited and some gifts were distributed among the audience.[532]

It is narrated from the book 'Uyunul Mu'jizat that when Imam Riza ('a) passed away, Imam Abu Ja'far ('a) was nearly seven. The Shi'ah in Baghdad and other cities had controversy about Imam Riza's ('a) successor. Rayyan Ibn Salt, Safwan Ibn Yahya, Muhad Ibn Hakim, Abdur Rahman Ibn Hajjaj, Yunus Ibn Abdur Rahman, and a group of other trustworthy Shi'ahs gathered in the house of Abdur Rahman Ibn Hajjaj and mourned for the martyrdom of Imam Riza ('a). Then Yunus Ibn Abdur Rahman stood and said, "We'd better stop crying and consult with each other in this regard to find out who should we refer to for our religious questions until Abu Ja'far grows up." At his time, Rayyan Ibn Salt was annoyed, rose, and said, "O Yunus! Apparently you are a believer, but are you a doubter really? If Imamate is devolved from the Almighty Allah, an infant can be like a scholar old man. And if it is not from Allah, thousand years of age will make no difference

---

[532] Al-'Irshad, Vol 2, p. 281; Al-Fusulul Muhimmah, p. 249; Biharul Anwar, Vol 50, p. 74; Kashful Ghummah, Vol 3, p. 143.

for an ordinary person. Our viewpoint should be so."

It was the hajj season then. Eighty of jurisprudents and scholars of Baghdad gathered and went to hajj. They also went to Medina to meet Imam Abu Ja'far ('a). They went into Imam Sadiq's ('a) house, because it was empty. Abdullah Ibn Musa came to visit them. So someone said, "He is the son of Messenger of Allah (s). Ask him your questions!" Some questions were posed and Abdullah answered them, but his answers were not true. Therefore, the Shi'ah scholars and jurisprudents got upset. They wanted to leave. They thought to themselves, "If Abu Ja'far could answer the questions properly, we did not hear these wrong answers from Abdullah."

Suddenly, a door opened and Muwaffaq came in. He said, "This is Abu Ja'far!" The audience rose, welcomed and greeted him. Imam Abu Ja'far ('a) entered in a garment, a turban, and a pair of slippers and sat. Some people asked him their questions and heard the answers from Imam Abu Ja'far ('a). All the answers were true and according to religious rules. The scholars were satisfied, prayed for Imam ('a), and said, "Your uncle, Abdullah, gave us untrue answers." Imam Muhammad Taqi ('a) stated, "La 'Ilaha illa Allah! (There is no deity but Allah) My uncle! It is very hard to be reckoned in the Hereafter because of giving verdicts about what one does not know, while there has been a more knowledgeable one among the people."[533]

In spite of short lifetime, scarce opportunities, hindrance by the enemies, and unawareness of some of the Shi'ahs, many traditions are left from Imam Muhammad Taqi ('a) and recorded in tradition books, which reveal his knowledge.

Imam Muhammad Taqi ('a) has also trained many narrators and students, including, Ayyub Ibn Nuh, Ja'far Ibn Muhammad Ibn Yunus, Hussayn Muslim Ibn Hassan, Mukhtar Ibn Ziyad 'Abdi, Muhammad

---

[533] Biharul Anwar, Vol 50, p. 99.

Ibn Hussayn Ibn Abi Talib, Shadhan Ibn Khalil Niyshaburi, Nuh Ibn Shu'ayb Baghdadi, Muhammad Ibn Ahmad Mahmudi, Abu Yahya Jurjani, Abul Qasim 'Idris Qumi, Ali Ibn Muhammad Ibn Harun, 'Is'haq Ibn 'Isma'il Niyshaburi, Ahmad Ibn 'Ibrahim Maraghi, Abu Ali Ibn Balal, Abdullah Ibn Muhammad Hazini, Muhammad Ibn Hassan Ibn Sham'un.[534]

Worship and Ethics

Imam Jawad ('a) had a short life, but he had a deep knowledge of theology, Creation, and Resurrection, just like his father and grandfathers. He observed the realities of the world via intuitive eye; his belief was beyond subjective themes. This is a necessity of Imamate. Therefore, Imam Jawad ('a) was just like his honorable father and grandfathers in worship, humiliation before Allah, sincere supplications, piety, alms-giving, and good ethics. Although the people did not attend to him much because of his young age and some other reasons, some scarce issues have been narrated about him.

Shiykh Mufid has written, "Imam Abu Ja'far ('a) left Baghdad with his wife, Ummul Fazl, and went toward Medina. In Kufah, the people welcomed him. Near the sunset, he reached the house of Musayyib. Imam ('a) landed from his horse and went to the mosque. There was a tree in the mosque yard that did not have fruit. Imam Jawad ('a) asked for water and performed wudu beside that tree. He performed the Evening Prayer with the congregation (jama'ah). In the first rak'ah, he recited the Surahs Al-Hamd and Al-Nasr and in the second rak'ah Surahs Al-Hamd and Al-'Ikhlas. Before the second ruku', Imam ('a) recited qunut. In the third rak'ah, he recited tashahhud and salam. Then he remained seated and recited zikrs for a while. After that, he rose and performed four rak'ahs of nafilah. Then he recited the

---

[534] Manaqib 'ali Abi Talib, Vol 4, p. 412.

supplications and performed sajdah shukr two times. He then left the mosque. The people went out too and found that the tree had fruits because of blessing of Imam Abu Ja'far's ('a) wudu. They ate the fruits that were very sweet, but had no stones."[535]

Here is one of the supplications that is narrated from Imam Muhammad Taqi ('a):

O Allah! Surely the oppression of Your servants has increased on the Earth to the extent that justice is died, solutions to problems are scarce, truth is decreased, righteousness is removed, goodness is hidden, evilness is apparent, piety is little, guidance is hindered, untruth is confirmed, corruption is high, enmity is strong, and injustice is spread.

O Allah! O Lord! These cannot be remedied except by Your sovereignty. Only Your Mercy can save us from them.

O Allah! O Lord! Eradicate oppression, cut the knob of injustice, perish evilness, honor those who dislike evilness, and perish evildoers.

O Allah! Hasten their ousting, humble them, and perish evilness, so that the scared people are immune and the grieved are calm. Feed the hungry, maintain the destroyed, and inhabit the outcast, return the misplaced, enrich the poor, lodge the refugee, honor the oppressed, humble the oppressor, gladden the sad, calm the scared, remove differences, make knowledge dear, spread health, gather the scattered, strengthen beliefs, and make people recite the Quran; surely You are Pious and Beneficent.

One of the sons of Hanifah, who was an inhabitant of Bast and Sajistan, has said, "At the beginning of caliphate of the Abbasside Mu'tasim, I accompanied Imam Abu Ja'far ('a), who was going to hajj. When eating food, I told Imam ('a), 'Our governor is a fan of you and the Prophet's (s) Ahlul-Bayt. He has obliged me to pay a tax, which I cannot afford. Can you recommend that he does not take the tax from

---

[535] Al-'Irshad, Vol 2, p. 288; Al-Fusulul Muhimmah, p. 252.

me?' Imam Muhammad Taqi ('a) said, 'I do not know him.' I said, 'He is fond of you and your letter will be helpful in this regard.' Imam ('a) asked for a piece of paper and wrote, 'In the Name of Allah, the Most Compassionate, the Most Merciful. The holder of this letter said that you have a good conduct. Your deeds are surely better than what he said. So do good to your brothers. Know that the Almighty Allah will ask you even about small amounts of things'"

When I reached Sajistan, the governor, Hussayn Ibn Abdullah Niyshaburi, heard the news of the letter and he came to welcome me two miles away from the city. I gave him Imam's ('a) letter. He took it, kissed it, and put it on his eyes. Then he asked me, 'What is your request?' I answered, 'There is a tax on me that I cannot afford to pay it.' So the governor ordered not to take the money from me. Then he told me, 'As long as I am in office, I will not charge taxes on you.' Afterwards, he asked about my family and my income and ordered to pay me an amount of money more than I needed for me and my family. As long as that man was the governor, I did not pay any tax. And he gave me alms as long as he was alive."[536]

Abu Hashim has said, "Abu Ja'far ('a) gave me a bag of three hundred dinars and told me, 'Give it to that cousin of mine. He will ask you to introduce him to someone to buy things for him.' When I gave the money to Imam's ('a) cousin, he told me, 'Introduce someone to me to buy things for me.'"[537]

Baznati has said, "Imam Abul Hassan Riza ('a) wrote in a letter to his son, Abu Ja'far ('a), 'O Aba Ja'far! I have heard that your servants take you out from the small door of the house. They are envious lest someone takes or sees goodness from you. My son! I swear you by myself that your coming and going be only from the big door of your

---

[536] Kafi, Vol 5, p. 111.

[537] Manaqib 'ali Abi Talib, Vol 4, p. 422.

house. Whenever you go out, bring some money with yourself. If someone asked help from you, grant him something. If your uncles and cousins asked you grant them not less than fifty dinars. More than this amount is up to you. If your aunts asked you, give them not less than twenty five dinars and more than that is up to you. I pray that the Almighty Allah give you a high stance. Give alms to others and do not fear poorness!'"[538]

The Tenth Imam; 'Ali Hadi

Birth and Martyrdom

Imam Ali Al-Naqi ('a) was born on fifteenth of Zi Hajjah in the year 212 A.H. in Siriya near Medina. His father was Imam Muhammad Taqi ('a) and his mother was called Samanah. His nickname was Abul Hassan and his titles were Naqi, Hadi, 'alim, Faqih, 'Amin, Mu'tamin, Tayyib, Mutawakkil, 'Askari and Najib. Imam Hadi ('a) was also called Abul Hassan Thalith (the third). According to some narrations, he was martyred on the third of Rajab in the year 254 A.H. in Samira' and buried in the same city. He was 42 then. He lived about eight years with his father and his Imamate lasted 33 years.[539]

Texts Proving His Imamate

As mentioned in previous sections, various reasons can be used for proving the Imamate of each of infallible Imams ('a), one of which is the traditions by each Imam about the Imam after himself. Here we only point out this kind of traditions.

'Isma'il Ibn Mihran has said, "The first time Imam Abu Ja'far ('a) was

---

[538] Biharul Anwar, Vol 50, p. 102.

[539] Kafi, Vol 1, p. 497; Al-'Irshad, Vol 2, p. 297; Biharul Anwar, Vol 50, pp. 113-117; Al-Fusulul Muhimmah, p. 295; Matalibus Su'ul, Vol 2, p. 144.

summoned to Baghdad, I told him, 'May I sacrifice for you! I am afraid of this travel for you. Who will be the Imam after you?' Imam ('a) told me, 'What you are fearful of does not happen this year.'"

When Mu'tasim summoned Imam Abu Ja'far ('a), I went to see Imam ('a) and told him, 'They are taking you to Baghdad. Who will be the Imam after you?' Imam ('a) wept so much that his holy beard got wet and said, 'This time my travel is dangerous. The Imamate after me will be for my son, Ali.'"[540]

Khiyrani has narrated from his father, "I had a mission to guard the house door of Imam Abu Ja'far ('a). 'Ahmad Ibn 'isa Ash'ari came every dawn to ask about Imam's ('a) health. And then when the envoy of Imam ('a) came to see my father, 'Ahmad Ibn 'isa left so that they could talk in private."

One night, the envoy of Imam Abu Ja'far ('a) came to see my father. 'Ahmad Ibn 'isa and I left them alone. 'Ahmad walked outside and listened to their conversation. The envoy of Imam Abu Ja'far ('a) told my father, 'Your master greeted you and said, 'My death is coming. The Imamate will be devolved to my son, Ali, after me. You will have to fulfill the same duties toward him as you did toward me.'"

The envoy of Imam Abu Ja'far ('a) went out after delivering the message. 'Ahmad Ibn 'isa returned to my father and asked, 'What did the envoy say?' My father said, 'It was good.' 'Ahmad said, 'I heard what he said completely.' My father told him, 'You did something unlawful! Don't you know that the Almighty Allah states in the Holy Quran, 'And spy not on each other.'[541] Now that you have heard the message of Imam ('a), maintain it until the day we will need it. But do not reveal it before that.'"

The next morning, my father wrote the message of Imam Abu Ja'far

---

[540] Al-'Irshad, Vol 2, p. 298.

[541] Surah Al-Hujurat(49): 12.

('a) in ten copies, leaving each of them with a trustworthy person. Then he said, 'If my death came, open the letters and follow the orders.' My father said, 'When Imam Abu Ja'far ('a) passed away, I did not left my house until I heard that the nobles of the tribe have gathered in the house of Muhammad Ibn Faraj to discuss the Imamate issue. Muhammad Ibn Faraj informed me of this gathering and asked me to join them. I rode my horse and went to them. I saw the noble men in his house who were talking about relation with the Imam. Most of them were doubtful of the Imamate issue. I told the trustworthy people who had a copy of Imam's message to bring them. I told the audience, 'This is s message Imam Abu Ja'far ('a) has sent me to convey to you.' Some of the audience said, 'We wish at least one other person testified to this.' I said, 'The Almighty Allah has destined that Abu Ja'far 'Ash'ari hear this message and can testify to it. You can ask him.' The audience asked 'Ahmad Ibn Muhammad about it, but he refused to testify to what he had heard. So I invited him to mubahilah (cursing). He got frightened of it and said, 'Yes, I heard the same issue, but it is an honor that I liked to be for an Arab man. Now, however, I cannot hide the truth after being invited to mubahilah.' After this testimony, all the audience surrendered to Imam Abul Hassan ('a).'"

After narrating this story, Shiykh Mufid has added, "There are many traditions about this issue. The book will get so lengthy if I want to mention all these traditions. The consensus of the companions about the Imamate of Imam Abul Hassan ('a) and lack of any other one who claims to be the Imam are sufficient for us."[542]

Saqar Ibn Abi Dilf has said, "I heard from Imam Abu Ja'far Muhammad Ibn Ali ('a), 'The Imam after me will be my son, Ali. His order will be my order, his speech will be my speech, and obeying him is like obeying me. The Imamate after him will be devolved to his son,

---

[542] Kafi, Vol 1, p. 324; Al-'Irshad, Vol 2, p. 300.

Hassan.'"543

Muhammad Ibn 'Uthman Kufi has said, "I told Imam Abu Ja'far ('a), 'If, Allah forbids, something happens to you, who should we refer to?' Imam ('a) answered, 'To my son, Abul Hassan.' Then Imam ('a) stated, 'Soon there will happen a break.' I said, 'Where should we go at that time?' Imam ('a) answered, 'To Medina.' I asked, 'Which Medina (city)?' Imam Abu Ja'far ('a) answered, 'Madinatur Rasul (the city of Prophet (s)).'"544

Umayyat Ibn Ali Qiysi has said, "I told Imam Abu Ja'far Thani ('a), 'Who will be your successor?' He answered, 'My son, Ali.' Then he added, 'Soon the wondering time will arrive.'"545

Muhammad Ibn 'Isma'il Ibn Bazi' has said, "Imam Abu Ja'far ('a) stated, 'The Imamate will reach my son, Abul Hassan, when he is seven.' Then he added, 'Yes, seven years and even younger, just as Prophet Jesus ('a).'"546

Harun Ibn Fazl has said, "I met Imam Abul Hassan ('a) on the day when his father, Imam Abu Ja'far ('a) had passed away. He said, 'We are Allah's and we will return to Him. My father Abu Ja'far has passed away.' He was then asked, 'How do you know that your father has passed away?' He answered, 'I experience a state of humility before the Almighty Allah that had never happened before.'"547

A group of people from Isfahan, including Abul Abbas Ahmad Ibn Nadhr and Abu Ja'far Muhammad Ibn 'Alawiyyah said, "In Isfahan, there was a Shi'ah man called Abdur Rahman. He was asked, 'Why did you accept the Imamate of Ali Naqi among all other people?' He

---

543 Biharul Anwar, Vol 50, p. 118.

544 'Ithbatul Wasiyyah, p. 193.

545 'Ithbatul Hudat, Vol 6, p. 209.

546 Ibid, p. 211.

547 Biharul Anwar, Vol 50, p. 138.

answered, 'I observed something in him that caused my belief in his Imamate. I was a poor man who dared to speak openly. One year, the people of Isfahan sent me to Mutawakkil, the Abbasside caliph, for petition. One day, when I was in the house of Mutawakkil, he summoned Ali Ibn Muhammad Riza ('a). I asked someone about the summoned person, who I thought Mutawakkil wanted to kill. He answered, 'He is an Alawi man. The Rafizah (the Shi'ah) believe in his Imamate.' I thought to myself, 'I stay here to know this man more.' At this time, Ali Naqi ('a) entered on his horse. The crowd opened his way and looked at him. When I saw him, I felt affection for him and prayed that the Almighty Allah save him from the evilness of Mutawakkil. When he reached me, he looked at me and said, 'Your prayer was accepted; your life will be long and you will own many children and much property.' I was shocked of the unseen tidings, but I said nothing to my companions about it. Then I returned to Isfahan. I gained much property. I have a million dirhams only in my house, not to mention what I possess outside. The Exalted Allah granted me ten children. Now I am more than seventy years old. I believe in the Imamate of the man who was aware of my thoughts and his prayer about me was accepted.'"[548]

Virtues

Shiykh Mufid has written, "After Imam Abu Ja'far ('a), his son, Abul Hassan Ali Ibn Muhammad ('a) reached the Imamate position, because he possessed all Imamate qualities. There was no other person as qualified as he was at that time for occupying this position. He was appointed to the Imamate by his father."[549]

Ibn Shahr 'ashub has described Imam Ali Al-Naqi ('a) this way, "His

---

[548] Biharul Anwar, Vol 50, p. 138.
[549] Al-'Irshad, Vol 2, p. 297.

face was more attractive than that of others and his speech was truer than that of others. He was the most perfect and the nicest of all the people. When he was silent, his dignity increased and when he talked his illumination appeared. He was from the family of prophet hood, Imamate, and caliphate of the Muslims. He was a branch from great prophet hood tree, but benefitting from him did not last long. He was the fruit of prophecy tree, which was selected a short time after getting ripe."[550]

Abu Musa has said, "I told Imam Hadi ('a), 'Teach me a special supplication for solving my problems.' Imam ('a) said, 'I recited this supplication most of the time and asked the Almighty Allah not to disappoint any prayer from His Mercy. (O my helper at the time of calamities, o my hope and my trustworthy friend and my supporter! O the One Being! I ask You o Allah by whoever of the servants You have created and You have not created anyone like any other o send greetings to them and do this and that[551] for me.)'"[552]

Sa'id Hajib has said, "A group of soldiers and I attacked the house of Abul Hassan ('a) at night by the order of Mutawakkil and we climbed over the wall to enter. He was performing prayer in a wool cloth and a head cover and was not afraid of our intrusion."[553]

Ibn Hajar has said, "Abul Hassan ('a) was the holder of his father's legacy regarding knowledge and generosity."[554]

Ibn Sabbagh Maliki has narrated from some scholars, "The virtues of Abul Hassan Ali Ibn Muhammad Hadi ('a) are like a tent that stands on the land of honor and whose ropes are attached to the stars. Any

---

[550] Manaqib 'ali Abi Talib, Vol 4, p. 432.

[551] The prayer's wish should substitute this phrase.

[552] Biharul Anwar, Vol 50, p. 127.

[553] Al-Fusulul Muhimmah, p. 264.

[554] Al-Sawa'iq Al-Muharriqah, Vol 1, p. 207.

virtue or excellence that is mentioned he possesses. He is worth any praise. Any gratitude or respect deserves him. His merits, virtues, and honor are rooted in his essence, keeping him away from vices, just as a cameleer maintains the little camels from dangers. His soul is pure, his ethics are good, and his conduct is excellent."[555]

Suliyman Ibn 'Ibrahim Qunduzi Hanafi has narrated from the book Faslul Khitab by Muhammad Khajah, "Abul Hassan Ali Hadi ('a) was a pious man, a jurisprudent, and an Imam. Mutawakkil was told, 'There are weapons in his (Abul Hassan's) house and he is going to obtain caliphate.' So Mutawakkil ordered some people to attack his house at night and enter it. They found Abul Hassan ('a) in a wool garment and a wool hat on his head, while he was sitting on the ground in the direction of the qiblah. There was nothing but sand beneath him. He was reciting the Holy Quran. The agents took Imam ('a) to Mutawakkil in the same state. When Mutawakkil saw Imam Hadi ('a), he respected Imam ('a) and placed Imam ('a) beside himself. Imam Abul Hassan ('a) talked to him. Then Mutawakkil cried and asked Imam ('a), 'O Abul Hassan! Do you have a debt?' Imam ('a) answered, 'Yes! I have a debt of four thousand dinars.' Mutawakkil ordered to give that amount of money to Imam Hadi ('a) and sent him to his house respectfully."[556]

Muhammad Ibn 'Ahmad has quoted from his father's uncle, "One day, I went to meet Imam Hadi ('a) and told him, 'Mutawakkil has quitted my salary, because he has understood that I am your companion. Please recommend him about me.' Imam ('a) answered, 'Everything will be all right.' At night, an agent came to my house from Mutawakkil and said that Mutawakkil has called me. When I went to Mutawakkil, he told me, 'O Abu Musa! I had completely forgotten you because of my engagements. How much money should I pay you?' I told him

---

[555] Al-Fusulul Muhimmah, p. 264.

[556] Yanabi'ul Mawaddah, p. 463.

what he always paid me. So he ordered to pay me twice as much as he regularly paid me. Then I asked Fat'h Ibn Khaqan (Mutawakkil's agent), 'Did Ali Ibn Muhammad come here or did he write a letter to Mutawakkil?' 'No,' he answered. Later, I went to see Imam Ali Ibn Muhammad ('a). He asked me if the money I received was satisfactory. I said, 'Yes, because of the blessings of your existence. But they said you did not go to Mutawakkil and did not ask him anything.' So Imam Hadi ('a) stated, 'The Almighty Allah knows well that we do not ask anyone to solve problems except Him. Allah has taught us that whenever we pray He will accept it. I fear that if we leave this conduct of us, Allah will abandon His Mercy too.'"[557]

Knowledge

As pointed out elsewhere in the present book, knowing all religious sciences and teachings is a prerequisite of the Imamate. The main philosophy of needing an Imam and the major duty of the Imam is maintaining and publishing religious teachings and sciences. There is no difference among the Imams in this regard. The sources of religious sciences have been present for all infallible Imams and they have attempted well to fulfill their duties. If there are fewer traditions from some of the Imams in tradition books, the reason is different time and place conditions and the hindrance made by oppressor rulers of the time and the enemies of Ahlul-Bayt ('a).

Like his father and honorable grandfathers, Imam Hadi ('a) was a perfect human, possessing all human virtues. He attempted much in teaching religious sciences to the Muslims, but unfortunately he faced limitations that hindered his ideal performance.

Imam Hadi ('a) lived for nearly forty years. He reached Imamate position at age eight and his Imamate lasted about thirty three years. At

---

[557] Manaqib 'ali Abi Talib, Vol 4, p. 442.

the beginning, he lived twenty two years in Medina. According to the history, the rulers in Bagdad watched Imam Hadi ('a) by their agents in Medina. Naturally, the Shi'ah and advocates of Imam ('a) faced limitations for gaining knowledge from him. The Abbasside caliph, Mutawakkil, was not satisfied with watching from distance and invited Imam Hadi ('a) to Baghdad; apparently with respect, but actually with cruel agents. He lodged Imam Hadi ('a) in 'Askar district –a military region– in Samira'. From that time, Imam Hadi ('a) was formally under severe guarding of secret agents, thus his relationship with the Shi'ah was nearly cut. Who dared give him money or learn sciences from him in those conditions? That is why the traditions narrated from him are scarce. However, there are some traditions from Imam Hadi ('a) about religious principles, ethics, preaching, and various jurisprudential issues in tradition books. Studying these traditions reveals the scientific stance of Imam Ali Ibn Muhammad ('a).

Imam Hadi ('a) trained many students, whose names are recorded in history, tradition, and rijal books. The author of Manaqib has named scholar companions of Imam Hadi ('a) this way: Dawud Ibn Ziyd Abu Salim Zankan, Hussayn Ibn Muhammad Mada'ini, Ahmad Ibn 'Isma'il Ibn Yaqtin, Bashar Ibn Bashar Niyshaburi Shadhani, Sulayman Ibn Ja'far Marwazi, Fat'h Ibn Yazid Jurjani, Muhamamd Ibn Sa'id Ibn Kulthum (a speaker), Mu'awiyah Ibn Hakim Kufi, Ali Ibn Muhammad Ibn Muhammad Baghdadi, Abul Hassan Ibn Raja' Abarta'i.

The Eleventh Imam; Hassan Askari

Birth and Martyrdom

Imam Hassan Askari ('a) was born on eighth of Rabi'ul Thani in the year 232 A.H. in Medina. His father was Imam Ali Ibn Muhammad ('a) and his mother was called Hadith or Susan. His nickname was Abu Muhammad and his titles were Samit, Hadi, Rafiq, Zaki, Naqi, Khalis, and 'Askari. He was martyred on the eighth of Rabi'ul Awwal in the year 260 A.H. in Samirra' and was buried beside his father's gravesite. He lived for twenty eight years and his Imamate lasted six years.[558]

Texts Proving His Imamate

It was mentioned before that there are two kinds of reason for proving Imamate; the general reasons for proving the Imamate of all infallible Imams ('a) and specific reasons for proving Imamate of each of the Imams. The first type of reasons was discussed in previous chapters of this book. The second type of reasons includes the traditions narrated from each Imam about the Imamate of the next Imam, which are cited here.

Abdul Azim Ibn Abdullah Hasani has said, "One day I went to meet Imam Ali Ibn Muhammad ('a). He told me, 'O Abul Qasim! Bravo! You are a real lover of us.' I told Imam ('a), 'I want to present my religious beliefs to you. If they were true, I will maintain them until my death.' So Imam ('a) told me, 'Go on!' I said, 'I believe that Allah is One and nothing is like Him…,' until I said, 'Muhammad (s) is Allah's servant and messenger and the last Prophet. There will be no prophet after him until the Resurrection. The Imam, caliph, and guardian of the ummah after Prophet Muhammad (s) will be Ali Ibn Abi Talib ('a)… Then the Imam will be Ja'far Ibn Muhammad ('a), then Musa Ib Ja'far ('a), then Ali Ibn Musa ('a), then Muhammad Ibn Ali ('a), and then you.' Ali Ibn Muhammad ('a) said, 'And after me my son, Hassan, will be the Imam of the Muslims. So how will the people be about his successor?' I asked, 'How will they be?' Imam ('a) answered, 'He will not be seen and saying his name will be haram, until he rises to establish justice in the earth after being filled with oppression.' Then Imam Ali Ibn

---

[558] Al-'Irshad, Vol 2, p. 313; Biharul Anwar, Vol 50, pp. 235-238.

Muhammad ('a) stated, 'O Abul Qasim! This is the religion Allah has selected for His servants. Maintain your belief in what you said. May the Exalted Allah keep you in the same belief!'"[559]

Abu Hashim Dawud Ibn Qasim Ja'fari has said, "I heard Imam Abul Hassan Sahib Askari ('a), 'My successor will be my son, Hassan. How will you behave about his successor?' I asked, 'May I sacrifice for you! Why do you ask it?' Imam ('a) answered, 'Because you will not see him and mentioning his name will be banned for you.' I asked, 'So how should we name him?' Imam Abul Hassan ('a) answered, 'Say, hujjat, the son of hujjat.'"[560]

Saqar Ibn Abi Dilf has said, "After Mutawakkil summoned my master, Imam Abul Hassan ('a), to Baghdad, I went to get some news from Imam ('a). Mutawakkil looked at me and asked, 'Why have you come here?' I answered, 'I have come with a good intention.' He said, 'Sit down!' Different thoughts came to my mind and I regretted going there. Mutawakkil sent others out and asked me again the reason of my going there. I said again, 'My intention is good.' He said, 'Perhaps you have come to see your master.' I said, 'O Amiral Mu'minin! Who is my master?' He said, 'Be quiet! Your master is the true master! Do not fear! I have the same belief as you have.' I said, 'Praise be to Allah!' He said, 'Do you want to meet your master?' I answered positively. So he told me, 'Wait until the messenger gets out.'"

When the messenger went out, Mutawakkil told his servant, 'Take Saqar to the prison of that Alawite man and leave these two alone!' The servant took me to a room and left. I saw Imam Abul Hassan ('a) on a piece of matting, while a grave was dug before him. I greeted him and sat. He told me, 'Saqar! Why did you come here?' I answered, 'I came to ask about you.' Then I looked at the grave and wept. Imam

---

[559] Kifayatul Athar, p. 282.

[560] Ibid, p. 284.

('a) looked at me and said, 'O Saqar! Do not be upset! I will get no harm.' I said, 'Praise be to Allah! O my master! There is a tradition from Prophet Muhammad (s) whose meaning I do not know.' Imam ('a) asked, 'What is it?' I said, 'What is the meaning of do not be the enemy of the days, so they will be your enemies?'"

Imam Abul Hassan ('a) answered, 'The heavens and the earth are created because of the blessing of us, the Ahlul-Bayt. Sibt (Saturday) is the name of Messenger of Allah (s). Ahad (Sunday) is Amiral Mu'minin ('a). Ithniyn (Monday) implies Hassan and Hussayn ('a). Thulatha' (Tuesday) refers to Ali Ibn Hussayn ('a), Muhammad Ibn Ali ('a), and Ja'far Ibn Muhammad ('a). Arba'a' (Wednesday) is Musa Ibn Ja'far ('a), Ali Ibn Musa ('a), Muhammad Ibn Ali ('a), and I. Khamis (Thursday) is my son, Hassan, and Jumu'ah (Friday) is his son. He will gather the advocates of the truth around himself and will fill the earth with justice after being filled with oppression. This is the meaning of the days. So do not be the enemy of these days, or else they will be your enemies in the Day of Judgment.' Then Imam ('a) said, 'O Saqar! Bid me and leave, because you will not be safe.'"[561]

Saqar Ibn Abi Dilf has also said, "I heard from Ali Ibn Muhammad ('a), 'After me my son, Hassan, will be the Imam and after Hassan his son will be the Imam and a Qa'im, who will fill the earth with justice after being filled with oppression.'"[562]

Yahya Ibn Yasar has said, "Four months before his demise, Imam Abul Hassan Ali Ibn Muhammad ('a) willed to his son, Hassan, and selected him as the Imam. A group of his relatives were witness to this."[563]

Ali Ibn 'Umar Nufili has said, "I was with Imam Abul Hassan ('a) in

---

[561] Kifayatul Athar, p. 285.

[562] Kifayatul Athar, p. 288.

[563] Al-Irshad, Vol 2, p. 314.

his house, when his son, Muhammad, passed us. I told Imam ('a), 'May I sacrifice for you! Will he be the Imam after you?' Imam Abul Hassan ('a) answered, 'No, your Imam after me will be my son, Hassan.'"[564]

Abdullah Ibn Muhammad 'Isfahani has said, "Imam Abul Hassan ('a) told me, 'Your Imam after me is the one who will perform prayer for my corpse.' At that time, Abu Muhammad ('a) was not known yet. When Imam Abul Hassan ('a) passed away, his son, Abu Muhammad ('a), performed prayer for his body."[565]

Ali Ibn Ja'far has said, "I was with Imam Abul Hassan ('a) when his son, Muhammad, passed away. Imam ('a) told his son, Hassan ('a), 'My son! Thank Allah, because the Almighty Allah has appointed you as the Imam.'"[566]

Ahmad Ibn Muhamamd Ibn Abdullah Ibn Marwan has said, "When Abu Ja'far Muhammad Ibn Ali ('a) passed away, I was present. Imam Abul Hassan ('a) came in and sat on a chair. His household was around him. His son, Abu Muhammad, was present too. When Imam ('a) completed shrouding and burying Abu Ja'far ('a), he looked at his son, Abu Muhammad ('a), and said, 'My son! Thank the Almighty Allah, because He has placed the Imamate in you.'"[567]

Ali Ibn Mahziyar has said, "I told Imam Abul Hassan ('a), 'If a bad happening occurred for you, who should we refer to?' Imam ('a) answered, 'My promise will be devolved to my eldest son, Hassan.'"[568]

Ali Ibn 'Umar Attar has said, "I went to see Imam Abul Hassan ('a), while his son, Abu Ja'far, was alive and we thought that he will be the successor to Imam ('a). I told Imam Abul Hassan ('a), 'May I sacrifice

---

[564] Ibid, p. 314.

[565] Ibid, p. 315.

[566] Al-'Irshad, Vol 2, p. 315.

[567] Ibid, p. 316.

[568] Al-'Irshad, Vol 2, p. 316.

for you! Which of your sons do you prefer?' Imam ('a) answered, 'None of my sons are selected before my verdict is issued.' Later on, I wrote a letter to Imam Abul Hassan ('a) and asked, 'Who will be the Imam after you?' Imam ('a) wrote in answer, 'My eldest son.' And Abu Muhammad ('a) was elder than Abu Ja'far."[569]

Sa'd Ibn Abdullah has narrated from some of the Hashemite, including Hassan Ibn Hussayn 'Aftas, "After the demise of Muhammad Ibn Ali Ibn Muhamamd ('a), we gathered in the house of Imam Abul Hassan ('a). A carpet was spread in the yard and people came to see Imam Abul Hassan ('a). We estimated the crowd to be one hundred and fifty people of Bani Abbas and 'ali Abu Talib, excluding the servants and other people. Then Hassan Ibn Ali ('a), who had tore his cloth collar out of sorrow, came and stood on the right side of his father. Imam Abul Hassan ('a) told him, 'O my son! Praise Allah, because he has devolved the Imamate to you.' So Hassan ('a) wept and said, 'Praise be to Allah, Lord of the worlds. I only ask Him all the blessings for us. We are Allah's and we will return to Him.' We asked who he was. It was answered that he was Hassan, the son of Imam Abul Hassan ('a), who was twenty then. So we knew him and found out that Imam Abul Hassan ('a) selected him as the next Imam."[570]

Muhammad Ibn Yahya has said, "After the demise of Abu Ja'far, I went to see Imam Abul Hassan ('a) and consoled him for the death of his son. Abu Muhammad was also there and was weeping. Imam Abul Hassan ('a) attended to him and said, 'The Exalted Allah has selected you in his place. So praise Allah!'"[571]

Shahwiyah Ibn Abdullah has said, "Imam Abul Hassan ('a) wrote in a letter to me, 'After the demise of Abu Ja'far, you were worried and

---

[569] Al-'Irshad, Vol 2, P. 316.

[570] Ibid, p. 317.

[571] Al-'Irshad, Vol 2, p. 318.

wanted to ask about my successor. Do not be worried, because the Almighty Allah does not let the guided people go astray. Your Imam will be Abu Muhammad. All the knowledge needed by the people is with him. Allah will make junior or prior anyone He likes. 'None of Our revelations do We abrogate or cause to be forgotten, but We substitute something better or similar.'[572]"[573]

Virtues

Shiykh Mufid has written, "After Abul Hassan Ali Ibn Muhamamd ('a), his son, Abu Muhammad Hassan Ibn Ali ('a), reached the Imamate position, because he possessed all the virtues. He was superior to all the people of his age in terms of knowledge, piety, wisdom, infallibility, brevity, generosity, and intense worship. Moreover, he was appointed to Imamate by his honorable father."[574]

Hussayn Ibn Muhammad 'Ash'ari and Muhamamd Ibn Yahya and other people have said that 'Ahmad Ibn Abdullah Ibn Khaqan was the official in charge of tax and state property in Qum and an enemy of the Ahlul-Bayt ('a). One day, the people talked about the Alawite and their beliefs in his presence. 'Ahmad Ibn Abdullah said, "I have seen no one among the Alawite better than Hassan Ibn Ali Ibn Muhammad in terms of conduct, speech, chastity, generosity, and greatness. Even the elderly, elites, ministers, and army commanders preferred him to themselves."

'Ahmad Ibn Abdullah has also said, "One day, my father had a general meeting and I was standing there. Suddenly, the doormen came in and said, 'Abu Muhammad Ibn Al-Riza ('a) is here.' My father told them, 'Let him in!' I was wondering how the doormen dared name someone

---

[572] Surah Al-Baqarah (2): 106.

[573] Al-'Irshad, Vol 2, p. 319.

[574] Ibid, p. 313.

using his nickname in my father's presence, because they could only name the caliph and the vice regent this way. Then a young handsome man came in formally. Seeing him, my father stood up and approached him. I had not seen my father welcome someone so warmly. My father hugged him, kissed his face, and placed him in his own place. Then my father sat before Abu Muhammad ('a) and began talking to him. When talking, my father frequently told Abu Muhammad, 'May I sacrifice for you!' I was very astonished of my father's behavior. Then a doorman came and said, 'Muvaffaq ('Ahmad Ibn Mutawakkil Abbasi) wants to see you.' Usually when Muvaffaq wanted to come to my father, the doormen and army commanders stood in two lines until he came in and went out. So my father told some of the audience, 'Keep Abu Muhammad behind you so that Muvaffaq cannot see him.' Then Muvaffaq came in, hugged my father, and went out after a while. I asked the doormen, 'Who was this person with who my father behaved so warmly and respectfully?' They answered, 'He is an Alawite man called Hassan Ibn Ali and his nickname is Ibn Al-Riza.' I was even more astonished of hearing this."

When my father performed the Night Prayer and went into his private room for doing administrative jobs, I went to him and asked, 'Who was the man you respected very much in your morning meeting?' My father answered, 'He was the Imam of the Rafizi, Hassan Ibn Ali, Ibn Al-Riza.' Then he continued, 'My son! If the caliphate is removed from the Abbasside, no one is more deserved for caliphate than him among the Hashemite. No one is like him in knowledge, chastity, conduct, piety, worship, and good morality. If you saw his father you found him a wise generous man.'"

I got angry of my father and decided to investigate about Ibn Al-Riza. I talked about him with the Hashemite, army commanders, secretaries, judges, jurisprudents, and other people. Everyone talked respectfully of him and preferred him to others. This way I understood his greatness."575

Muhammad Ibn 'Isma'il Alawi has said, "Abu Muhammad ('a) was in the prison of Ali Ibn 'Utamish, a foe of the Ahlul-Bayt, who ordered to treat Abu Muhammad harshly. After a few days, he became an advocate of Imam Abu Muhammad ('a), honoring him and recalling him as a virtuous person."576

Muhammad Ibn 'Isma'il Ibn Ibrahim Ibn Musa Ibn Ja'far has said, "A group of Bani Abbas went to see Salih Ibn Wasif, head of Abu Muhammad's ('a) prison and told him, 'Treat Abu Muhammad harshly in the prison.' He answered, 'What should I do? I hired two of the rabbles to guard him, but after some days they reached a high position in worship, prayer, and fasting.'"

Then he called the two guards and told them, 'Woe to you! Why don't you treat this prisoner severely?' They answered, 'What can we say about someone who is fasting everyday and worshipping every night? He does not talk to anyone and is not engaged in anything but worship. When he looks at us we tremble and we cannot control our awe.' When those people from Bani Abbas heard this, they became disappointed and went away."577

Abu Hashim Ja'fari has said, "I wrote a letter to Imam Abu Muhammad ('a) and complained about my tight prison and harsh anklet. He wrote in answer, 'You will perform the Noon Prayer at your house today.' I was freed from the prison on the same day and performed my Noon Prayer at home. I could hardly make a living. I wanted to mention this in my letter to Imam ('a), but I couldn't. When I reached my house, Imam Abu Muhammad ('a) sent me one hundred dinars and wrote to me, 'Do not be ashamed of asking your requests. Ask me

---

575 Al-'Irshad, Vol 2, p. 321.

576 Ibid, p. 329.

577 Ibid, p. 334.

and I will fulfill your request insha'allah.'"[578]

Muhammad Ibn Abi Za'faran has quoted from the mother of Imam Abu Muhammad ('a), "One day Abu Muhammad ('a) told me, 'In the year 260, there will happen a severe problem for me. I fear that a calamity will happen for me.' I became very upset and wept. So he told me, 'There is no way. This will happen. Do not be impatient!'"

In Safar of the year 260, the mother of Imam ('a) got very anxious. He exited Medina often to get some news. She was then informed that Mu'tamid has imprisoned Abu Muhammad ('a) and his brother, Ja'far. Mu'tamid frequently asked about Imam ('a) from Ali Ibn Jarir, the prison guard. He answered that Abu Muhammad ('a) was engaged in worship; fasting in the days and performing prayer at nights. One day, Mu'tamid asked about Imam Abu Muhammad ('a) again and heard the same news. He told the guard, 'Go and free him. Say my hello to him and tell him to return to his house.'"

The prison guard said, 'When I reached the prison gate, I saw a donkey prepared for mounting of Imam Abu Muhammad ('a). I went in and saw Imam ('a) in his clothes and shoes ready to go out. Seeing me, he rose and I gave him his freedom verdict. He went out, mounted the donkey, but he did not go. I asked the reason and he answered, 'I will not go without my brother, Ja'far. Go and tell Mu'tamid that Ja'far and I came out of one house; if we don't return together, problems will arise. I conveyed Imam Abu Muhammad's ('a) message to Mu'tamid and he replied, 'I free Ja'far for your sake, though I had imprisoned him because of his crimes against himself and you.' So Mu'tamid freed Ja'far too and they returned home together.'"[579]

It is narrated that Buhlul saw Imam Hassan Askari ('a) as a child, who looked at the children's playing and cried. Buhlul thought that he

---

[578] Al-'Irshad, Vol 2, p. 330.

[579] Biharul Anwar, Vol 50, p. 313.

cries because he does not have playthings. So he went to Imam ('a) and said, "Do not cry! I will but playthings for you." Imam ('a) answered, "O stupid! We are not created for playing." Buhlul asked, "So why are we created?" Imam ('a) answered, "For knowledge and worship." Buhlul asked again, "What is the reason?" Imam ('a) answered, "The Almighty Allah has stated in the Holy Quran, 'Did ye then think that We had created you in jest, and that ye would not be brought back to Us (for account?'"580

Then Buhlul asked Imam Hassan Askari ('a) to preach him. Imam ('a) recited a poem in answer and then he fainted. When he was sober again, Buhlul told him, "You are a child and have no duty. Why are you scared?" Imam ('a) answered, "I saw my mother firing large woods with small ones. I fear that I may be the small woods of the Hell." 581

Muhammad Ibn Ali Ibn Ibrahim Ibn Musa Ibn Ja'far has said, "Once our living became harsh. My father said, 'Let us go to Abu Muhammad ('a). I have heard much about his generosity.' I told my father, 'Do you know him?' He answered, 'No, I have not seen him nor do I know him.'"

We went to Imam Abu Muhammad ('a). While going, my father said, 'I need five hundred dirhams. Two hundred for clothing, two hundred for paying debts, and one hundred for life expenses.' I thought to myself, 'I wish he can give me three hundred dirhams; one hundred for buying a donkey, one hundred for life expenses, and one hundred for buying clothes. Then I am going toward Jabal.'"

When my father and I reached the house of Imam Abu Muhammad ('a), a servant came out and said, 'Ali Ibn Ibrahim and his son, Muhammad, you can come in!'"

We went to see Imam Abu Muhammad ('a) and greeted him. He told

---

580 Surah Al-Mu'minun (23): 115.

581 Nurul Absar, p. 183, Al-Sawa'iqul Muharriqah, p. 207.

my father, 'O Ali! Why did you come to me so late?' My father said, 'I was ashamed to come to you in such a state.'"

When coming out, the servant of Imam ('a) gave a bag of money to my father and told him, 'There is five hundred dirhams in this bag; two hundred for clothing, two hundred for paying debts, and one hundred for life expenses.' Then he gave me a bag too and told me, 'Three hundred dirhams is inside this bag; one hundred for buying a donkey, and two hundred for life expenses. You should not go to Jabal, but to Sura.'"

I regretted from going to Jaabal, went to Sura' instead, and married there. After some time, one thousand dinars was sent to me by Imam Hassan Askari ('a)."[582]

Imam's Knowledge

Like his honorable father and grandfathers, Imam Hassan Askari ('a) knew all religious sciences, rules, and teachings. He possessed the sources of Imamate sciences and Divine infallibility. He considered his duty to publish and maintain religious sciences and did his best in fulfilling this duty.

Of course, the Imams ('a) did not live in similar conditions. Each of the Imams ('a) fulfilled his duty according to his chances. Unfortunately, the sciences and teachings narrated from Imam Hassan Askari ('a) are not as much as what is narrated from his grandparents, especially Imam Baqir ('a) and Imam Sadiq ('a). The reason for this is twofold:

Imam Hassan Askari ('a) spent his lifetime in Samirra', a military district, and the caliphs agents watched him openly or hidden. In fact, his speech, conduct, and his guests were completely limited. Therefore, Imam Askari ('a) could not publish as much traditions as his father

---

[582] Kafi, Vol 1, p. 506.

and grandfathers. Nevertheless, many traditions are narrated from him and recorded in tradition books about monotheism, prophet hood, Resurrection, Imamate, ethics, preaching, and various fields of jurisprudence.

It is probable that many traditions of Imam Askari ('a) and other infallible Imams ('a) are missed throughout the ages and have not reached us. Despite his limitations during his short six-year term of Imamate, Imam Hassan Askari ('a) trained many students and tradition narrators, whose names are recorded in related books.[583]

The Twelfth Imam; Mahdi

Birth and Martyrdom

Hujjat Ibn Al-Hassan ('a) was born on the night of fifteenth of Sha'ban in the year 255 A.H. in Samira'. His name is the name of the Prophet of Islam (s), Muhammad, and his nickname is the Prophet's (s) nickname, Abul Qasim. His father was Imam Hassan Askari ('a) and his mother was Narjis. When his father was martyred, Imam Mahdi ('a) was only five. Being only five, he possessed knowledge and wisdom and he reached the Imamate position, just as Prophet Yahya ('a) reached prophet hood at childhood and Prophet Jesus ('a) became prophet in cradle.[584]

The titles of Imam Mahdi ('a) are Hujjat, Qa'im, Mahdi, Khalaf Salih,

---

[583] A researcher has collected the traditions narrated from Imam Hassan Askari (a.s) in various fields in a book called Musnad Al-Imam Al-Askari (a.s). The narrators of his traditions as recorded in this book exceed 149 people.

[584] Al-'Irshad, Vol 2, p. 339; 'A'lamul Wura, Vol 2, p. 214.

Sahib Al-Zaman, and Sahib.[585]

People Who Saw Imam Mahdi ('a) in his early days

Some close companions of Imam Askari ('a) had seen his son or heard the news about him.

Hakimah Khatun, the paternal aunt of Imam Hassan Askari ('a), has said, "On the birth night of Imam Qa'im ('a), I was in the house of Imam Hassan ('a) and present at the birth time. I saw the newborn son then and several times after that night."[586]

Fat'h –Mulla Zarari– has said, "I heard from Abu Ali Ibn Mutahhar, 'I saw the son of Imam Hassan Askari ('a).' He also described the height of Imam's ('a) son."[587]

'Amr Ahwazi has said, "Imam Abu Muhammad ('a) showed his son to me and told me, 'He is your guardian.'"[588]

'Ibrahim Ibn Muhamamd has narrated from Abu Nasr Tarif, the servant, "I saw the son of Imam Hassan ('a)."[589] Nasim, the servant of Imam Hassan ('a), has said, "Two nights after the birth of Sahib Al-Zaman ('a), I saw him. I sneezed, so he told me, 'Allah bless you!' And I became happy."[590]

Abu Ja'far 'Amri has said, "When our master was borne, Imam Abu Muhammad ('a) called Abu 'Umar. When he came, Imam ('a) told him, 'Buy ten thousand trays of dates and ten thousand trays of meat and divide them among Bani Hashim. Buy a certain number of sheep and

---

[585] 'A'lamul Wura, Vol 2, p. 213.

[586] Al-'Irshad, Vol 2, p. 351.

[587] Ibid, p. 352.

[588] Al-'Irshad, p. 353.

[589] Ibid, p. 354.

[590] 'A'lamul Wura, Vol 2, p. 217.

give away as 'aqiqah for my son.'"⁵⁹¹

Abu Ghanim, the servant, has said, "The child of Abu Muhammad ('a) was borne. Abu Muhammad named him Muhammad. On the third day after the birth, Abu Muhammad ('a) showed his son to his companions and told them, 'He is your guardian after me and the caliph after me. He is the Qa'im, who is waited for by the world people, and will fill the world with justice, after being filled with oppression.'"⁵⁹²

Muhammad Ibn Hassan Karkhi said that he heard from Abu Harun, "I saw Sahib Al-Zaman; his birth was on a Friday in the year 256 A.H."⁵⁹³

Muhammad Ibn 'Ibrahim Kufi has said, "Abu Muhammad ('a) sent a slain sheep for one of his companions with this message, 'This is 'aqiqah for my son, Muhammad.'"⁵⁹⁴

Hassan Ibn Mandhar has said, "One day Hamzah Ibn Abul Fat'h came to me and told me, 'Good tidings! Last night the child of Abu Muhammad ('a) was born and he ordered that we hide the news of it.' I asked about his name. He answered, 'His name is Muhammad and his nickname is Ja'far.'"⁵⁹⁵

Hassan Ibn Hussayn 'Alawi has said, "I went to meet Imam Abu Muhammad Hassan Ibn Ali ('a) in Samirra' and congratulated him on the birth of his son, Qa'im."⁵⁹⁶

'Ibrahim, a friend of Imam Abu Muhammad ('a) has said, "My master, Abul Hassan ('a), sent four sheep for me with this message, 'Give them away as 'aqiqah for my son, Mahdi. Eat from them and feed other

---

⁵⁹¹ Biharul Anwar, Vol 51, p. 5.

⁵⁹² Ibid.

⁵⁹³ Ibid,p. 15.

⁵⁹⁴ Ibid,p. 15.

⁵⁹⁵ Biharul Anwar, Vol 51, p. 15.

⁵⁹⁶ Ibid, p. 16.

Shi'ahs with them.'"⁵⁹⁷

Texts Proving His Imamate

Shiykh Mufid has written in this regard, "The traditions from Prophet Muhammad (s), Ali Ibn Abi Talib ('a), the infallible Imams ('a), and his father, Imam Hassan ('a) about Imamate of Imam Mahdi ('a) were previously mentioned. His honorable father had introduced him as the Imam and appointed him to Imamate among his trustworthy Shi'ah companions."⁵⁹⁸

Shiykh Mufid has also written, "One of the reasons for Imamate of Qa'im, Muhammad Ibn Hassan ('a), is the logical reason for necessity of existence of an infallible Imam, who is independent of the knowledge of other people, in every time. In fact, someone should be present to enjoin goodness and forbid evilness, punish the criminals, guide the misguided people, enforce the hudud, execute Divine rules, appoint the governors, maintain the Islamic land from the danger of enemies, and establish Jumu'ah and 'id prayers."

It is proved that such a person should be infallible and an Imam introduced by the previous Imam. Or he should prove his Imamate by doing a miracle for the people."

After the demise of Imam Hassan Askari ('a), there was no one possessing all these characteristics except his son, Mahdi ('a). Therefore, his Imamate is proved and there is no need to cite traditions in this regard."⁵⁹⁹

'Is'haq Ibn Sa'd 'Ash'ari has said, "I went to see Imam Abu Muhammad Hassan Ibn Ali Askari ('a) and told him, 'O son of Messenger of Allah! Who will be the Imam and caliph after you?' Imam Askari ('a)

---

⁵⁹⁷ Ibid, p. 28.

⁵⁹⁸ Al-'Irshad, Vol 2, p. 339.

⁵⁹⁹ Al-'Irshad, Vol 2, p. 242.

rose and entered his house rapidly. Shortly afterwards, he returned with a child on his shoulder. He was a three-year-old son with an illuminating face. Then Imam ('a) stated, 'O 'Is'haq Ibn Sa'd! If you were not dear to Allah and the Imams, I did not show you my son. This son has the same name and nickname as the Prophet of Islam (s). He is the person, who will fill the world with justice after being filled with oppression and injustice. O 'Is'haq! He is like Khizr and Zul Qarnayn! By Allah that he has an occultation in which only the people are saved, who have a constant belief in Imamate –by Allah's Mercy– and pray for my son's hasty reappearance.' I asked, 'Does he have a sign to assure my heart?' Then the child said in fluent Arabic, 'I am Allah's remnant on His earth and the avenger of His enemies.'"

I was happy of hearing this and went out. I returned on another day and asked Imam Askari ('a), 'O son of Messenger of Allah! I got very happy of your news. You really did bless me. Now tell me what the tradition of Khizr and Zul Qarnayn is?' Imam ('a) answered, 'Occultation.' I asked again, 'Will he have a long occultation?' He answered, 'By Allah yes! His occultation will be so long that most of the believers in Imamate will change belief, except the people in whose hearts Allah has inspired our affection and the real belief. His occultation will be by Allah's order and a secret of His secrets. Remember what I told you and keep it from the aliens. Praise Allah so that you will be with us in the Hereafter.'"[600]

Muhammad Ibn Ali Ibn Bilal has said, "Imam Abu Muhammad Hassan Ibn Ali ('a) informed me of his successor two years before his demise. He also introduced his successor to me three days before his demise."[601]

'Amr 'Ahwazi has said, "Abu Muhammad ('a) showed his son to me

---

[600] 'A'lamul Wura, Vol 2, p. 248.

[601] 'A'lamul Wura, Vol 2, p. 250.

and told me, 'He will be your guardian after me.'"[602]

Muhammad Ibn 'Uthman 'Amri has said, "Abu Muhammad ('a) showed his son to us in his house. We were forty people. He told us, 'He will be your Imam and caliph after me. Obey him and do not create dispute, or else your religion will be lost. Beware that you will not see him again.' Only a few days later, Abu Muhammad ('a) passed away."[603]

Musa Ibn Ja'far Ibn Wahab Baghdadi has said, "I heard from Imam Abu Muhammad Hassan Ibn Ali ('a), 'It is as if I see you in dispute over my successor! Everyone who accepts the infallible Imams after the Messenger of Allah (s), but denies my son, is like someone who accepts the prophet hood of the prophets (s), but denies the prophet hood of Muhammad (s). Obeying the last person of us is like obeying the first one of us and denying the last of us is like denying the first one of us. My son will have an occultation in which the people will doubt about his existence, except the people who are saved by the Almighty Allah.'"[604]

Muhammad Ibn 'Uthman 'Amri has said, "I heard from my father that Abu Muhammad Hassan Ibn Ali ('a) was asked about the tradition from his grand fathers, 'The earth will not be void of Allah's hujjat until the Resurrection.' and that 'Everyone who dies without knowing the Imam of his age has died a pagan death.' Imam Abu Muhammad ('a) answered, 'This is the truth just as the day is true.' So he was asked, 'Who will be the hujjat and the Imam after you?' Imam ('a) answered, 'My son, Muhammad, will be the Imam and hujjat after me. Everyone who dies without knowing him has died a pagan death. Beware that my son will have an occultation in which the ignorant will wander

---

[602] Ibid, p. 252.

[603] Ibid.

[604] Ibid.

and the followers of untruth will perish. Anyone who defines the time of my son's reappearance is a liar. He will rise. It is as if I see white flags swinging above his head in Najaf.' '"[605]

Some of the companions have narrated that when the wife (formerly servant) of Abu Muhammad got pregnant, Imam ('a) told her, "You will soon give birth to a son, named Muhammad. He will be the Qa'im after me."[606]

Saqar Ibn Abi Dilf has said, "I heard from Ali Ibn Muhammad Ibn Ali ('a), 'The Imam after me will be my son, Hassan. After Hassan, his son will be Qa'im, who will fill the earth with justice after it has been filled with injustice and oppression.'"[607]

More Proofs

In addition to the mentioned traditions, there are many other traditions that can be used for proving the existence of the twelfth Imam ('a). These traditions are of several types.

The first type; the traditions from the Messenger of Allah (s) about the twelve caliphs from Quraysh after himself.

'amir Ibn Sa'd Ibn Waqqas has said: I wrote in a letter to Jabir Ibn Samarah, 'Inform me of what you heard from the Messenger of Allah (s).' He wrote in answer, 'On a Friday, I heard from the Messenger of Allah (s), 'This religion will continue until the Resurrection, until twelve caliphs from Quraysh will rule.'"[608]

Such traditions reveal that:

-The religion (Islam) will exist until the Resurrection.

-Twelve caliphs from Quraysh will rule as the Prophet's (s) succes-

---

[605] 'A'lamul Wura, Vol 2, p. 352.

[606] Kifayatul 'Athar, p. 290.

[607] Ibid, p. 288.

[608] Sahih Muslim, Vol 3, p. 1453.

sors.

There are some probabilities about the instances of these twelve caliphs, none of which are acceptable. The only acceptable explanation is the belief of the Imamiyah, the Shi'ah. According to this belief, the Imams and caliphs after Prophet Muhammad (s) are twelve people from Quraysh and Bani Hashim, the twelfth of which is Imam Muhammad Ibn Hassan Askari ('a), who is alive but hidden. He will reappear and rise in the destined time and fill the world with justice.

The second type; the traditions about the twelve infallible Imams and their last one, Qa'im and Mahdi.

Salman Farsi has said, "I went to see the prophet (s) and saw Hussayn ('a) on his lap. The Prophet (s) kissed Hussayn's ('a) eyes and mouth and said, 'You are Sayyid, the son of Sayyid, and the father of Sayyids. You are the Imam, the son of Imam, and the fathers of Imams. You are hujjat, the son of hujjat, and the father of nine hujjats, the ninth person of which is Qa'im.'"[609]

The third type; the traditions about twelve Imams, including the names of each Imam.

Jabir Ibn Abdullah Ansari asked the Messenger of Allah (s), "O Messenger of Allah! Who are the Imams from the progeny of Ali Ibn Abi Talib ('a)?" Prophet Muhammad (s) answered, "Hassan and Hussayn, the youth of the Paradise, then Sayyidul 'abidin in his time, Ali Ibn Hussayn, then Baqir, Muhammad Ibn Ali. O Jabir! You will meet him, so say my hello to him! Then Sadiq, Ja'far Ibn Muhammad, then Kazim, Musa Ib Ja'far, then Riza, Ali Ibn Musa, then Taqi, Muhammad Ibn Ali, afterwards Naqi, Ali Ibn Muhammad, then Zaki, Hassan Ibn Ali, and after him his son, Qa'im, Mahdi, who will fill the world with justice as it was filled with oppression."[610]

---

[609] Yanabi' Al-Mawaddah, p. 308.

[610] Ghayatul Maram, Vol 1, p. 163.

Sahl Ibn Sa'd Ansari has said, "I asked Fatimah ('a), the daughter of Messenger of Allah (s), 'Who are the Imams?' Fatimah ('a) said, 'The Messenger of Allah (s) told Ali ('a), 'O Ali! You will be the Imam and caliph after me. You are more deserved than the believers to interfere in their affairs. When you pass away, your son, Hassan will be the most deserved one. After Hassan's demise, Hussayn will be the most deserved one. After Hussayn's ('a) demise, his son, Ali Ibn Hussayn ('a) will be the most deserved one. When Ali Ibn Hussayn ('a) passes away, his son, Muhammad, will be the most deserved one. When Muhammad passes away, his son, Ja'far, will be the most deserved one. After Ja'far's demise, his son, Musa, will be the most deserved one. When Musa passes away, his son, Ali, will be the most deserved one. When Ali passes away, his son, Muhammad, will be the most deserved one. After Muhammad's demise, his son, Ali, will be the most deserved one. When Ali passes away, his son, Hassan, will be the most deserved one. After Hassan's demise, his son, Qa'im, Mahdi, will be the most deserved one. He will conquer the East and the West of the world.'[611]

The fourth type; the traditions about twelve infallible Imams.

Abu Tufayl has narrated from Imam Ali ('a) from Messenger of Allah (s), "You are my guardian for anyone who dies from my Ahlul-Bayt and my successor among my ummah. Fighting you is like fighting me and making peace with you is like making peace with me. You are the Imam and the father of the Imams. Eleven Imams, all purified and infallible, will be born from your progeny. One of them will be Mahdi, who will fill the world with justice. Woe to those who conflict them!"[612]

The fifth type; the traditions about the existence of Ahlul-Bayt until the Last Day.

---

[611] Ghayatul Maram, Vol 1, p. 216.

[612] Ghayatul Maram, Vol 1, p. 193.

Prophet Muhammad (s) stated, "The stars are safety for residents of the heavens. If all the stars expire, the residents of heavens will die too. My Ahlul-Bayt are safety for residents of the earth. If my Ahlul-Bayt perish, the earth people will perish too."[613]

Abdullah Ibn Sulayman 'amiri has narrated from Imam Sadiq ('a), "The earth will never be empty of Allah's hujjat, who distinguishes between halal and haram and guides the people to the right path."[614]

Abu Hamzah has said, "I asked Imam Sadiq ('a), 'Will the earth be void of Imams?' Imam Sadiq ('a) answered, 'No. If the earth gets void of Imams, it will collapse.'"[615]

Washa' has said, "I asked Imam Riza ('a), 'Will the earth be without Imams one day?' Imam Riza ('a) answered, 'No.' I said again, 'It is narrated for us that the earth will never be without Imams except if Allah becomes angry with His servants.' Imam Riza ('a) stated, 'No. The earth will never be without Imams, otherwise it will collapse.'" [616]

Such traditions reveal that the existence of Imam –an infallible complete human as the goal of creation– is necessary for continuation of the life on earth. As the earth will never be without an Imam, our age is not without an Imam, though he is hidden from sights.

This also confirms the belief of the Shi'ah that the Imam of our age is the progeny of Imam Hassan Askari ('a), who was born in the year 255 A.H. He is hidden from sights and is fulfilling his duties until the ground is ready for his reappearance and reforming the world.

Continuous News about the Existence of Mahdi

---

[613] Al-Mustadrak, Hakim Niyshaburi, Vol 3, p. 150.

[614] Al-Ghaybah, Al-Nu'mani, p. 68.

[615] Ibid, p. 69.

[616] Ibid, p. 69

From the time of Prophet Muhammad (s) until the age of Imam Askari ('a), there had been news about the existence of Mahdi and Qa'im. Many traditions are narrated in this regard and recorded in tradition books, some of which are cited here.

Jabir Ibn Abdullah Ansari has narrated from the Messenger of Allah (s), "Mahdi will be one of my progeny; his name is my name and his nickname is my nickname. He is more similar to me than anyone else in terms of creation and ethics. He will have an occultation in which the people will go astray about him. Then he will reappear like the rising of a star and will fill the world with justice, as it had been filled with oppression and injustice."[617]

Imam Hussayn ('a) has narrated from his father, Ali Ibn Abi Talib ('a), "O Hussayn! Someone from the ninth generation of your progeny will be the very Qa'im (riser for the sake of truth), the revitalizer of religion, and spreader of justice." Imam Hussayn ('a) asked, "O Amiral Mu'minin! Will this really happen?" Imam Ali ('a) answered, "Yes, by Allah Who appointed Muhammad to prophet hood and selected him from among all the people. Spread of justice by him will be after his occultation and bewildering of the people. Only the sincere believers will maintain their belief in religion during that occultation; the people who have a promise with Allah about our affection, whose belief is in their heart, and are confirmed."[618]

Imam Hassan ('a), after his peace contract with Mu'awiyah, told the protesters, "Don't you know that none of us, the Imams, can escape oath of allegiance with the monarch of our age, except Qa'im, behind who Jesus, son of Mary, will perform prayer? The Exalted Allah will hide his birth and he will be hidden until his reappearance. Then he will not be forced to take oath of allegiance with anyone. He will be a

---

[617] Kamalad Din, Vol 1, p. 403.

[618] Ibid, p. 421.

progeny from the ninth generation of my brother, Hussayn. He will spend his long life in occultation. Then he will reappear while he resembles a forty year old one, by Allah's power. And Allah has power over all things."[619]

Hussayn Ibn Ali Ibn Abi Talib ('a) stated, "Qa'im (riser) of this ummah will be a progeny from my ninth generation. He will have an occultation and his legacy will be divided during his lifetime."[620]

Sa'id Ibn Jubayr has said, "I heard from Ziynul 'abidin Ali Ibn Hussayn ('a), 'Qa'im will have a tradition from Noah and that is long life.'"[621]

Muhammad Ibn Muslim Thaqafi has said, "I heard from Abu Ja'far Muhamamd Ibn Ali ('a), 'Qa'im will win by scaring his enemies and will be confirmed by Allah. The earth will surrender its treasures to him. His sovereignty will envelop the East and the West. The Almighty Allah will win Islam over other religions by him, though the disbelievers do not like it. He will organize all the earth. Prophet Jesus (s) will descend the heavens and perform prayer with him.'"[622]

Safwan has said, "I heard from Imam Sadiq ('a), 'Anyone who accepts all the Imams but denies Mahdi ('a) is like someone who accepts all the prophets, but not Prophet Muhammad (s).' Imam Sadiq ('a) was then asked, 'O son of Messenger of Allah! Whose son is Mahdi?' Imam ('a) answered, 'A progeny from the fifth generation of the seventh Imam. He will be hidden from you and saying his name will be forbidden for you.'"[623]

Yunus Ibn Abdur Rahman has said, "I asked Imam Musa Ibn Ja'far

---

[619] Kamalad Din, Vol 1, p. 433.

[620] Ibid, p. 434.

[621] Ibid, p. 439.

[622] Ibid, p. 439.

[623] Ibid, Vol 2, p. 2.

('a), 'Are you Qa'im?' He answered, 'I am Qa'im (riser) for the truth, but Qa'im, who will eradicate Allah's enemies and will fill the earth with justice as it had been filled with injustice, will be the fifth person from my progeny. He will have a long occultation, because he is fearful of his life. During his occultation, some people will forget their belief and some will be constant in their beliefs.' Then he said, 'Good for our Shi'ahs who will resort to us in occultation time, love us, and dislike our enemies! They are from us and we are from them. They are happy with our Imamate and we are happy of their being Shi'ah. Goof for them! By Allah that they will be with us in the Hereafter.'"[624]

Rayyan Ibn Salt has said, "I asked Imam Riza ('a), 'Are you Sahibul 'Amr?' He answered, 'Yes, I am Sahibul 'Amr, but not the Sahibul 'Amr who will fill the earth with justice after being filled with oppression. How can I be Sahibul 'Amr with my weak body? Qa'im is the person who appears, in his old age, like a young strong man. He is able to eradicate a large tree and if he shouts before mountains, the stones collapse. He possesses the stick of Moses ('a) and the signet of Solomon ('a). He will be the fourth generation of my progeny. Allah will hide him from sights then he will reappear and will fill the earth with justice after it had been filled with injustice and oppression.'"[625]

Abdul 'Azim Hassani has said, "I went to see Imam Muhammad Ibn Ali Ibn Musa ('a). I was going to ask about Qa'im and whether he is Mahdi ('a) or not when Imam ('a) told me, 'O Abul Qasim! Our Qa'im will be Mahdi ('a) who should be waited for in his occultation time and obeyed after his reappearance. He is from the third generation of my progeny. By Allah, Who appointed Muhammad (s) to prophet hood and allocated Imamate to us, if only one day is remaining from the world, Allah will last it until Mahdi ('a) reappears and fills the earth

---

[624] Kamalad Din, Vol 2, p. 30.

[625] Kamalad Din, Vol 2, p. 48.

with justice as it was filled with oppression. Allah will organize the affairs for Mahdi ('a) in a single night, as He did for Moses ('a). Moses went away to bring fire, but he returned as a prophet.' Then Imam Riza ('a) stated, 'The best deed of the Shi'ah is waiting for Mahdi's ('a) reappearance.'"[626]

Saqar Ibn Abu Dilf said, "I heard from Imam Ali Ibn Muhammad Ibn Ali ('a), 'The Imam after me will be my son, Hassan, and after Hassan his son will be Qa'im, who will fill the earth with justice after being filled with oppression.'"[627]

'Ahmad Ibn 'Is'haq 'Ash'ari has said, "I went to see Imam Abu Muhammad Hassan Ibn Ali ('a). I was going to ask him about his successor, when Imam ('a) told me, 'O 'Ahmad Ibn 'Is'haq! The Exalted Allah will never leave the earth without hujjat until the Hereafter. Because of the blessings of the hujjat calamities do not happen for the earth inhabitants, it rains, and blessings come out of the earth.' I asked, 'O son of Messenger of Allah! Who will be your caliph and the Imam after you?' Imam Hassan Ibn Ali ('a) rapidly went to his house and came out after a while. He held a three-year old son on his shoulders, whose face illuminated like the full moon. So Imam ('a) told me, 'O 'Ahmad! If you were not dear to me, I did not show my son to you. He has the same name and nickname as the Prophet of Islam (s). He is the very person, who will fill the earth with justice after it is filled with oppression and injustice.'"[628]

The mentioned traditions and many more similar ones reveal that the honorable Prophet (s) and infallible Imams ('a) had frequently informed the people of existence of the twelfth Imam, Mahdi, or Qa'im, to prepare them for accepting him. In fact, it has happened as

---

[626] Kamalad Din, Vol 2, p. 49.

[627] Ibid, p. 55.

[628] Ibid.

they had informed. What was begun by the Prophet (s) was continued by infallible Imams ('a).

Foretelling the Occultation

As is clear from previous traditions, the Occultation of the twelfth Imam ('a) has always been discussed among the Shi'ah until the age of the eleventh Imam ('a) and Prophet Muhammad (s) and his Ahlul-Bayt, the infallible Imams ('a) announced it. The occultation had been considered a characteristic of Mahdi ('a). In addition to these traditions, many other traditions explicitly mention the Occultation.

The honorable Prophet (s) stated, "By Allah, Who appointed me for giving good tidings, Qa'im from my progeny will hide because of a promise. Then most of the people will say, 'Allah does not need the Household of Muhammad.' Some others will doubt about his birth altogether. So everyone who is present in occultation time should attempt in maintaining his religion and avoiding satanic temptations; he may get you out of my religion, as he drove your parents away from Paradise before. Allah has given guardianship of the disbelievers to Satan."[629]

Imam Sadiq ('a) stated, "If you heard the news of your Imam's occultation do not reject it."[630]

Tabarsi has written, "The news of occultation of Imam of the age ('a) had been issued before he, his father, and his grandfather were born. The Shi'ah narrators have recorded these news in books authored in the times of Imam Baqir ('a) and Imam Sadiq ('a). One of trustworthy narrators and authors is Hassan Ibn Mahbub Zarrad. He has recorded the traditions about Occultation of Imam Mahdi ('a) in his book more than one hundred years ago. As it was cited in traditions, the

---

[629] 'Ithbatul Hudat, Vol 6, p. 386.
[630] Ibid, p. 350.

Occultation was materialized."[631]

Muhammad Ibn 'Ibrahim Ibn Ja'far Nu'mani, who was born during Short Occultation of Imam Mahdi ('a), wrote in his book Al-Ghaybah, which was written when Imam ('a) was about eighty years old, "The infallible Imams ('a) had declared the Occultation of Imam of the age ('a) before. If his occultation had not happened, it was a reason for denying the Shi'ah belief. However, the Almighty Allah revealed the truth of Imams' ('a) traditions by materializing the Occultation."[632]

In addition to Hassan Ibn Mahbub, some other companions of Imams ('a) have authored books about Imam Mahdi's ('a) Occultation before his birth, including:

1. Ali Ibn Hassan Ibn Muhammad Ta'i Tatari, a companion of Imam Musa Ibn Ja'far ('a) has written a book about Occultation. He was a trustworthy jurisprudent.

2. Ali Ibn 'Umar 'A'raj Kufi, another companion of Imam Musa Ibn Ja'far ('a) wrote a book about Occultation.

3. 'Ibrahim Ibn Salih 'Anmati has authored a book about Occultation.

4. Hassan Ibn Ali Ibn Abi Hamzah, who lived in the age of Imam Riza ('a), wrote a book about Occultation.

5. Abbas Ibn Husham Nashiri 'Asadi, one of the companions of Imam Riza ('a), has written a book about Occultation.

6. Ali Ibn Hassan Ibn Fazzal, a companion of Imam Hadi ('a) and Imam Askari ('a) has written a book about Occultation.

7. Fazl Ibn Shadhan Niyshaburi, the companion of Imam Hadi ('a) and Imam Askari ('a) wrote a book about Qa'im of Prophet Muhammad's (s) Household and his Occultation.

As a result, the existence of the twelfth Imam in his occultation is certain, because:

---

[631] 'A'lamul Wura, Vol 2, p. 257.

[632] Al-Ghaybah, Nu'mani, p. 6.

I. Based on logical reasoning proved before and many traditions from infallible Imams ('a), the existence of Imam and hujjat is necessary for continuation of human race and the earth will never be without Allah's hujjat.

II. Many frequent traditions mention that the number of Imams will be twelve.

III. According to the traditions and the testimony of history, eleven of the Imams have reached Imamate and passed away after some time. Therefore, it can be concluded that the twelfth Imam is the son of Imam Hassan Askari ('a), the eleventh Imam, and is living in Occultation.

Imam Mahdi's ('a) Virtues

Unfortunately, Imam Mahdi ('a) has lived in Occultation from childhood and has not interacted with the people directly, so his innate virtues, ethical qualities, knowledge, are not narrated for us. However, based on the prerequisites of the Imam it should be said that Imam Mahdi ('a) possesses all virtues of other infallible Imams ('a). He is infallible too, away from all sins and faults. He knows all sciences and teachings necessary for an Imam. The sources of his knowledge are the sources of knowledge of other Imams, too.

Imam Mahdi's ('a) social, ethical, and worshipping conduct is the same as the conduct of Messenger of Allah (s) and infallible Imams ('a), though the details about him are not narrated for us. After his reappearance, all his virtues will be revealed, insha'allah.

Imam Baqir ('a) stated, "Knowledge of Allah's Book and tradition of the Prophet (s) grows in the heart of our Mahdi ('a) as a plant grows in a ready piece of land in its best form. Every one of you who witnessed the time of his reappearance should say, 'Greetings to you, O Ahlul-Bayt of Mercy and prophet hood, the treasures of knowledge and prophecy! Greetings to you O Baqiyyatullah (Allah's remnant) on the earth!'"⁶³³

Imam Baqir ('a) also stated, "When our Qa'im rises, he will put his hand on the people's heads; he will make them smart and will complete their minds and thought."[634]

Imam Sadiq ('a) said, "Knowledge is divided into 27 parts. Whatever is revealed to the prophets (s) and the people have learned is only two parts out of 27 parts. When our Qa'im rises, he will reveal the remaining 25 parts and teaches them to the people. These 25 parts plus what the prophets (s) have revealed equals the 27 parts of knowledge."[635]

Of course, such traditions do not imply that the knowledge of Imam Mahdi ('a) is superior to that of Prophet Muhammad (s)! Rather, the Prophet (s) and all infallible Imams ('a) are equal regarding their knowledge and virtues. The difference is that the time conditions and people's understanding had not been prepared for accepting the complete sciences before Imam Mahdi's ('a) time.

Short Occultation and Long Occultation

According to the Imamiyyah (Shi'ah) belief, the twelfth Imam ('a) has had two occultation periods; the Short Occultation and the Long Occultation. The former began from the birth of Imam Mahdi ('a) and ended in the year 329 A.H. During this period, Imam Mahdi ('a) was hidden from most of the people; however, he interacted with the Shi'ah through some elites, answering religious questions and fulfilling their needs. Imam Mahdi's deputies for interacting with the people were four trustworthy persons, called na'ib (deputy), as cited below:

The first na'ib of Imam Mahdi ('a) was 'Uthman Ibn Sa'id. He was a

---

[633] Biharul Anwar, Vol 52, p. 317.

[634] Ibid, p. 328.

[635] Biharul Anwar, Vol 52, p. 336.

trustworthy companion of Imam Hadi ('a) and Imam Hassan Askari ('a). He was one of the people to who Imam Hassan Askari ('a) showed his son and said, "You will not see him again. In Occultation time, obey 'Uthman Ibn Sa'id, who is deputy of your Imam." [636]

The second na'ib of Imam Mahdi ('a) was Muhammad Ibn 'Uthman. After his father, 'Uthman Ibn Sa'id, Muhammad Ibn 'Uthman was appointed as deputy by Imam of the age ('a). 'Uthman Ibn Sa'id said before his demise, "My son, Muhammad, will be my successor and the deputy of your Imam ('a) after me."[637]

After 'Uthman Ibn Sa'id, his successor was confirmed by Imam Mahdi ('a) in a letter.[638]

The third na'ib of Imam Mahdi ('a) was Hussayn Ibn Ruh. Muhammad Ibn 'Uthman introduced him as his successor and deputy of Sahibul Amr before his demise. He told his companions, "I have a mission from Imam of the age ('a) to appoint Hussayn Ibn Ruh as na'ib after myself. Refer to him for your affairs and questions."[639]

The fourth na'ib of Imam Mahdi ('a) was Ali Ibn Muhammad Samari. He was a reliable Shi'ah. Hussayn Ibn Ruh appointed Ali Ibn Muhammad Samari as his successor and deputy of Imam Mahdi ('a) before his demise.[640]

Ali Ibn Muhammad Samari was the last deputy of Imam Mahdi ('a). He passed away in the year 329 A.H. Before his demise, he recited the letter Imam Mahdi ('a) had sent to him for the people, "Your death will come in six days. Organize your affairs, but do not set a successor to yourself. From this time, my Long Occultation begins. I will not

---

[636] Biharul Anwar, Vol 51, p. 346.

[637] Rijal Mamaqani, Vol 1, p. 30.

[638] Biharul Anwar, Vol 51, p. 349.

[639] Ibid, p. 355.

[640] Ibid, Vol 51, p. 360.

reappear until a long time passes, the hearts become stubborn, the earth becomes replete with oppression, and the Almighty Allah allows me to reappear. From this time on, anyone who claims seeing me is a liar, so deny him." [641]

The short Occultation and existence of Imam Mahdi's ('a) deputies lasted for nearly seventy four years. In this period, the Shi'ah were in contact with Imam ('a) through his deputies. Sometimes the people asked their questions and received response letters, called towqi', from Imam Mahdi ('a). Some other times, Imam ('a) primarily sent letters to the Shi'ah and issued verdicts and orders.

Some miracles have been narrated in this regard that need more time and space to be mentioned. The purpose of Short Occultation was preparing the Shi'ah for accepting the Long Occultation.

Imam Mahdi's ('a) Long Occultation began from the demise of Imam's ('a) last deputy, Ali Ibn Muhammad Samari, in the year 329 A.H. and will last until Imam's ('a) reappearance. The honorable Prophet (s) and his Household, infallible Imams ('a), had announced these two Occultation periods before.

'Is'haq Ibn 'Ammar has said, "I heard from Imam Sadiq ('a), 'Qa'im will have two Occultation periods; a short one and a long one. In the former, close Shi'ahs know about his place, but in the latter one only a few close sincere companions know about his place.'"[642]

The living place of Imam Mahdi ('a) is not clear. He may live and interact with ordinary people in disguise.

The Philosophy of Occultation

Some people may ask, "Why did Imam of the age ('a) become absent? Couldn't he live somewhere in the world, like other people, lead the Islamic ummah, and publicize religious rules and verdicts, until the

---

[641] Ibid, pp. 360-361.

[642] 'Ithbatul Hudat, Vol 7, p. 69.

situation became ready for his world uprising and reform and Allah allowed him to reappear? Then he could demolish the oppressor governments and establish a just Islamic one instead."

The answer is that this is a good, but unfortunately impractical, hypothesis. Some points worth mentioning in this regard:

The mission of promised Mahdi ('a) is different from missions of other Imams ('a). The other Imams ('a) had no duty to have armed fighting for establishing Islamic government, enforcing religious rules and verdicts, combating oppression, supporting the deprived oppressed people, and establishing complete justice. The promised Mahdi ('a), however, has such important duties and this duty is one of his characteristics. Prophet Muhammad (s) and infallible Imams ('a) have introduced Imam Mahdi ('a) this way.

The government of Imam Mahdi ('a) is an international Islamic one, not limited to a single country, tribe, or language. Establishing such a government is not an easy work. It needs preparation in two ways; first, having complete military equipments superior to the world's military forces, and second, preparing majority of world's people mentally for accepting such a government and attempting to materialize it.

It has been proved logically and through traditions that the existence of the Imam is necessary for continuation of human generation. In fact, the world will never be without Allah's hujjat.

According to many frequent traditions, the number of infallible Imams ('a) after Prophet Muhammad (s) will be twelve; eleven of them have lived in this world, so the last one –Qa'im (riser) for the truth and the promised Mahdi– should be alive until the Day of Judgment.

The honorable Prophet (s) and infallible Imams ('a) have frequently announced the existence of Mahdi ('a) and his uprising, saying, "When the world is replete with oppression and injustice, Mahdi ('a) will revolt and eradicate injustice and oppression with the aid of his companions, establishing the government of justice."

Based on what was mentioned so far, it should be discussed if Imam of the age could live like an ordinary person somewhere in the world and fulfill his duties as much as possible. What would happen in the world in such an assumption?

In such situation, Imam Mahdi ('a) always faced two groups of people; first, the oppressed weakened people, who have always consisted the majority of the people throughout history and have waited for Imam Mahdi's ('a) reappearance. These people always complain about difficulties and ask for world uprising, because they see Mahdi ('a) among them. Then if Imam ('a) accepts their request and begin his rise, he will not be victorious. Since the grounds had not been prepared for a world rising, Imam ('a) would be killed and the world people would lose their hujjat and Imam.

If Imam Mahdi ('a) does not accept the request of oppressed people, they would get disappointed and scattered. As a result, the only way for him is to be absent.

The second group is monarch governments of the world, which are dominant in most parts of the world. Unfortunately, they avoid no crime for continuing their dominance and would remove any probable threat to it.

This group has heard that the promised Mahdi ('a) would rise for defending the oppressed people's right and fighting tyranny. If they see Imam ('a) with his long unconventional life, they feel the danger and undoubtedly assassinate him. Therefore, the earth would become void of hujjat.

In conclusion, the occultation of Imam of the age ('a) is necessary for preventing the mentioned happenings.

The Signs and Benefits of Absent Imam ('a)

In discussing the necessity of an Imam's existence some major duties of the Imam were mentioned in previous chapters, including:

Recording and maintaining religious sciences, teachings, verdicts, and rules.

Publishing and propagating them among the Muslims.

Establishing and administering Islamic government and enforcing judiciary, political, social, economic, and cultural verdicts of an Islamic country for people's problems.

Now it may be asked, "These needs necessitate the existence of the Imam. However, none of these are fulfilled by absent Imam ('a). So what is his benefit?"

The answer is that Imam Mahdi ('a) has no difference with other infallible Imams ('a) in fulfilling the first duty; he records and maintains religious verdicts. In fact, after Prophet Muhammad (s) religious sciences and teachings have remained intact with the Imams ('a) throughout the ages.

Concerning the other two duties of the Imam, though the people of occultation time cannot use the existence of absent Imam ('a), Imam ('a) has no fault in this regard. Rather it is the fault of people, who have not prepared the conditions for Imam's ('a) reappearance and establishment of Islamic government. Therefore, Imam Mahdi ('a) is forced to live a hidden life until the grounds are prepared for his reappearance and rising.

Moreover, there is no obvious reason for Imam's ('a) not interfering in scientific, cultural, political, and social issues of Islamic ummah. It is probable that Imam Mahdi ('a) gives direct or indirect scientific aid to some individuals, groups, or officials in urgencies and crises. Such helps cannot be denied.

In addition to mentioned uses of Imam Mahdi ('a), there are two other major benefits:

The first use of existence of Imam Mahdi ('a) is continuation of human race and protection of the earth. This is proved by two kinds of reasons; reasons found in traditions and logical reasons.

Reasons from traditions: There are many traditions saying that the existence of hujjat and Imam is necessary for continuation of human race and inexistence of him is the cause of devastation of the earth and extinction of human race. These traditions have been cited previously in this book.

Logical reasons: Some reasons have been pointed out in kalam and philosophy books for necessity of existence of Imam. Defining these reasons –proved in related books– requires a related introduction, which cannot be mentioned in this book. Only a summary of proved results are cited here:

Human is composed of physical body and spiritual soul. The body and soul combine to create a thing called human. Human has two levels of existence. The superior level is the everlasting heavenly human essence and the inferior one is physical. So the latter level can move and develop.

Human soul can go one of two ways; the direct path of humanity and development of human virtues to reach the Almighty Allah, or deviation from the true path and developing vices and evilness. Going to either of the two routes depends on individual humans.

The creation of human being and the world has not been vain and purposeless. The purpose is development of human soul, passing the rout to Allah, and reaching physical and spiritual perfection.

Human is not needless in finding the true path of humanity and seeking true salvation, rather he needs his Creature and guidelines of the prophets (s). Therefore, it is said that Allah's Mercy necessitates that He send a program for human salvation in this world and the Hereafter by His prophets (s). Religious rules and verdicts are revealed for the same reason; to show direct path to humanity and meeting the Almighty Allah.

True belief, good ethics, and virtuous deeds are factors of soul development that bring about human salvation in the Hereafter. Evil belief and conduct and wrongdoing lead human to decline.

The route of human spiritual development is not credential, but real. Human essence moves in a real route. It goes either toward perfection or away from humanity and toward viciousness.

Thus, it can be concluded that there should always be a perfect human among the people who moves toward humanity, inside framework of religion, and possesses good ethics and conduct. Such a person is the purpose of creation. This brilliant human seeks the way toward absolute perfection and receives Allah's blessings. He absorbs other people seeking this way with his spiritual attractions, benefitting them from Allah's blessings revealed to pure soul of an Imam.

Such a noble person is the goal of creation, leader of humanity, and Allah's hujjat. His existence causes the existence of human race and his inexistence causes extinction of humans and demolishing of the earth.

Therefore, it can be said that the major use of existence of the Imam is human survival. His absence or presence does not make any difference in manifestation of this effect. The absent Imam is compared to the sun behind the clouds in some traditions.

Sulayman has said, "I told Imam Ja'far Sadiq ('a), 'How do the people benefit from the absent Imam?' Imam ('a) answered, 'Just as they benefit from the sun behind the clouds.'"[643]

This tradition needs a little explanation. It is proved in astrology that the sun is the center of solar system. The sun gravity maintains the earth from collapsing. The earth rotates around the sun, creating day and night and different seasons. The sun light illuminates the earth and its heat is the cause of life for humans, animals, and plants. These benefits are effective in days, at nights, and in cloudy weather.

The second use of existence of Imam of the age ('a) is strengthening

---

[643] Biharul Anwar, Vol 52, p. 92.

hope of waiting for his reappearance and preparation for participating in plans for world reformation. His plan includes ousting monarch governments and eradicating their oppression forever, establishing a single Islamic government and developing justice, promoting Islam throughout the world above other religions, complete eradication of infidelity, and enforcement of Islamic verdicts and removing poverty and deprivation forever.

A little attention reveals that realization of these goals is not possible except in case of all-out world preparation. This great victory is possible with fighting and attempting not with miracle. Nowadays, world oppressors have developed military industries and mass destruction weapons. True believers in promised Mahdi ('a) and his world reformation should prepare themselves for his rising and a difficult war. First, waiters for Imam Mahdi ('a) should develop their souls in a way that Imam ('a) wants all the people to be. Second, they should prepare world people mentally for accepting Islam and a single world government. Third, they should attempt to compensate their industrial and military shortcomings and become superior to other forces. This is the meaning of waiting for reappearance that is mentioned in some traditions. It is also considered another use of believing in the existence of the absent Imam ('a).

Traditions about Imam Mahdi ('a) in Sunni Books

The traditions about promised Mahdi ('a) are not only observed in Shi'ah books, rather many Sunni scholars have cited such traditions in their books, including the following:

Ali Ibn Abi Talib ('a) has narrated from Prophet Muhammad (s), "If only one day is remaining from the age of the world, the Almighty Allah will send a man from my Household to fill the earth with justice as it had been filled with oppression and injustice."[644]

Ummi Salamah has said, "I heard from Messenger of Allah (s), 'Mahdi ('a) is from my Ahlul-Bayt and a progeny of Fatimah (s).'"[645]

Ali Ibn Abi Talib ('a) has narrated from the Prophet (s), "Mahdi ('a) is from my Ahlul-Bayt. The Exalted Allah will prepare the conditions for his rising over night."[646]

There are tens of other similar traditions in books of Sunni narrators.

These traditions indicate that the belief in promised Mahdi ('a) is not especial to the Shi'ah Muslims; rather it is an Islamic belief emerged from the Prophet (s) and believed by the Sunni Muslims too. The difference, however, is that the Shi'ah Muslims consider Imam Mahdi ('a) as a known progeny of Prophet Muhammad (s) and his daughter, Fatimah (s), and his grandson, Imam Hussayn ('a), and also the son of Imam Hassan Askari ('a). The Shi'ah also believe that Imam Mahdi ('a) has been born in the year 255 A.H., is alive now, and lives in absence. He will reappear in latter ages of the world when the conditions are ready for his rising. The Sunni Muslims believe that the promised Mahdi ('a) is not a known figure. He is the progeny of the Prophet (s) and Fatimah (s) and will rise in latter ages to fill the world with justice. In fact, they believe that he will be born in the very latter ages of the world for reforming the world.

This belief comes from the Sunni books, which do not mention the birth of Mahdi ('a), his father, Imam Hassan Askari ('a), and his Short and Long Occultations. Though these sources do not deny the beliefs of the Shi'ah.

---

[644] Sunan Abi Dawud, Vol 2, Kitabl Mahdi; Fusulul Muhimmah, p. 275.

[645] Sunan Abi Dawud, Vol 2, Kitabl Mahdi. Sunan Abi Majah, Vol 2, Bab Khurujul Mahdi.

[646] Sunan Abi Majah, Vol 2, Bab Khurujul Mahdi, p. 1367.

Finally, it should be pointed out that the birth and absence of Imam Mahdi ('a) are not cited in Sunni books, but some Sunni narrators have acknowledged the birth of Imam Hassan Askari ('a) and recorded in their books, including:

Muhammad Ibn Talhah Shafi'i in the book Matalibus Su'ul, Muhammad Ibn Yusuf in the book Kifayatul Talib, Ibn Sabbagh Maliki in the book Al-Fusulul Muhimmah, Yusuf Ibn Qazawughli in the book Tadhkirah Khawas Al-Ummah, Shablanji in the book Nurul Absar, Ibn Hajar in the book Al-Sawa'iqul Muhaarriqah, Muhammad Amin Baghdadi in the book Saba'ik Al-Zahab, Ibn Khalkan in the book Wafiyyat Al-'A'yan, Sha'rani in the books Al-Yawaqit and Al-Jawahir, Khajah Parsa in the book Fasl Al-Khitab, Abul Falah Hanbali in the book Shadharat Al-Zahab, Muhammad Ibn Ali Hamawi in the book Tarikh Mansuri.

Long Life of Imam Mahdi ('a)

One of important issues about Imam Mahdi ('a) is his long life. He is born in the year 255 A.H. and is alive until now (1423 A.H.)[647]. The time of his reappearance and later his demise is not known. Anyway, this lifetime is so long and extraordinary in present age. It may be unacceptable for some people and requires scientific discussion.

The reasons and factors of lifetime, oldness, and death need broad research by a group of scientists and experts in related fields, such as biology, medicine, dietetics, hygiene, human sciences, sociology, etc. The findings of such scientists reveal the secrets of long life, which can help humans live healthier longer lives. Discovering the secrets of long life will be useful for everyone, especially the advocates of Imam Mahdi ('a).

---

[647] The present book was written in the year 1423 A.H. and translated in the year 1432 A.H.

Some issues should be pointed out here:
The average human lifetime has not been identical throughout the ages and across world countries. The differences are the result of type and quality of nutrition, observing hygiene basics, prevention of contagious diseases, life milieu, and development of medical sciences.

Some people have lived longer than the average lifetime of others, for example up to one hundred years. Exceptionally, some people have lived up to nearly 150 years. Some rare examples of people living until 200 years of age or a little more than that have been reported. The interesting point is that no scientist has ever defined a limit for human age that cannot be passed.

Although the Almighty Allah does the world affairs through natural causes, His Power is not limited to known causes; rather He can do anything through causes and means unidentified by humans, as is the case about miracles. Therefore, it can be said that if the existence of a special human until a long time later is necessary, the Almighty Allah can prepare essential natural or even odd causes for it. As a result, a person's exceptional hundreds or even thousands years of age cannot be denied.

The causes of old age and death are not clear for us. There is no reason for aging and lack of physical ability of all the people in the same age.

In the history, there have been people living for hundreds of years, thousand years, or even longer. Of course, proving such long lifetimes needs absolute reason. However, they cannot be denied altogether.

One of the people with a long life has been Prophet Noah ('a). The Holy Quran states that Noah ('a) lived 950 years. He invited his people to monotheism, but they always opposed him. Finally, severe rain and storm killed all the disbelievers. Only Prophet Noah ('a) and his followers boarded a ship and were saved from death.

(We (once) sent Noah to his people, and he tarried among them a thousand years less fifty: but the Deluge overwhelmed them while they (persisted in) sin. But We saved him and the companions of the Ark, and We made the (Ark) a Sign for all peoples!)

This verse shows that Prophet Noah ('a) have been fulfilling his mission for 950 years. It is not clear when he had been appointed to prophet hood or how much he had been alive after the storm happening. However, it can be concluded that he had lived more than a thousand years.

In sum, the Holy Quran that is an undeniable document has confirmed a lifetime more than thousand years. If we accept it, longer lifetimes cannot be denies either.

Imam Mahdi's ('a) Reappearance Time

No time is defined for reappearance and world rising of Imam Mahdi ('a). Rather, the infallible Imams ('a) have rejected anyone who clarifies a time for it.

Fuzayl has said, "I asked Imam Baqir ('a), 'Is there a specified time for reappearance of Mahdi ('a)?' Imam Baqir ('a) said three times, 'The definers of a time for it are liars.'"[648]

Muhammad Ibn Muslim has said, "Imam Sadiq ('a) stated, 'Do not hesitate to deny anyone who determines the time of Mahdi's ('a) reappearance, because we do not define a time for reappearance.'"[649]

Such traditions show that Prophet Muhammad (s) or infallible Imams ('a) have not given news of Imam Mahdi's ('a) reappearance time, thus preventing any probable misuses. Therefore, if someone quotes the reappearance time from an Imam or other people, we should deny him.

---

[648] Biharul Anwar, Vol 52, p. 103.

[649] Ibid, pp. 104-117.

The Signs of Imam Mahdi's Reappearance

Some signs and conditions to happen before Imam Mahdi's ('a) reappearance are recorded in tradition books. However, most of them have a weak unreliable document. They may have been altered and need exact review.

Perhaps the most important condition of reappearance is preparation of world milieu, which may reveal the closeness of reappearance time of Imam Mahdi –May Allah hasten his reappearance. Some issues need to be kept in mind in this regard.

Characteristics of Imam Mahdi's ('a) Government

The government of Imam Mahdi ('a) will not be an ordinary one, but an exceptional government with these qualities:

His government will be completely religious and Islamic. In that government, Islam will rule completely. Heavenly rules and verdicts are enforced and benefitted from in all social affairs.

The government of Imam Mahdi ('a) will be international. At that time, conventional boundaries related to countries, languages, and races will disappear; one government will rule the world and all the people will cooperate in this government.

Disbelief will be eradicated and Islam will overcome other religions. The holders of heavenly religions will live together peacefully.

Tyrant governments will be ousted; oppression will be eradicated in the world and justice will be expanded everywhere.

Present Conditions of the World

Nowadays, many of the world people are disbelievers or infidels. The tyrant rulers and governments are ruling countries, controlling science and industry, especially extraordinary military industries. In sum, the ruling is in control of oppressors, who suppress independence and freedom movements.

Conditions of Victory

One of the major conditions of victory of revolutions and movements is materialization of all its necessary prerequisites. International movement of Imam Mahdi ('a) is not an exception. Though Imam Mahdi ('a) and his followers will benefit from Allah's support in this movement, their victory will come with jihad and bloodshed, not with miracle.

Bashir has said, "I told Imam Abu Ja'far ('a), 'The people say that when Mahdi ('a) rises, the affairs will be organized for him naturally and there will not be any bloodshed, even a little bit.' Imam Abu Ja'far ('a) replied, 'By Allah that it is not so. If it was possible, it would have happened for the Prophet (s), when his tooth was broken and his forehead was wounded in the war. By Allah the movement of Sahibul 'Amr will not win, except that sweat and blood flow in the battlefield.' Then Imam ('a) touched his forehead."[650]

With regard to Imam Mahdi's ('a) great and expanded world plan, present and future state of military industries and tyrant monarchs in the world, and the fact that his movement will win with war, it can be concluded that realization of such great victory needs all-out world preparation. Without such preparation, Imam Mahdi ('a) will not reappear, nor will his movement win.

Preparing the world situation for reappearance of Imam Mahdi ('a) is the duty of Muslims, lovers of promised Mahdi ('a), and real waiters for reappearance. Realization of this great happening requires that: They observe refinement of their souls, development of good ethics, avoidance of sins, especially oppression, observing justice, practical adherence to Islamic rules and verdicts, defense of the oppressed deprived people, and expansion of justice. In fact, Imam Mahdi ('a) will rise for the same purposes.

---

[650] Biharul Anwar, Vol 52, p. 358.

They introduce Islamic rules and values in various worshipping, ethical, political, social, cultural, and economic aspects for the world people and prepare them mentally for accepting Islam.

They attempt in acquiring knowledge, technology, and military industries to compensate their previous lag and become superior to other powers.

They update their military force with developed weapons to confirm their power in the world and endanger their enemies so that they dare not attack Muslims.

They try to establish an Islamic government in a strong developed country, solve their economic, political, social, and cultural problems, and fight injustice, poverty, and prejudice to show the world people that complete enforcement of Islamic rules is the best way for managing the world.

Fulfilling these duties is the very real waiting for Imam Mahdi's ('a) reappearance, recommended to Muslims of Occultation time in tradition books. If the Muslims behave this way, the ground will gradually prepare for Imam Mahdi's ('a) reappearance and can be considered a sign of his reappearance, inshallah.

www.ingramcontent.com/pod-product-compliance
Lightning Source LLC
LaVergne TN
LVHW091720070526
838199LV00050B/2484